LEGENDARY LOCALS

OF

ARVADA

COLORADO

TANYA LONG

LEGENDARY LOCALS

ISBN 978-1-4671-0129-5

Legendary Locals is an imprint of Arcadia Publishing
Charleston, South Carolina

Printed in the United States of America

Library of Congress Control Number: 2013947417

For all general information, please contact Arcadia Publishing:
Telephone 843-853-2070
Fax 843-853-0044
E-mail sales@arcadiapublishing.com
For customer service and orders:
Toll-Free 1-888-313-2665

Visit us on the Internet at www.arcadiapublishing.com

Dedication
In loving memory of my great-grandmother Elizabeth Shannon and my grandparents Sam and Ruth Robertson

On the Front Cover: Clockwise from top left:
Bill Ashton, former president of the Arvada Historical Society and Arvada West High School teacher (Courtesy Arvada Historical Society; see page 91), Marcetta Lutz, local historian and writer (Courtesy Arvada Historical Society; see page 66), E.E. Benjamin, builder of the iconic 1925 Arvada Flour Mill (Courtesy Arvada Historical Society; see page 33), George Swadley, one of Arvada's first settlers and one of the town's most popular residents (Courtesy Arvada Historical Society; see page 11), the Hackberry Tree, a local landmark for over 100 years (Courtesy Arvada Historical Society; see page 16), Gertrude Weaver Barlow, the granddaughter of Arvada pioneer Thomas Weaver (Courtesy of Arvada Historical Society; see page 9), Vesta Miller, the second woman to be Arvada's mayor (Courtesy Arvada Historical Society; see page 108).

On the Back Cover: From left to right:
Erecka O'Hara (center), Arvada Woman of the Year for 2010 (Courtesy Arvada Chamber of Commerce; see page 71), an early 1900s picnic held at the George Swadley farm (Courtesy Arvada Historical Society; see page 11).

LEGENDARY LOCALS

OF

ARVADA

COLORADO

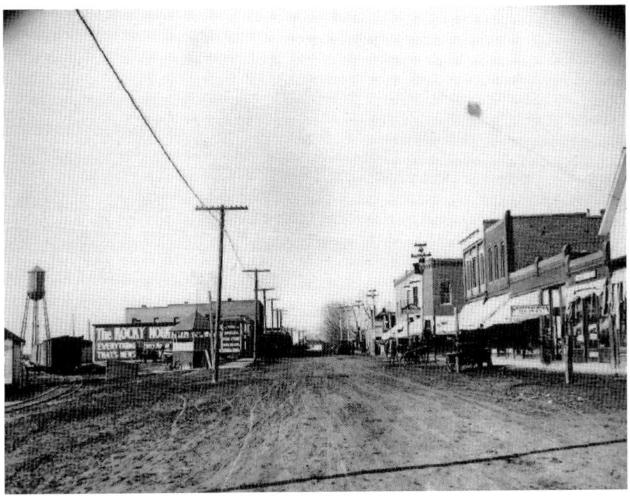

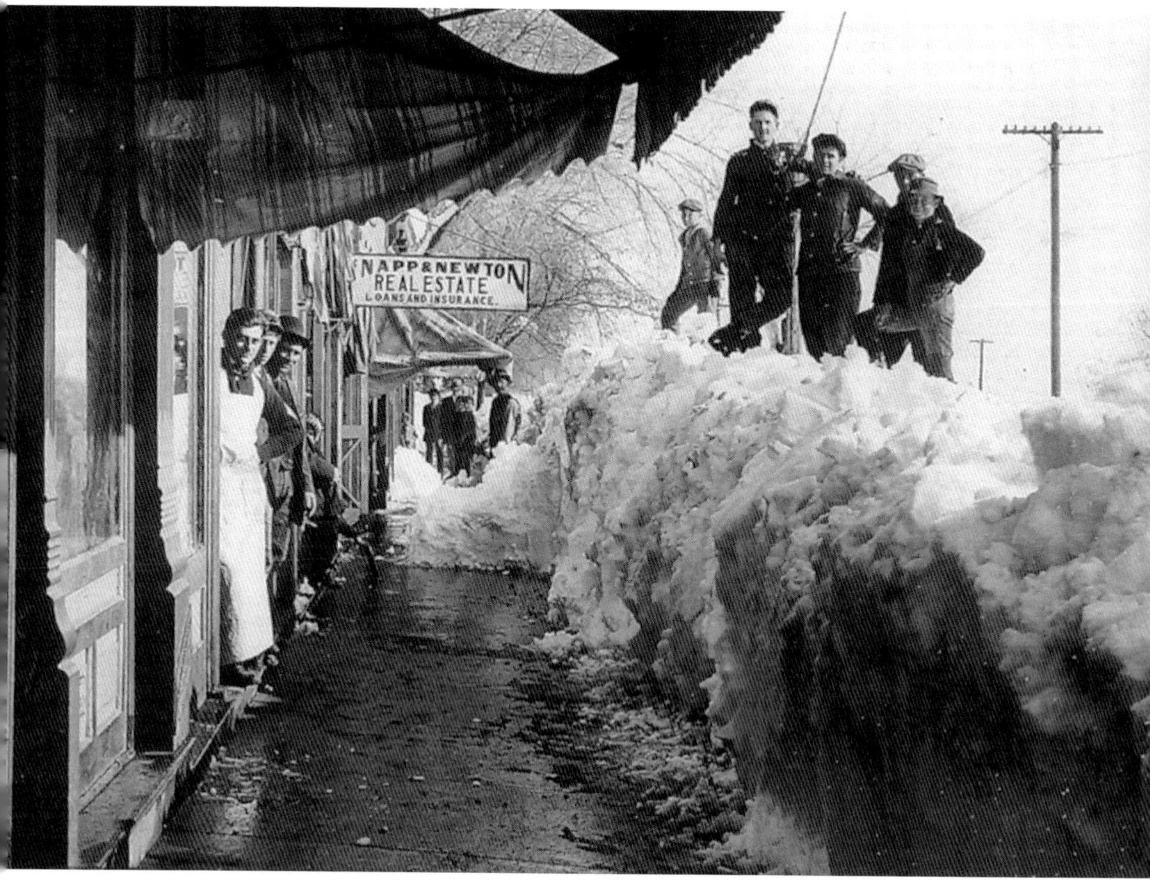

Blizzard of 1913
Shown is the Arvada blizzard of December 4, 1913. (Courtesy Arvada Historical Society.)

Page 1: Grandview Avenue
This view was taken looking west on Grandview Avenue in the early 1900s. (Courtesy Arvada Historical Society.)

CONTENTS

ACKNOWLEDGMENTS

Thank you to the Arvada Historical Society, Arvada Chamber of Commerce, Bonnie Thomas, Stan Stewart, Matthew Prythero, Betty Szekely, Beverly Shirley, Deb and Dee Williams, the Sedlmayr family, Nick Skinner Jr., KATV-8, Arvada Presbyterian Church, Erin Vosgien, Larry Peterson, and the City of Arvada.

All photographs were provided by the Arvada Historical Society unless otherwise noted.

Thanks and love to my family for supporting my dreams and to Fidel Lucero for his encouragement and words of wisdom.

INTRODUCTION

In 1850, California was admitted to the Union as the 31st state, Millard Fillmore was sworn in as the 13th president of the United States following the death of President Tyler, and *The Scarlet Letter* by Nathaniel Hawthorne was published. On June 22 of that year, Lewis Ralston, a Georgia prospector, found about a third of an ounce of gold (worth about $5 in 1850 money) in a tributary of Clear Creek in what would become central Colorado. At that time, Cheyenne and Arapaho tribes still roamed the area, and Anglo inhabitants were few. On June 23, Ralston and his fellow travelers continued on to the California gold fields but not before the creek where the gold discovery was made was christened Ralston Creek. Out of this first documented gold strike in the Rocky Mountain area grew a settlement called Ralston Point, where agriculture instead of gold flourished.

On December 1, 1870, Benjamin Wadsworth and Louis Reno plated the former Ralston Point, now called Arvada. At the time, the population was 100 residents. With the arrival of the Colorado Central Railroad, Arvada acquired its first post office, with Wadsworth as the first postmaster. From there, the business district made up of Railroad Street (Grandview Avenue) and Centre Street (Olde Wadsworth Boulevard) sprang up.

Incorporation in 1904 led to major improvements to the town. A town marshal was hired, electric and telephone service soon was provided, and a town board was launched to administer and enforce city ordinances. In 1910, the Arvada Water Tower began providing residents with quality artesian water. Education has been vital to Arvada since the earliest pioneers settled in the area. In 1863, the area's first school was started in a log cabin on the John Wolff homestead near present-day I-70 and Wadsworth Bypass. The first schoolhouse in Arvada proper was built in 1882, and the brick building at the corner of Olde Wadsworth and Fifty-seventh Avenue still stands. Today, Arvada has 4 high schools, 5 middle schools, 22 elementary schools, and 2 charter schools.

Arvada in the 1920s and 1930s was known as the celery capital of the world. In 1922, Pascal celery grown by Albert Bacher was sent to the White House to be enjoyed by President Harding with his Thanksgiving dinner. Four years later, Pres. Calvin Coolidge dined on celery raised by S.A. Lombardi.

In 1925, an Arvada tradition began. To celebrate the first paved road between Denver and Arvada, the Arvada Chamber of Commerce planned a fall celebration. Agriculture exhibits, a football game, raffle tickets dropped from an airplane, and a street dance were among the events planned. All signs pointed to a great festival for October 17. Then, on the night of October 16, the snow came. An overnight blizzard covered the town. In their best "the show must go on" fashion, the people of Arvada went to work clearing the streets and setting up so the first Arvada Harvest Festival could proceed.

That's the kind of pluck and determination Arvadans have always been made of. With ingenuity, hometown pride, talent, industriousness, compassion, and character, the Arvadans have changed history not only in their own hometown but also often in the world.

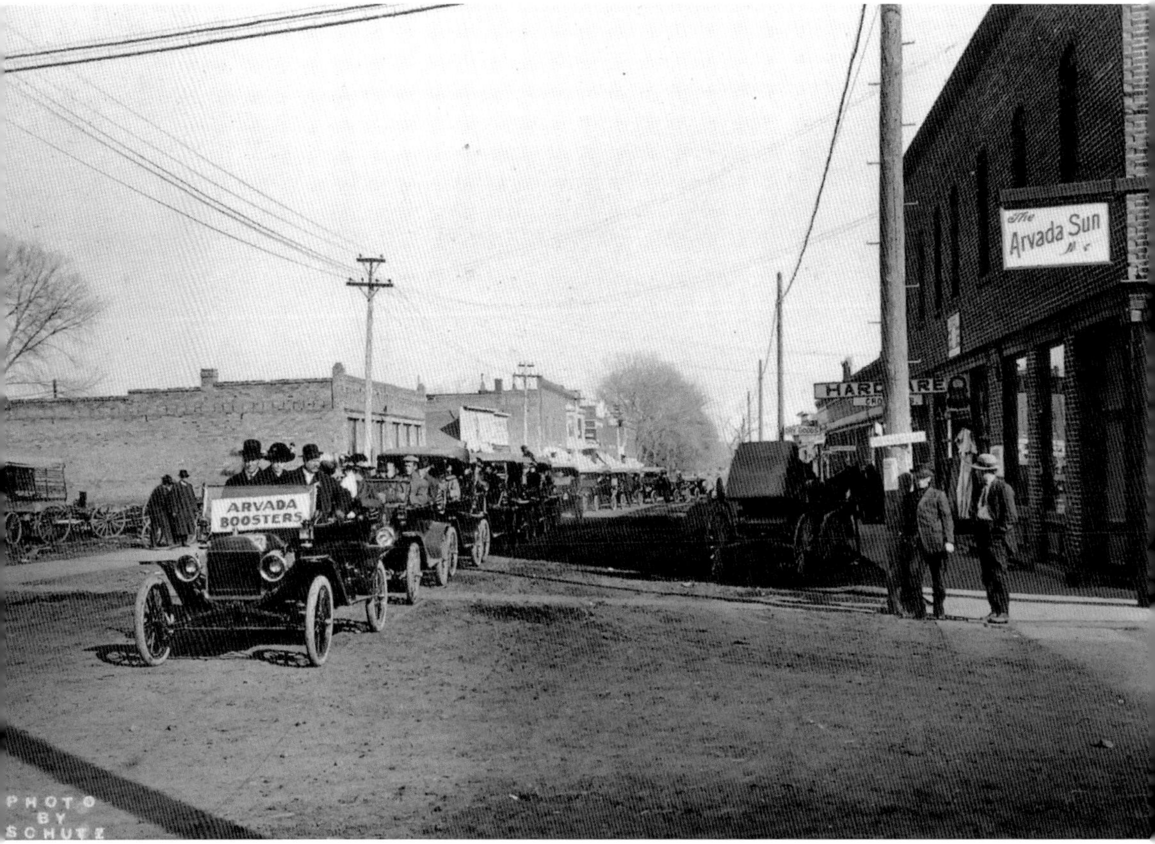

A.L. Davis
Arvada businessman A.L. Davis leads an Arvada Boosters parade down Grandview Avenue in 1915.

CHAPTER ONE

Pioneers

From the Native Americans who called the banks of Clear Creek home to the gold-seekers and early settlers of the 1850s, Arvada has been inhabited by a host of diverse individuals.

The legendary Hackberry Tree stood silent watch over the early settlers. John B. Wolff established the area's first school. Benjamin Wadsworth, who, along with Louis Reno, platted the town of Arvada in November 1870, named the town after his brother in law. The first city park in Arvada was formed from land bequeathed to the city in 1919 by pioneer Clemancy McIlvoy. Farmers and ranchers like George Swadley, Thomas Weaver, John Juchem, and George Bayer made their mark on the burgeoning community. These pioneers also donated land for schools and churches and held political office.

If not for these individuals' dreams of a better community and love of their hometown, Arvada would not be blessed with the many landmarks, homes, and legends that make up its rich history.

Thomas Weaver Family

In 1880, Thomas and Emma Weaver, along with their four children, homesteaded on 160 acres north of Arvada. Many times thereafter, Thomas left his family to seek his fortune in gold. In those times—according to Harriet Weaver Bueb, Thomas and Emma's granddaughter—it was up to Emma to keep the farm up and running. Thomas Weaver donated an acre of his land to became the old North School at present-day Sixty-eighth Avenue and Saulsbury Street. It was there the Weaver children and grandchildren attended school. Harriet's father, John, a successful rancher and operator of the Lone Tree Dairy, took over the farm as an adult. John and his wife, Anna, had three children. Gertrude was born in 1893 and Harriet in 1896, and the lone boy, Thomas, came along 12 years later.

After her high school graduation from Arvada in 1911, Gertrude attended Teacher's College in Greeley. Her first teaching job was in 1914 in Antonito, Colorado, in the extreme southern part of the state. It was there that the raven-haired Gertrude was introduced to Robert Edward Barlow, son of a local cattleman. The couple married at the Weaver Ranch on July 7, 1915. Less than three weeks later, on Sunday, July 25, Gertrude Weaver Barlow died in a New Mexico cattle camp under mysterious circumstances that are still not solved almost 100 years later. Harriet Weaver married William Bueb in 1918, and the couple became the third generation of Weavers to live on the original homestead. Harriet passed away in 1974.

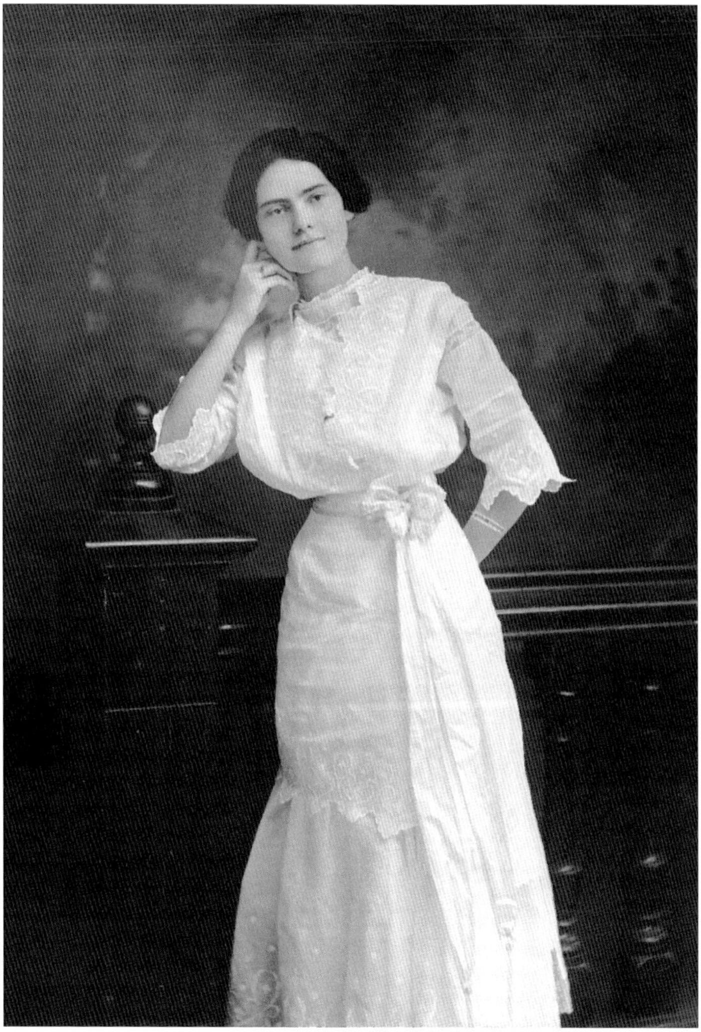

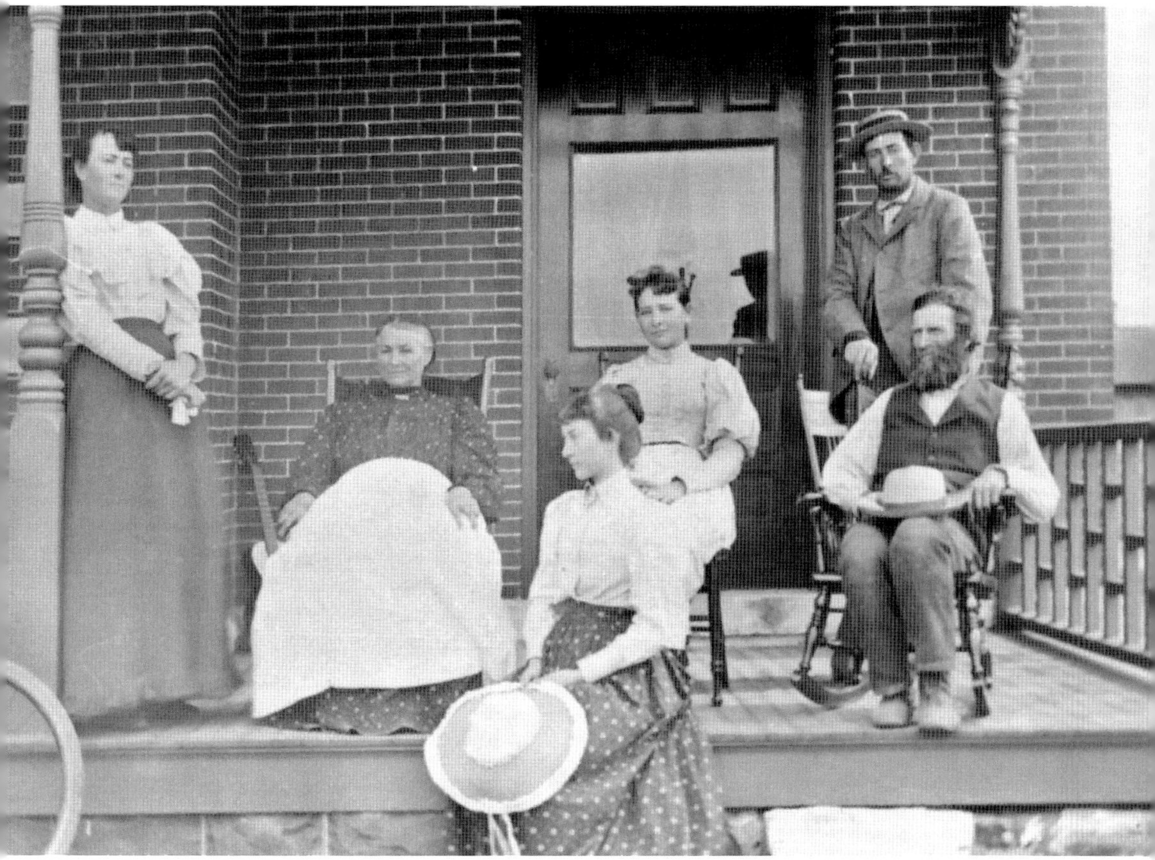

George Swadley
One of the most prolific and innovative of Arvada's early pioneers, George Swadley fully served his community for over 40 years.

Born in Virginia in 1837, Swadley apprenticed as a carpenter until the 1850s gold rush fever hit. Heading west, he settled near Ralston Point (present-day Arvada) in the winter of 1859. In the fall of 1860, Swadley purchased a $50 log cabin that had once belonged to Horace Greeley and moved it on 80 acres of land he owned. In October 1866, George Swadley married Mary Ellen Pollack. The couple moved into a nine-room, two-story frame house that Swadley had built north of his log cabin. The next few years saw Swadley prosper as a farmer. He developed a strain of corn called Swadley corn. He built a large brick house in 1894. The family became well known for holding annual pioneer picnics on their land. George and Mary Ellen were parents to five children: Clara Belle, William, Laura, Sarah, and John. John passed away at the age of five months. George Swadley passed away on January 12, 1906. At the time of his death, Swadley was president of the First National Bank of Arvada.

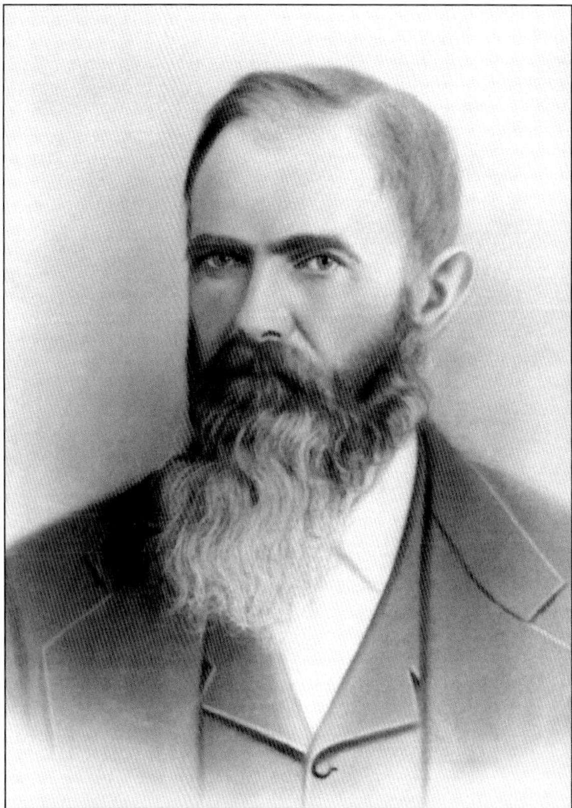

Benjamin Wadsworth
The town of Arvada was founded on a parcel of land owned by Benjamin Wadsworth, who was born in New York in 1827. In 1859, he was in Empire, Colorado, where he bought and sold mining claims. Wadsworth and his family settled in what would become Arvada in 1869. Along with Louis Reno, Wadsworth platted the town of Arvada in 1870. It was Mary Ann Wadsworth, Benjamin's wife, who gave the town the name Arvada, after her brother in law, Hiram Arvada Haskin. Wadsworth became the town's first postmaster. Besides farming, Wadsworth was also involved in real estate in Arvada. In 1876, Wadsworth donated the land for a two-room schoolhouse, the first school in Arvada Township. The building of the Arvada Methodist Church was another of Wadsworth's endeavors. In April 1893, Wadsworth went to Denver in his wagon to have a broken stained-glass church window fixed. On his return to Arvada, a stray dog bit his horse's nose, causing the wagon to jump and Wadsworth to fall out, hitting his head on a curb. He died from his injuries on April 12, 1893.

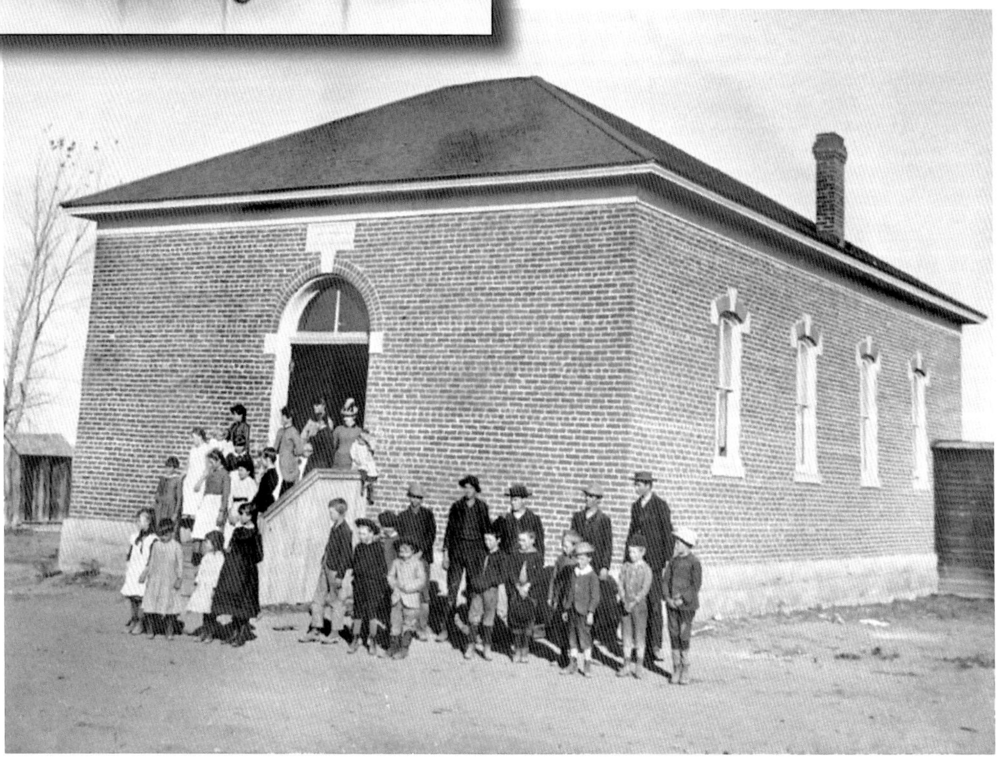

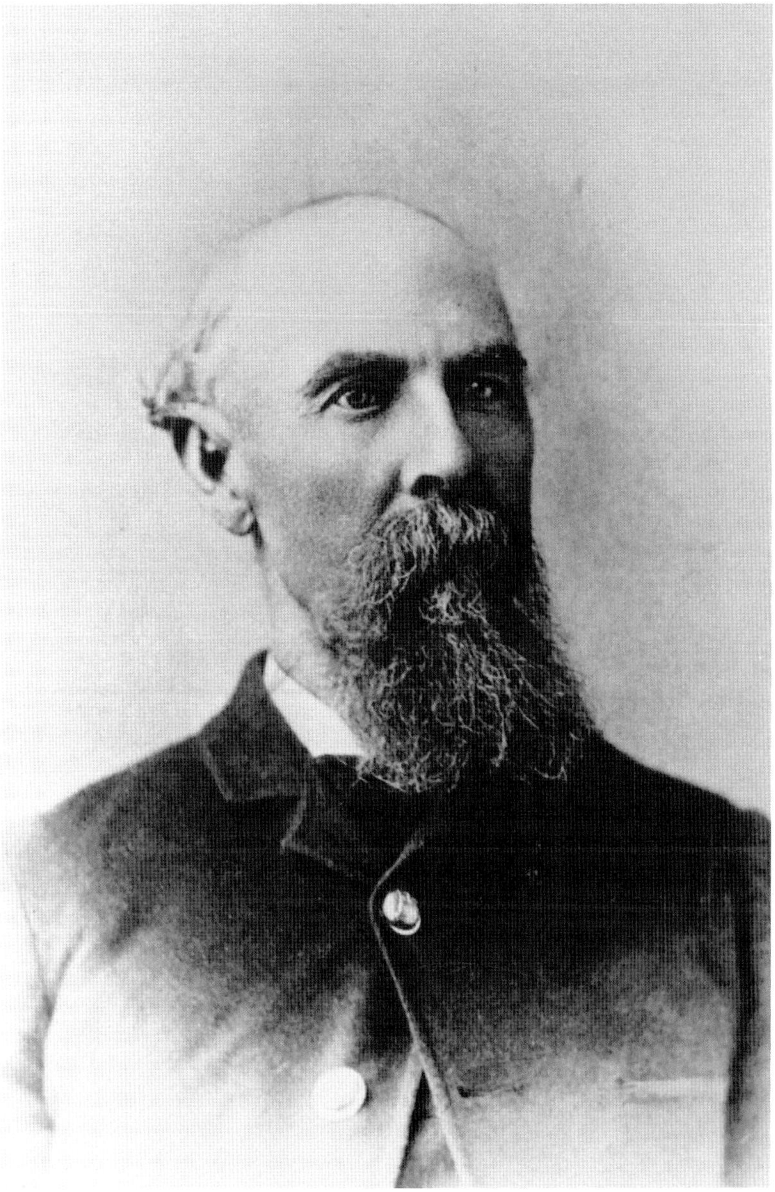

Louis Reno

Arvada cofounder Louis Reno was integral in establishing Arvada as a successful town in the late 1870s. Born in Pennsylvania on February 2, 1833, Reno served as a drummer boy in the Union army from 1861 until 1863. His brother John had already ventured west and settled in Colorado. It was John's letters home to his family of the beauty and opportunities in Colorado that led Louis, his father, stepmother, and five half sisters to settle there in 1863. Louis began homesteading on 40 acres of land west of that owned by Benjamin Wadsworth. Reno and Wadsworth saw the potential in the land they called home, and in 1870, they platted the town of Arvada. Reno wed Matilda Otto in 1877, and the couple had five children. The youngest child died at five months of age, and Matilda passed away from cancer some time later. Reno made his living in real estate, selling off lots of his original 40 acres. He supported incorporation and lived to see Arvada's in 1904. Louis Reno died on May 15, 1906.

Clemancy McIlvoy

The Arvada park and house that bears the name of McIlvoy was donated to the city by Clemancy McIlvoy, who—along with her husband, Dennis—made the town her home in her golden years.

Clemancy Davis was born on November 19, 1834, in Indiana. She wed Dennis McIlvoy in 1854. Shortly after their wedding, the newlyweds headed west in search of gold. Clemency is said the have been the first white woman in the mining town of Central City, Colorado. After coming up empty in Colorado, the McIlvoys followed the gold trail to Montana. Again, luck did not shine on the McIlvoys. They decided to settle in Colorado. First they homesteaded on a farm that sat at present day Sixty-fourth Avenue and Miller Street. In 1897, Dennis and Clemancy moved to Arvada.

The couple then built the house that stands at 7307 Grandview Avenue. It is said that the property sported a beautiful garden area tended to lovingly by Clemancy. With her cane hanging over her arm, a cigar in her mouth, and her dog by her side, Clemancy would happily greet the neighborhood children. To the youngsters of Arvada, Dennis and Clemancy came to be known as Uncle and Auntie Mac. Clemancy would spend hours entertaining the kids with stories of her gold rush and pioneer days.

Dennis passed away in March 1913, leaving Clemancy to tend to the old homestead. On May 12, 1919, Clemancy bestowed the deed to three acres of property north of her residence to the City of Arvada with the understanding that the land was to become a public park. The formal opening of McIlvoy Park was held on August 11, 1922.

Clemancy never got to see her dream of a park come to fruition. She passed away at her home on July 14, 1921, after suffering a fall. The McIlvoy house has been used as a public library and an American Legion post and now is home to the Arvada Historical Society.

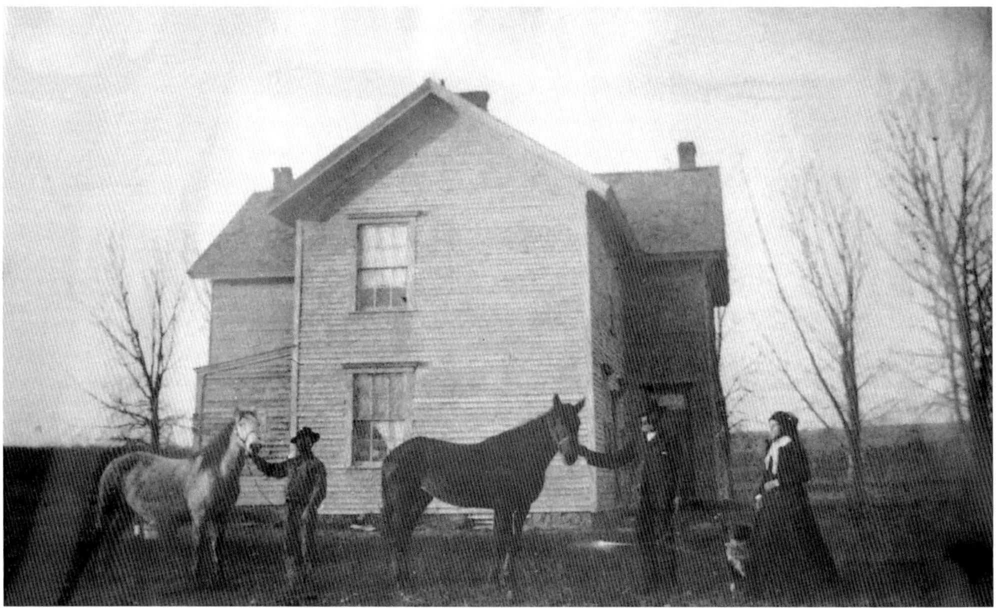

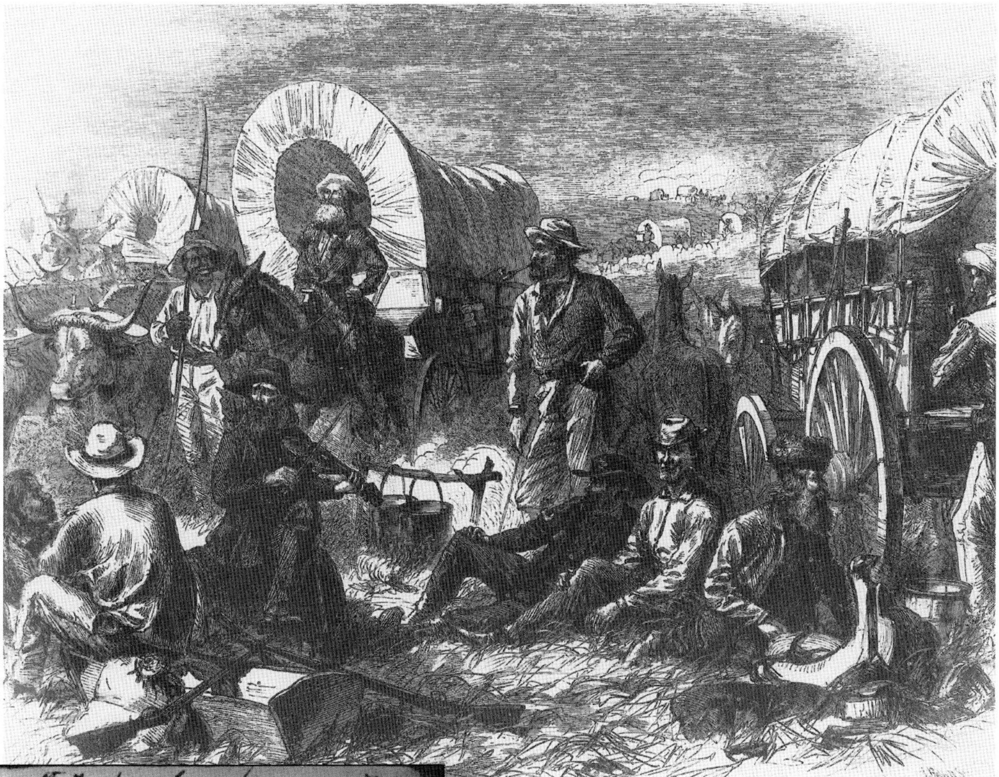

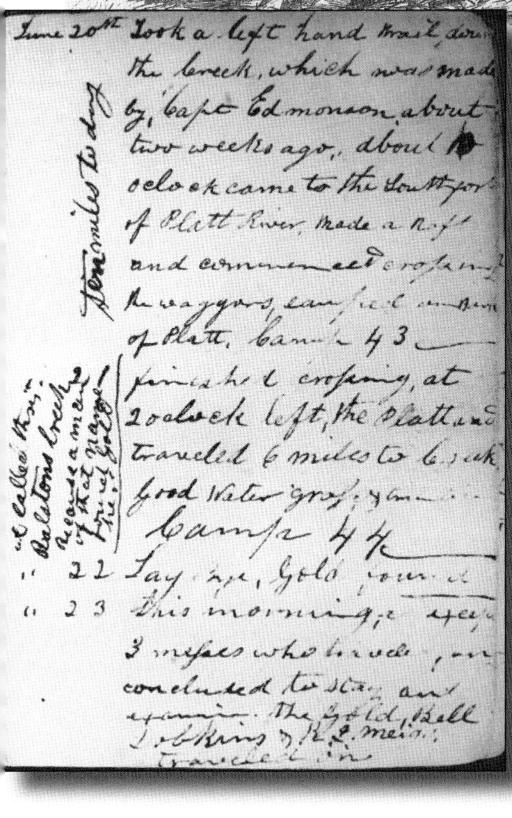

June 20th Took a left hand trail, down the creek, which was made by, Capt Edmonson, about two weeks ago, about 10 oclock came to the South fork of Platte River, made a raft and commenced crossing the waggons, [illegible] of Platte. Camp 43 —
finished crossing, at 2 oclock left the Platte and traveled 6 miles to Creek, good Water grass [illegible]
Camp 44 —
" 22 Lay up, Gold found
" 23 this morning [illegible] 3 messes who traveled [illegible] concluded to stay and examine. The Gold, Bell [illegible] & R.L. men [illegible] traveled in

Ten miles to day

we called this; Ralstons Creek because a man of that name found gold

Lewis Ralston

Arvada grew out of Colorado's first documented gold discovery on June 22, 1850. Bit by gold fever, Lewis Ralston, a Georgia farmer, headed west with a wagon train that included many Cherokees. During a layover of the wagon train on the banks of Clear Creek, Ralston dipped his gold pan in the water and panned out about a third of an ounce of gold. The group named this creek after Ralston and continued its journey westward. Lewis returned to Ralston Creek in 1858 with the Green Russell party. After dismal results panning for gold, and because of the constant fear of Indian attacks, Ralston and others headed back to Georgia. Never again did Ralston journey west, and he never saw what became of the town named Ralston Point, which became Arvada in 1870.

Schneider Family

German-born Moritz and Julia Schneider settled in Arvada in 1885. Settling on 10 acres that were purchased from Arvadan Thomas Sellman for $200 each, the Schneiders soon built their first home. Eight children were born to Moritz and Julia, and all except Mary, the eldest, were born in Arvada. The family made their living from selling the produce they raised, going daily in the summer and weekly in the fall and winter to the market in Denver. One of the Schneiders' sons, Emil, served on the Jefferson County Board of Commissioners in 1948 and 1952. A devoted Catholic, Emil helped dig the foundation for St. Anne's Catholic Church in 1920, and he and his wife, Marie, sang in the St. Anne's choir for 50 years. In 1955, Emil sold five acres of the family land and donated another five acres for the site of Spirit of Christ Catholic Church in north Arvada. Emil Schneider passed away in January 1989 at the age of 97.

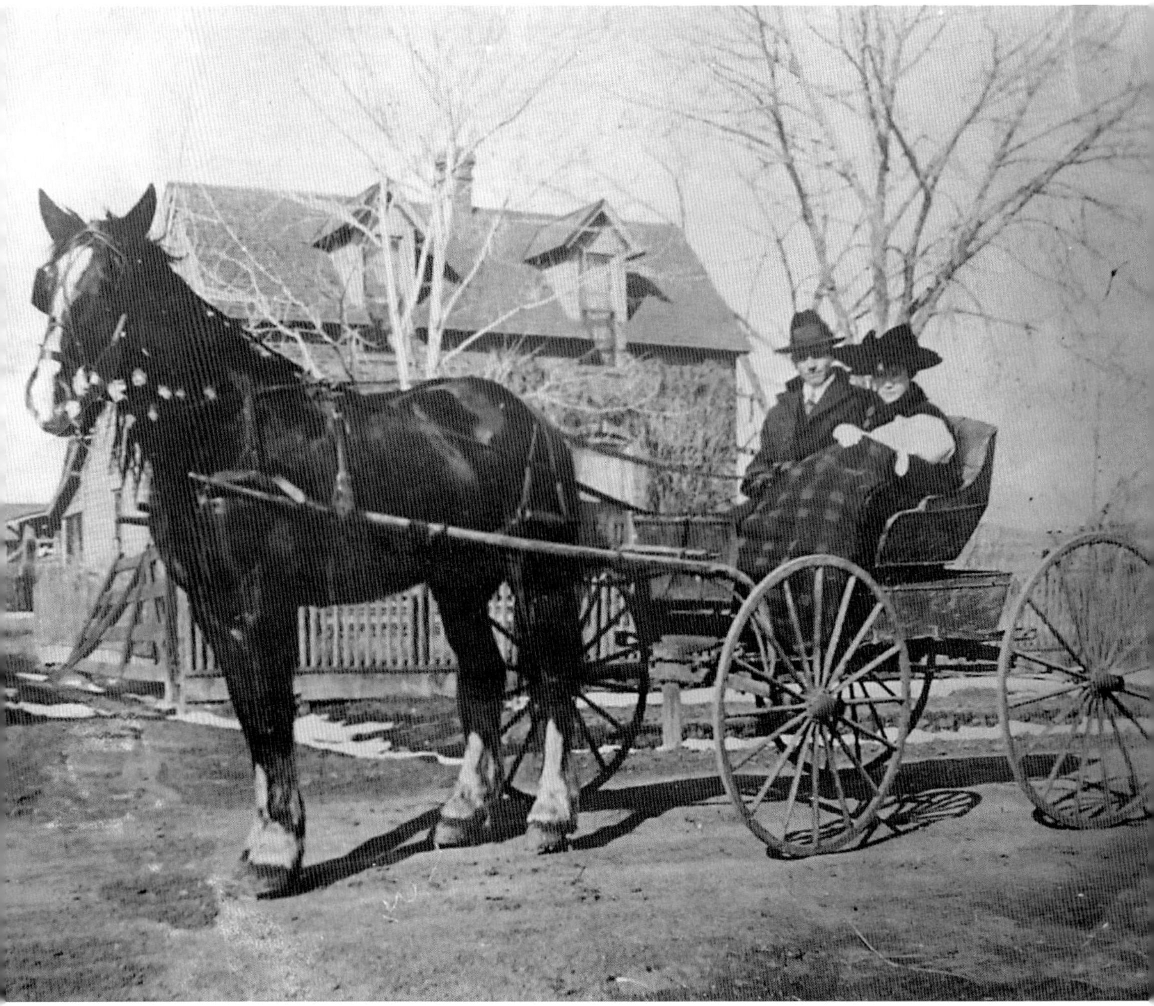

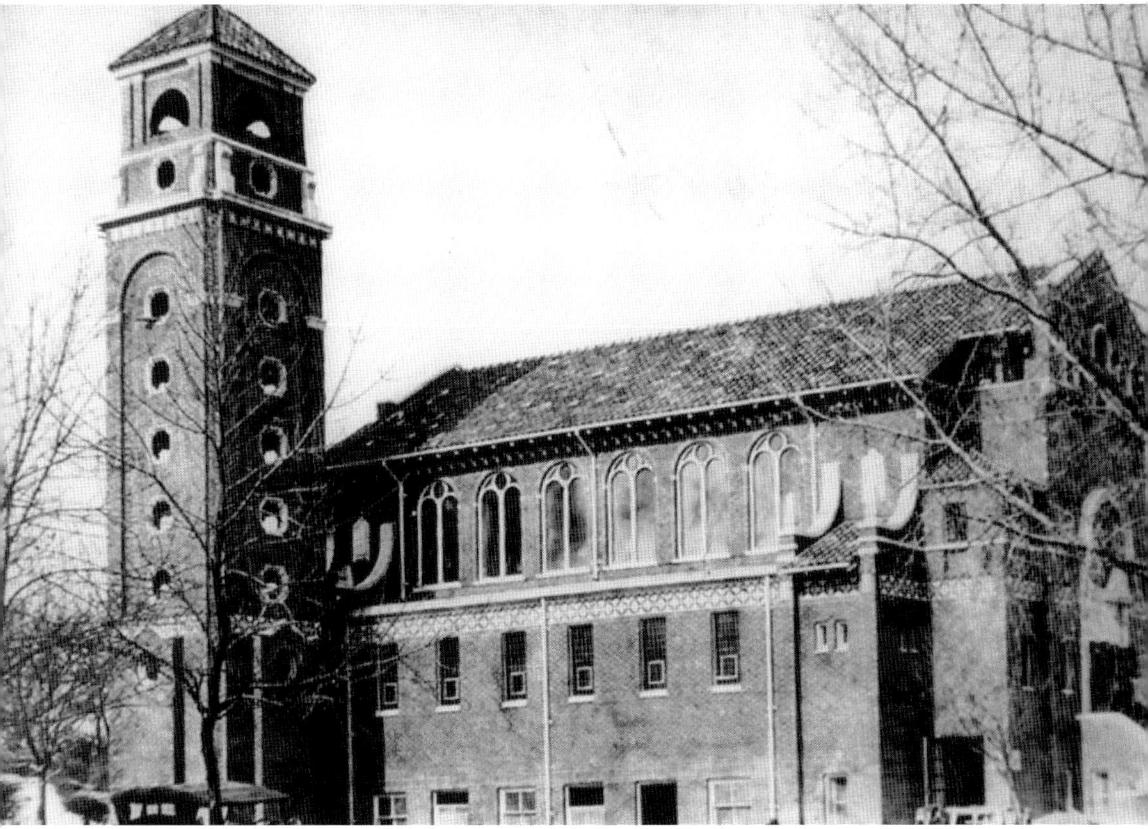

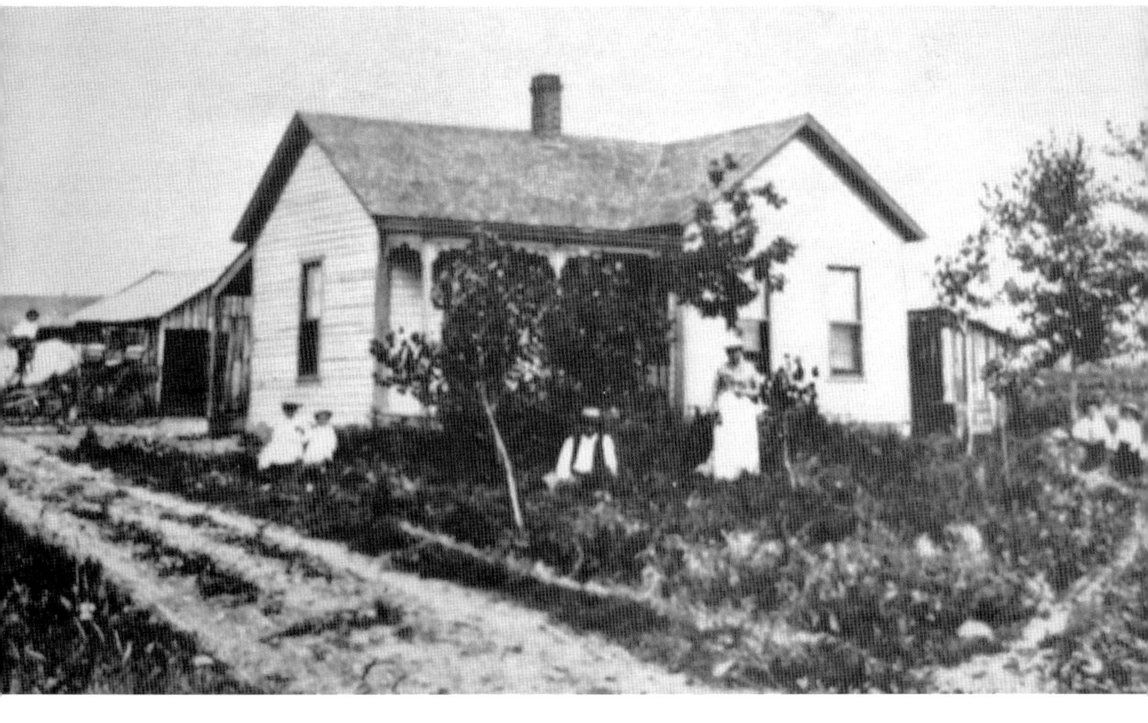

Juchem Family
John Juchem, the royal gardener for Germany's Frederick Wilhelm IV, quarreled with the king in 1858 and was fired. To avoid being conscripted into the Prussian army, John fled to America. Settling in the area that would become Arvada, John used his gardening skills to raise produce. Buying land, he built a cabin and reserved water rights, the first to do so in the area, it is said. In 1862, John traveled to St. Louis, where he wed Anna Woeber. The newlyweds traveled for six weeks by covered wagon to John's cabin in Colorado. Sometime in the 1860s, Juchem built a large home at current day Fifty-second Avenue and Garrison Street in Arvada. The Juchem ranch consisted of 400 acres of land. John Juchem was one of the area's most prosperous farmers. Henry Juchem, John and Anna's only son, became a politician as an adult and operated the Juchem Red and White Grocery Store in Arvada for many years.

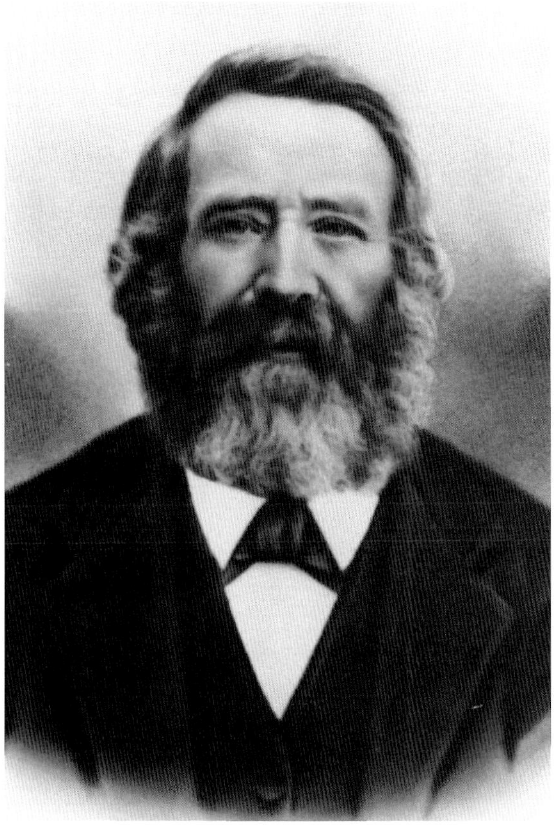

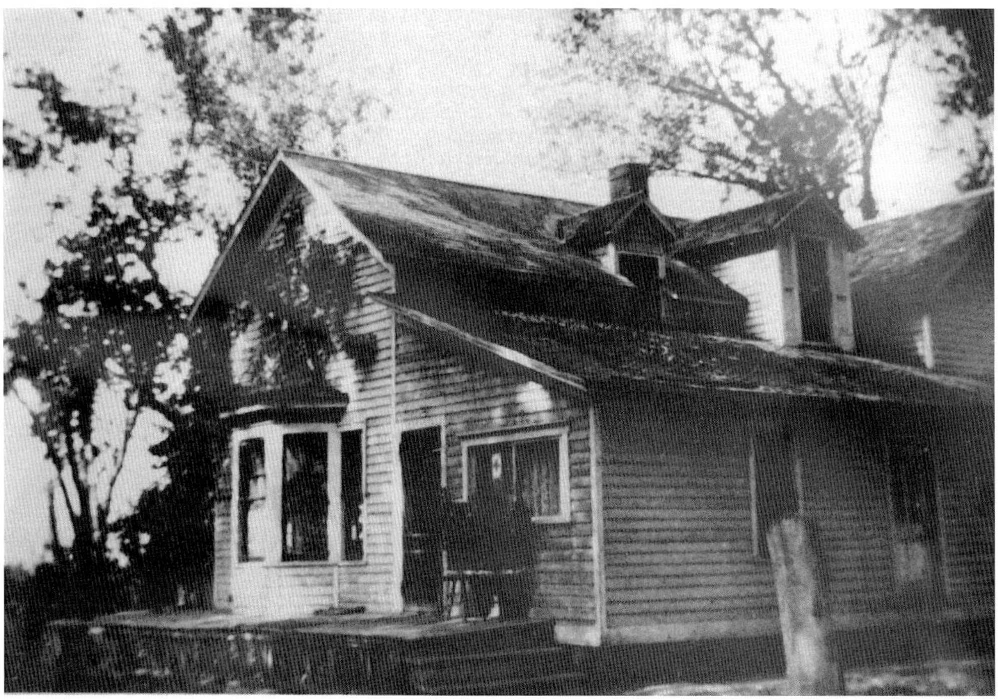

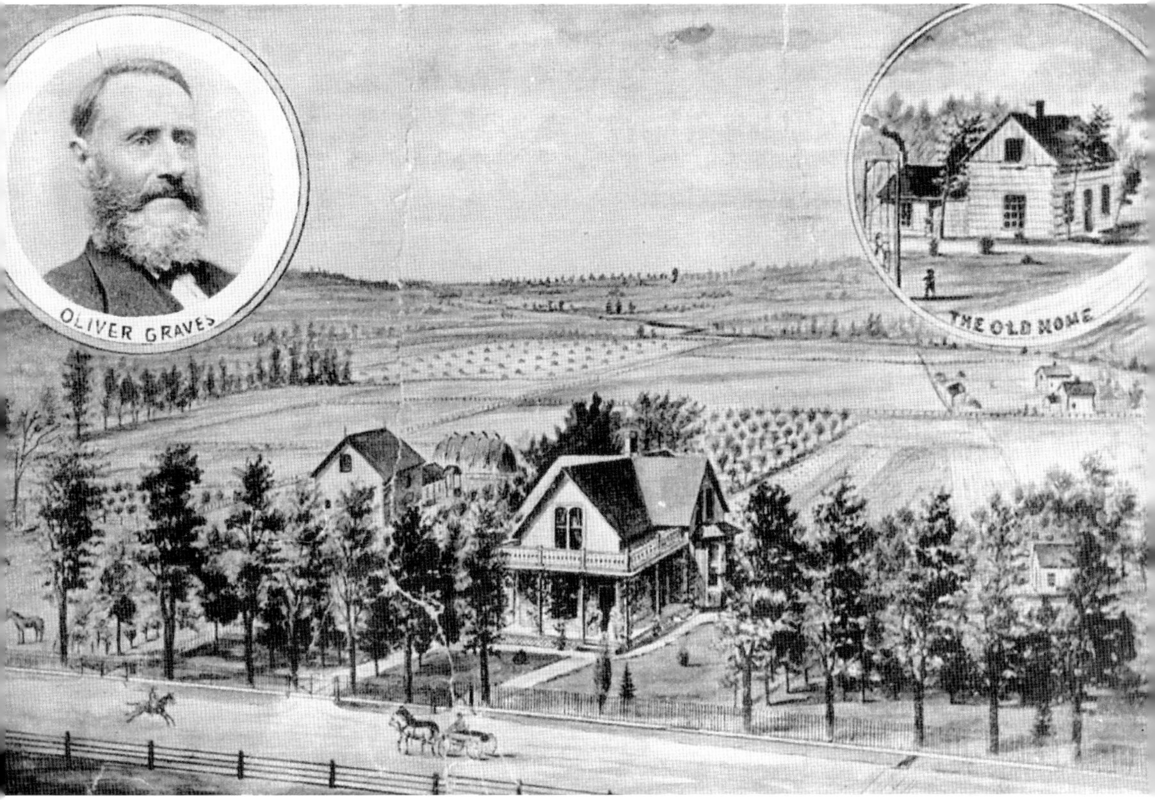

Graves Family

One of Arvada's earliest settlers, Oliver Graves, and later his son William became well-established citizens. Oliver Graves moved his family to Colorado from Illinois in 1860 by covered wagon. On this journey, Indians became enamored of Graves's daughter Emily and asked to "buy" her. The natives left telling Graves they would return the following day for Emily. The Graves family traveled all night and the next day without stopping to distance themselves from the Indians. The family arrived intact in Colorado soon after.

Upon his settling in Arvada in January 1861, Oliver Graves made a ranch claim of 160 acres south of Grandview Avenue on what is currently Marshall Street. The family became known for Graves Grove, a lovely spot with beautiful flowers that became a place for town gatherings, picnics, and parties. In 1867, Oliver Graves became a member of the school board. The first Methodist church services in Arvada took place at the Graves log cabin in 1863.

Oliver and his wife, Lucy, had nine children. Of those nine, three had passed away before the family came to Colorado. Graves's son William apprenticed as a blacksmith in his youth and worked in both Golden and Denver in that trade. Coming back to Arvada to help with the family farm, William went into the threshing business, buying and renting out the farming implement.

He also opened a blacksmith shop on the corner of Grandview Avenue and Wadsworth Boulevard in 1868. William Graves was elected Jefferson County commissioner in 1892 and served as the president of the Arvada School Board for 15 years.

Oliver Graves died on May 4, 1896. William passed away on May 17, 1912, at the age of 66.

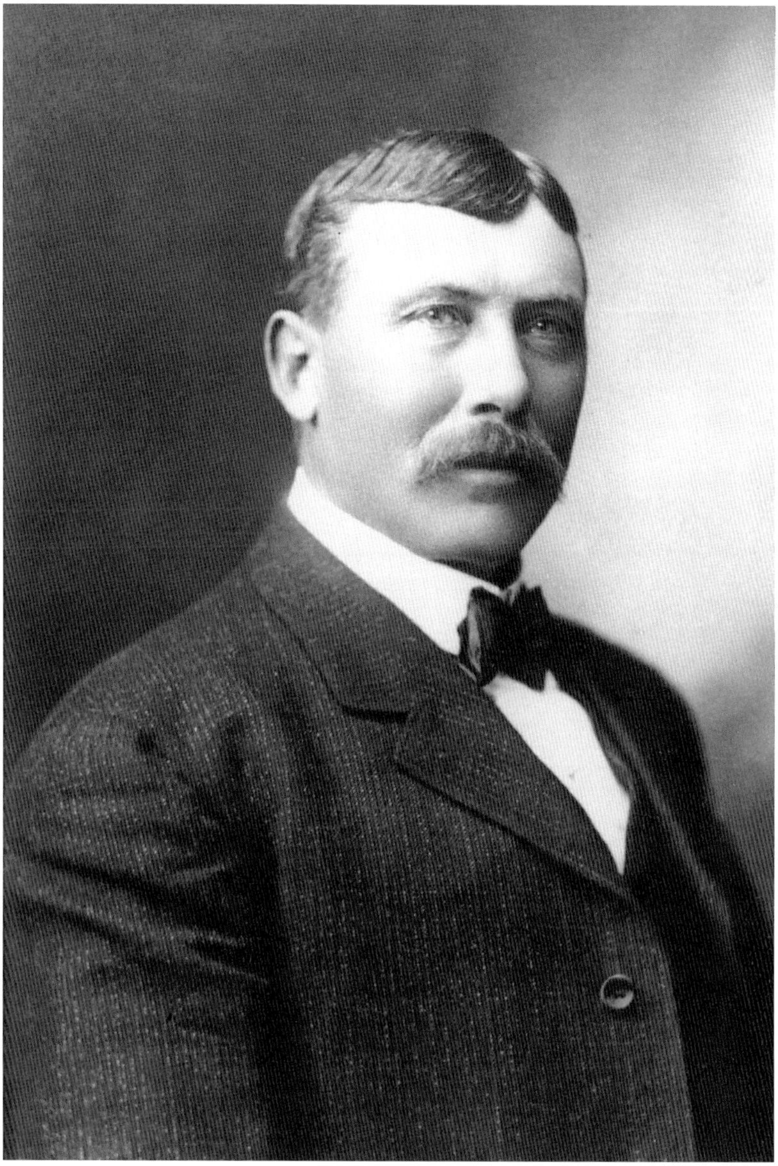

Bayer Family

This early Arvada family started the original Arvada Dairy. George and Karoline Bayer came to Colorado in 1891 from Buffalo, New York. Soon after their arrival in Arvada, George started the Arvada Dairy from their farm at present day Fifty-fifth Avenue and Pierce Street. The milk wagon left the farm at 4:00 a.m. every morning to deliver milk to an area of western Denver known as Berkley at the time. The area that the Bayers owned for their cattle to graze was south of the C&S tracks at Marshall Street. The Bayers also raised strawberries and raspberries, which were sold in Denver. In a memoir written by Frank Bayer, George and Karoline's son, he recalled seeing Orville Wright flying in an exhibition flight from Golden to Denver in 1902. Part of the route went over the Bayer farm. Karoline Bayer's father, Gottlieb Gunther, bought the land on which St. Anne's Catholic Church stands now in 1896. One of Frank's uncles, Louis Zeller, built the Wiebelt block on Grandview Avenue and owned a threshing machine that was used in the area.

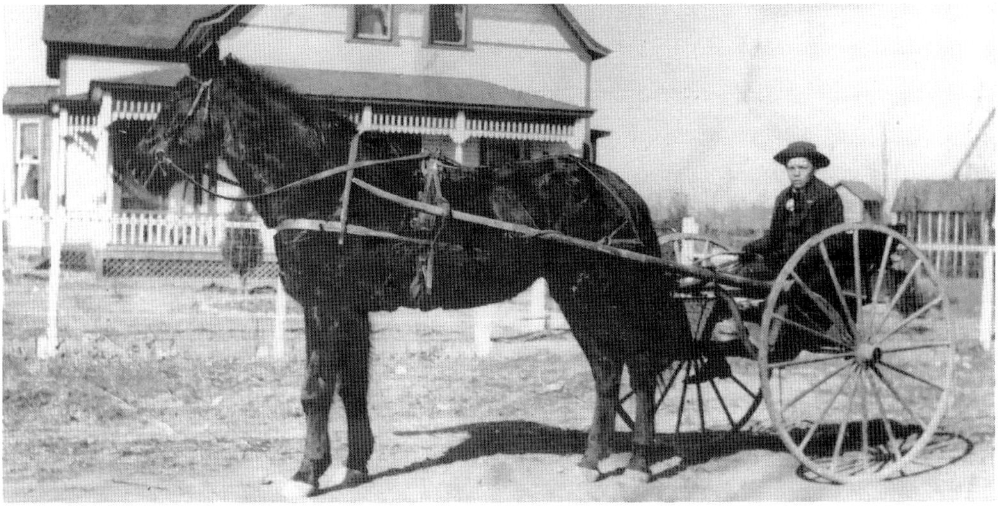

Aldis Bruce

An Arvada native, Bruce came from a pioneering Arvada family. John Bruce came to Arvada in the late 1880s to visit his sister. He met and married Eunice Ann Forsyth on March 27, 1889. Three children were born to John and Eunice Ann: Grace, Lyman, and Aldis, born on January 2, 1892. At a young age, Aldis delivered the *Denver Post*, his brother delivered the *Rocky Mountain News* and their father delivered a third Denver paper, the *Denver Republican*. Aldis attended school in Arvada. In 1914, Aldis was employed by J.T. Kennedy at his store on Grandview Avenue. In 1922, Aldis married Gertrude Lucas. The couple had one daughter, Eunice. In a 1977 interview, Bruce said he had worked many different jobs, including harvesting sugar beets, doing some "cowboying," and driving a laundry truck.

In that same interview, he spoke of his memories of his Arvada childhood. "The town was a cow pasture, I mean that. We raised pretty near everything ourselves. We had a cow or two, not only my family, but others, too. When we were done milking them, we'd let them go right in town. They grazed all around town. That's why I say Arvada was a cow pasture." Aldis Bruce passed away in 1981.

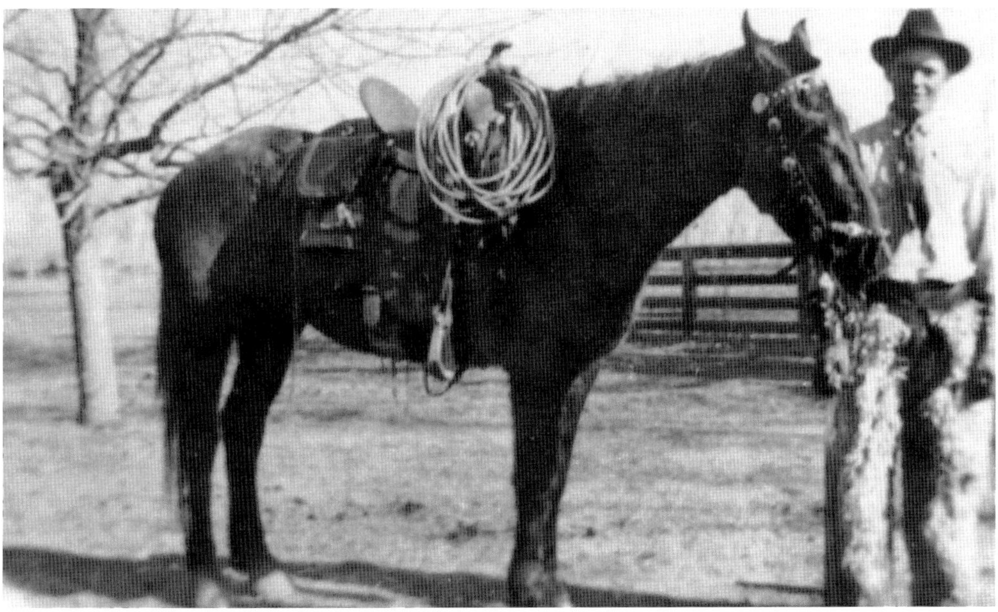

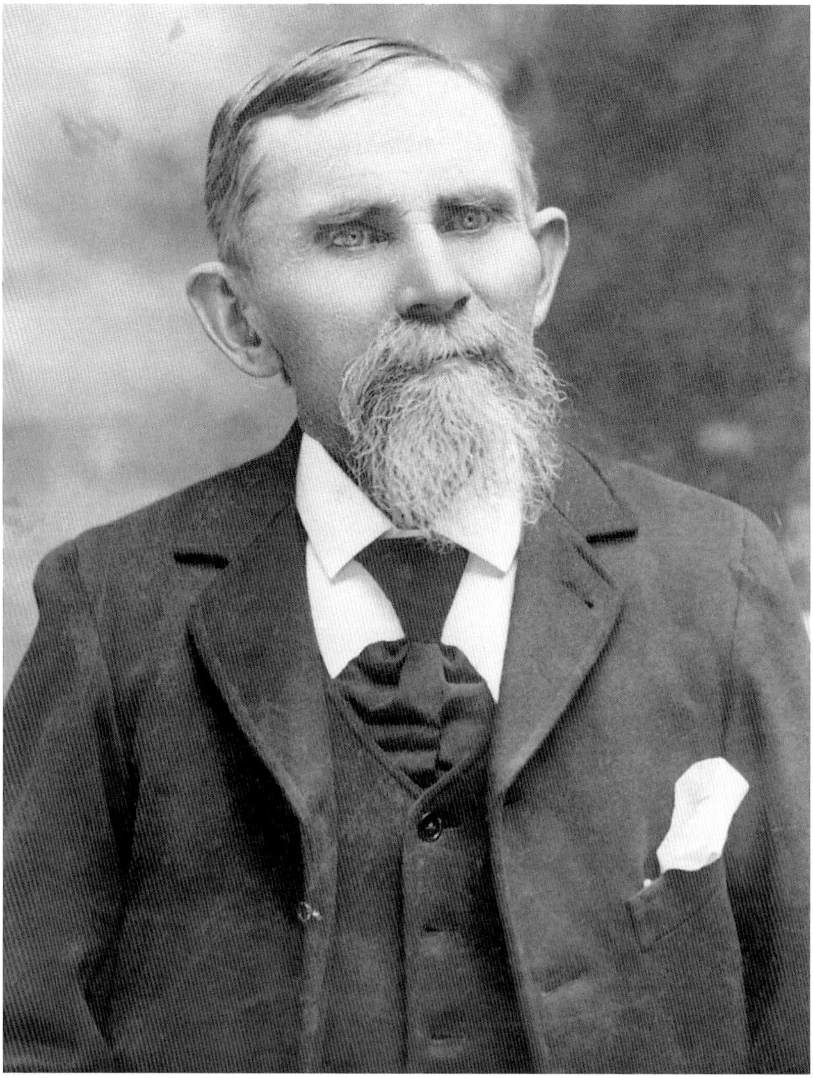

Thomas Sellman

Thomas Sellman settled in Arvada when it was still known as Ralston Point in 1865.

Thomas C. Sellman was born in Ann Arbor, Michigan, on February 25, 1835. After his parents' deaths, Sellman headed west in a wagon train. The trip from Michigan to Denver took 11 months, from September 1864 to August 1865. After reaching Colorado, Sellman proceeded to current-day Arvada, where he worked for the Rand family. The 1870 US census stated Sellman was still living in the Rand household. The 1880 census found Sellman on his own, and under occupation, it reads, "huckster." In 1869, Thomas Sellman was elected as the county assessor for Jefferson County, an office he held for two years. He also served as justice of the peace and road overseer. A lifelong bachelor, Sellman raised brothers Ike and James Truitt on his 160-acre farm northwest of Arvada. Sellman was a member of the Odd Fellows Lodge, and according to his obituary in the *Arvada Enterprise*, fellow members held birthday parties for him late in his life at which "he expressed great pleasure in being so honored." Thomas Sellman suffered from a fall in July 1915 that he never recovered from. He was tended to by the Truitt brothers for the last four years of his life.

Thomas C. Sellman passed away on August 31, 1919, in Arvada.

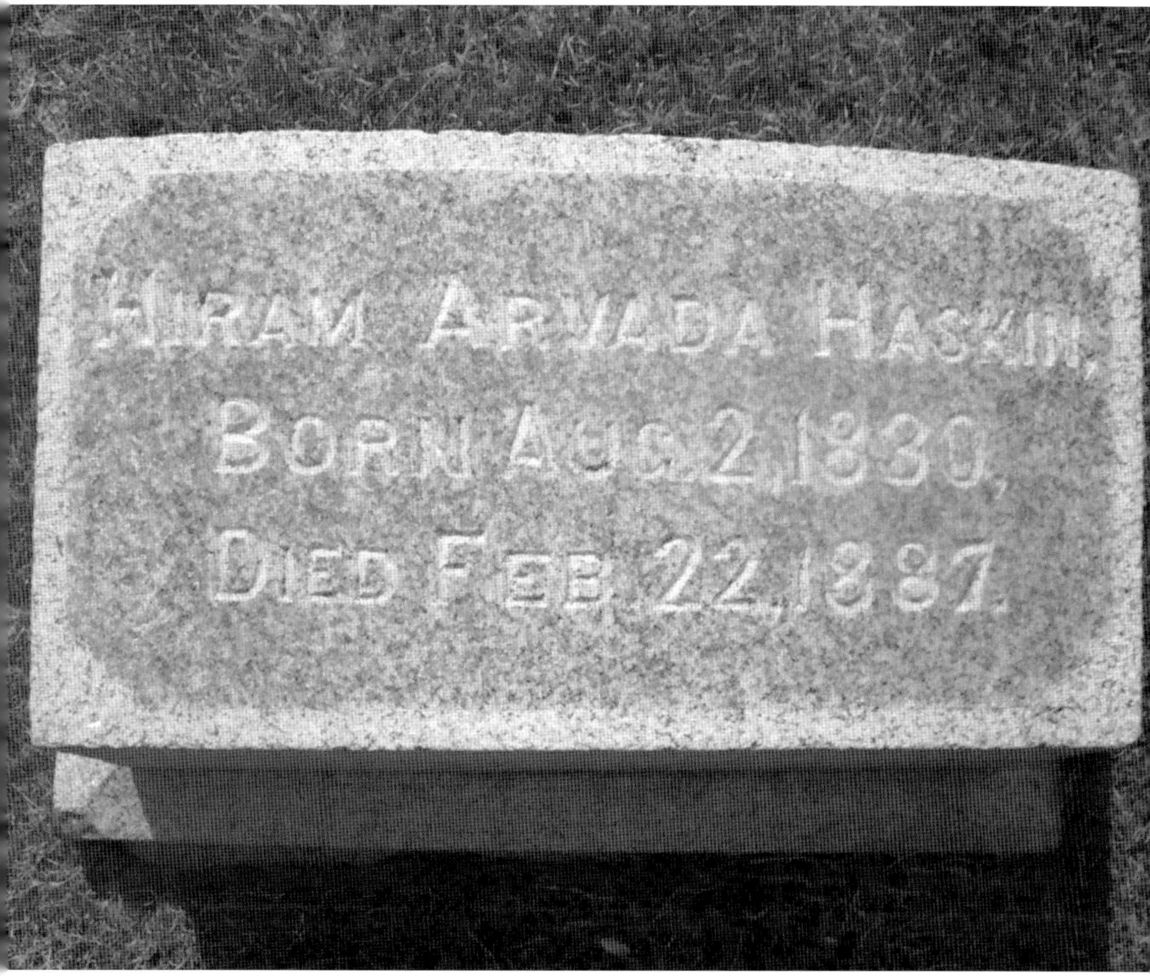

Hiram Arvada Haskin

Arvada's namesake, Hiram Arvada Haskin was the brother-in-law of town cofounder Benjamin Wadsworth.

Born August 2, 1830 in Essex County, New York, Haskin came to Colorado Territory in 1859. He wed Eliza Grove, it is believed, in the early 1860s. Hiram's profession was mining, and the couple lived in Georgetown and Empire, Colorado. Hiram and Eliza adopted their daughter Carrie in April 1867 in Idaho Springs. Hiram and Benjamin Wadsworth were partners in various mining ventures. It is unclear if the Haskin family ever lived in Arvada, but the 1880 US census states that Carrie Haskin was a member of the Wadsworth household that year.

Eliza Grove Haskin died on November 10, 1879. Hiram Arvada Haskin passed away on February 22, 1887. Both are buried in the Arvada Cemetery. (Author's collection.)

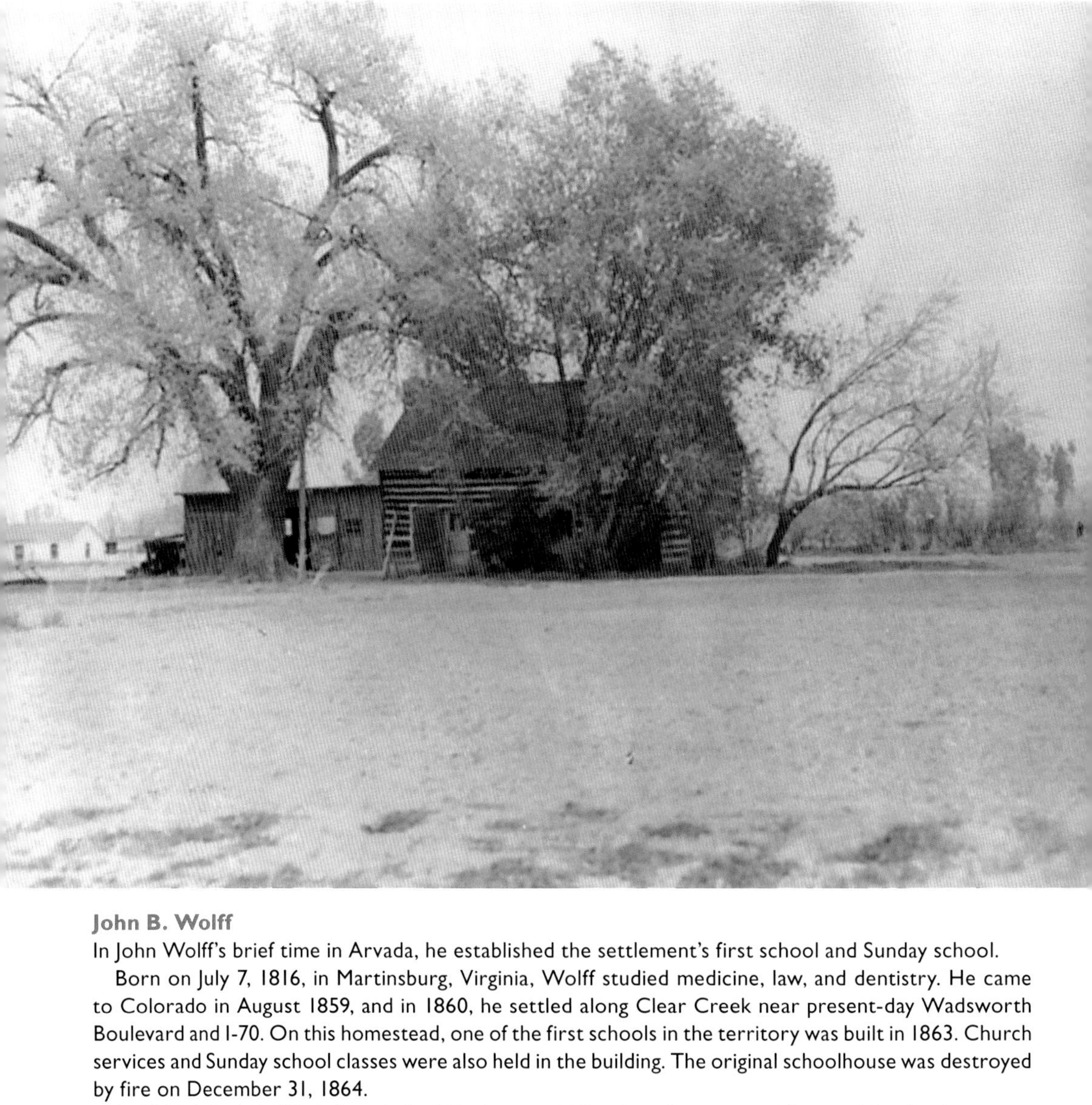

John B. Wolff

In John Wolff's brief time in Arvada, he established the settlement's first school and Sunday school.

Born on July 7, 1816, in Martinsburg, Virginia, Wolff studied medicine, law, and dentistry. He came to Colorado in August 1859, and in 1860, he settled along Clear Creek near present-day Wadsworth Boulevard and I-70. On this homestead, one of the first schools in the territory was built in 1863. Church services and Sunday school classes were also held in the building. The original schoolhouse was destroyed by fire on December 31, 1864.

In 1868, John Wolff left Arvada for Washington, DC, where he practiced law until his death.

Hackberry Tree

Legend has it that an Indian chief was killed in battle and buried north of present-day Arvada upon a hill. From a seed in the chief's medicine pouch grew a hackberry tree that could be seen for miles around. A landmark that guided travelers on stagecoaches and wagon trains, the "Lone Tree" on the hill became an Arvada icon. In 1937, it was decided that the route of Wadsworth Boulevard would go straight north instead of curving around Hackberry Hill, where the tree stood. An outcry from residents led to the decision to move the tree to McIlvoy Park. On January 26, the night before the tree was to be transported to the park, a road worker, Fred Fox, snuck in and cut the over-130-year-old tree down. In 1974, when Fox confessed to the vandalism, he stated that he cut the tree down because he was fed up with the townsfolk's effort to save the landmark.

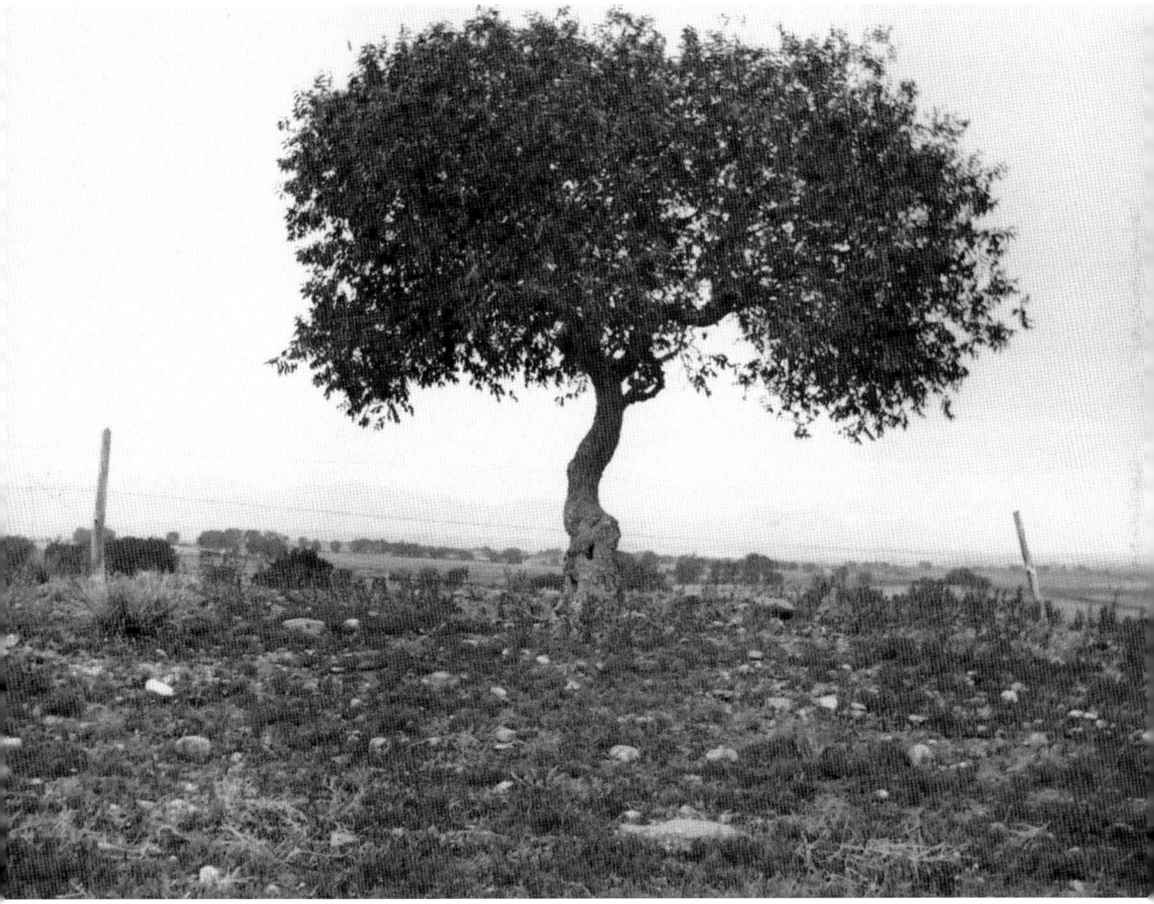

John Churches

John Churches was a leading citizen of Arvada in its early years. His farm is now a national and state historic site.

Born in England on August 8, 1823, John Churches and his wife, Mary Ann, settled on a 160-acre homestead in the Ralston Valley in 1862. Churches began farming and raising cattle and horses. He also turned their home into a way station for a stagecoach route. Churches constructed one of the area's first irrigation ditches. John and Mary Ann helped form the Enterprise Grange No. 25 in 1887. The building still stands at 11427 West Seventy-fourth Avenue. In 1998, the Churches Ranch was added to the National Register of Historic Places.

John Churches died on August 12, 1910.

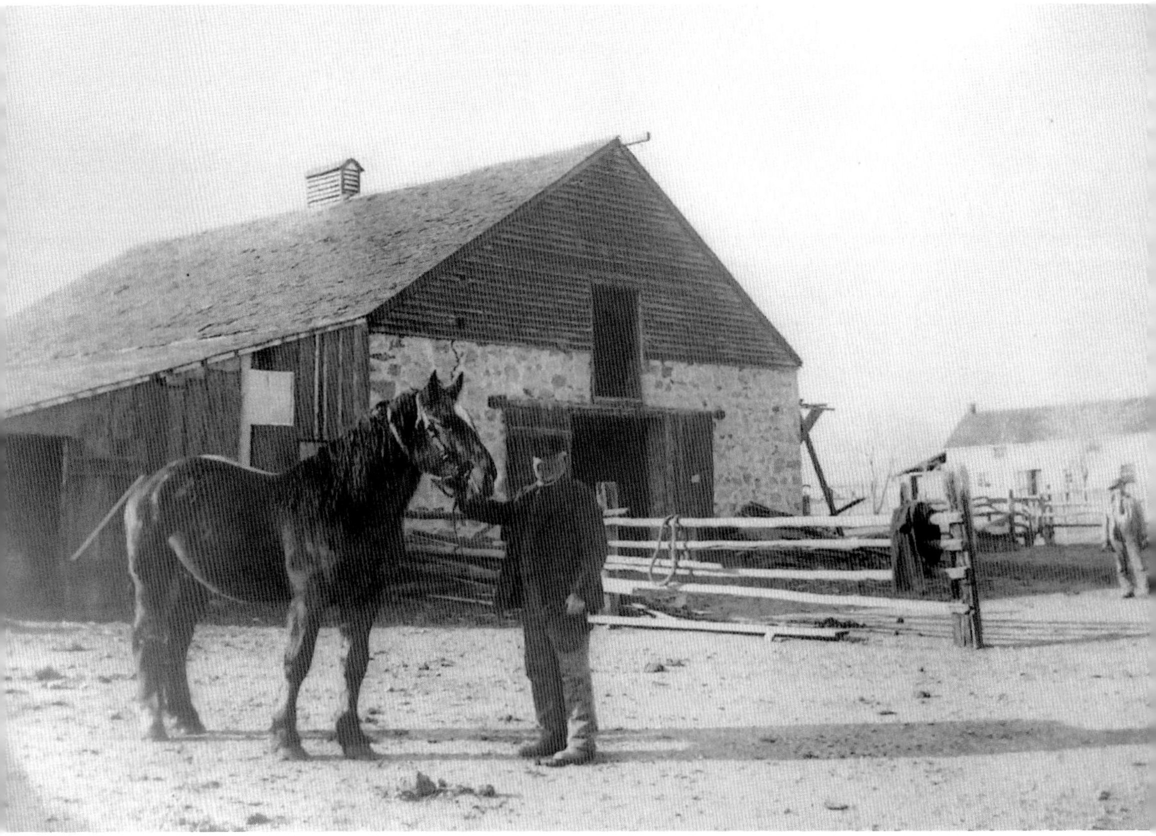

CHAPTER TWO

Business and Commerce

When it was still known as Ralston Point in the 1860s, the settlement that would become Arvada was dotted with ranches, farms, and the occasional business, such as a blacksmith shop.

Early businessman Hiram Burton not only ran a successful establishment but also served as the town justice of the peace and the county coroner. Albert Barth was instrumental in bringing the modern convenience of the telephone to Arvada. A.L. Davis opened the first Ford auto dealership in Jefferson County. William Peterson ran the town pool hall/lunch room on Grandview Avenue. He also mentored thousands of local young men. Others who ran eating establishments in Arvada included Lee Beghtol, Nick Skinner Sr., and Bernard Haug, who ran the area favorite Bernard's Restaurant for over a quarter of a century. Today, Tom Jacobson and Luke Heesaker are making their own mark in the Arvada business community.

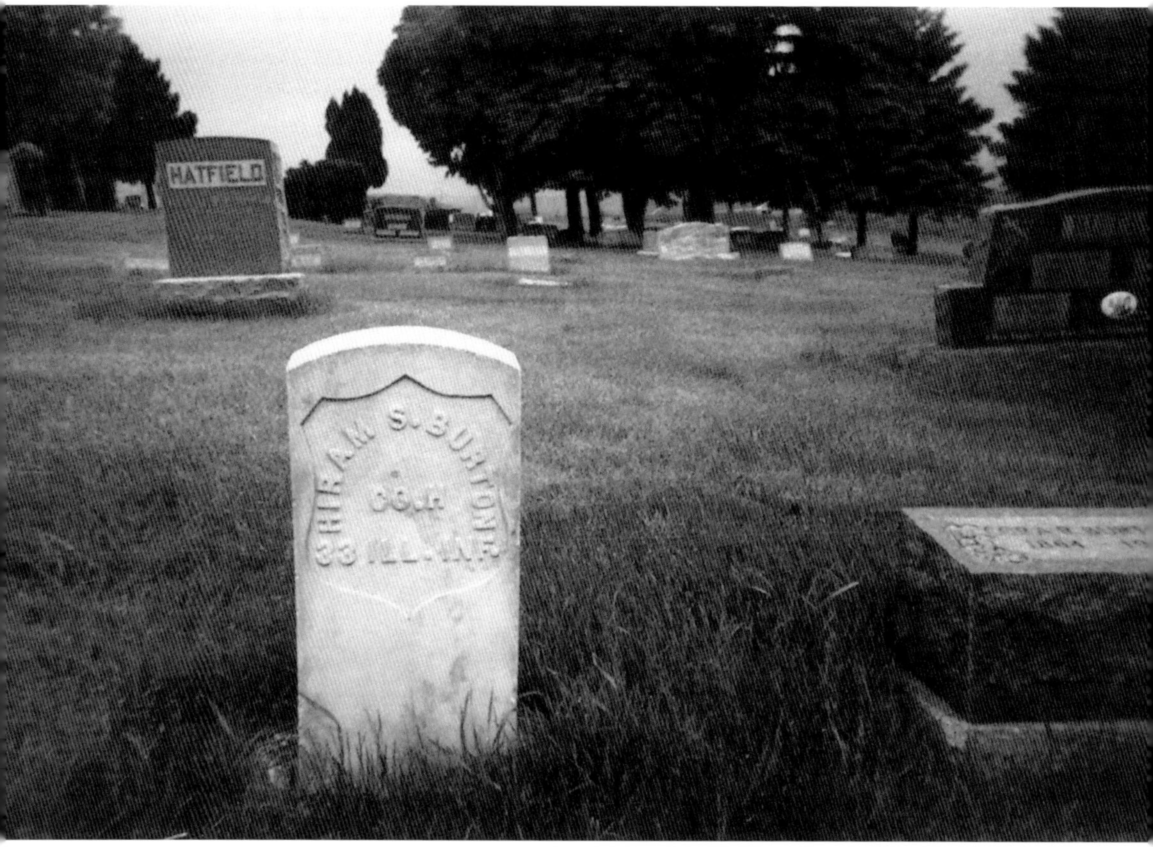

Hiram S. Burton

Hiram Burton was one of Arvada's first businessmen and served the town and country in many ways.

Born in Ohio on March 11, 1846, Hiram Burton served from 1863 to 1865 in the 159th Regiment Ohio Infantry. As a drummer boy, young Burton showed "remarkable courage for a lad of 16 years old." Hiram and his first wife, Sarah, settled in Arvada. By 1902, Burton had constructed a building for his undertaking establishment on Grandview Avenue that he ran with Michael Chinn. Burton served as a Jefferson County justice of the peace for nine years and was county coroner for many years. A member of the Arvada Odd Fellows Lodge, the Arvada Presbyterian Church, and the Arvada Town Board, Burton also found time to dabble in both the insurance and real estate trades. At the time of his death on October 1, 1925, Hiram Smith Burton was Arvada's last resident Civil War veteran. He was 79 years of age at the time of his passing. (Author's collection.)

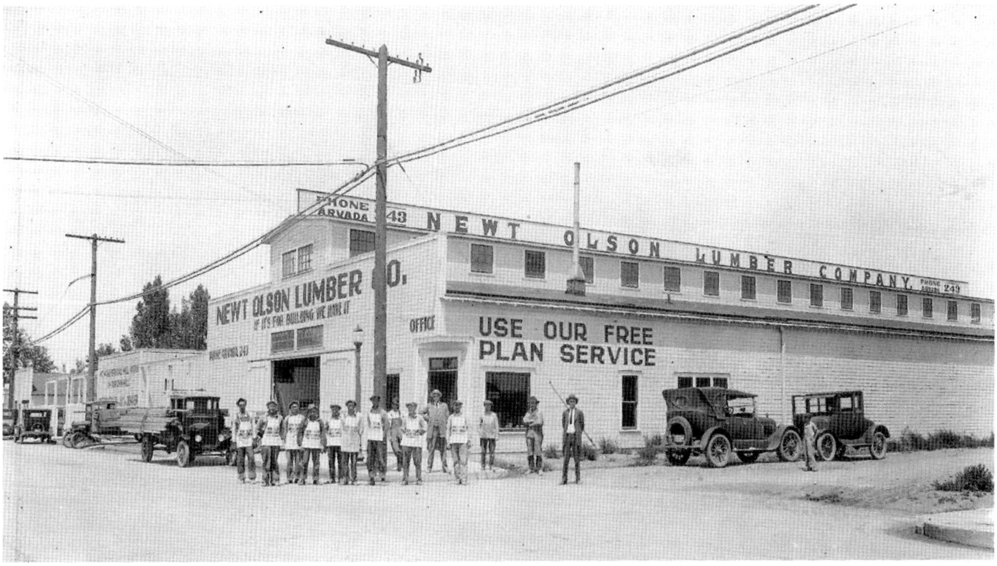

Newt Olson

Born to a Norwegian mother and a Swedish father in Iowa in 1887, Newt Olson came to Arvada from Wyoming in 1922. The Newt Olson Lumber Co. was in operation from 1922 until 1945 on the corner of present day Fifty-seventh Avenue and Olde Wadsworth Boulevard. In addition to running the business, Olson was a charter member of the Arvada Chamber of Commerce in 1925 and was integral in the creation of the Arvada Harvest Festival. After 23 years in Arvada, Newt and his wife, Bertha, moved to California for Bertha's health. Prior to this move, Olson sold his lumber company to J.W. Metz. Newt Olson passed away in 1950.

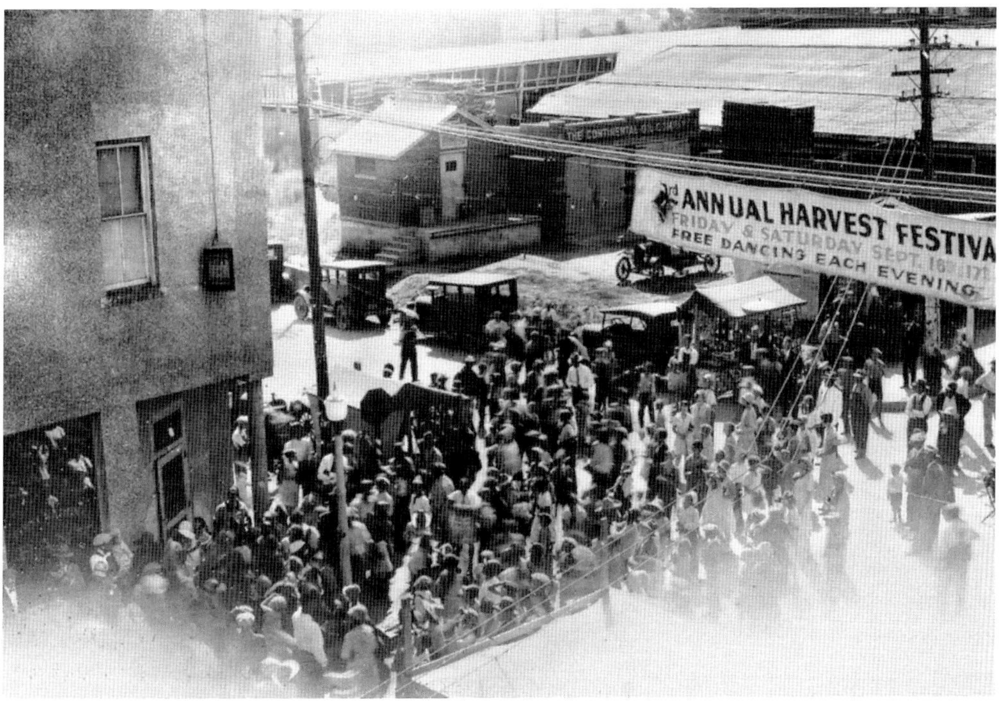

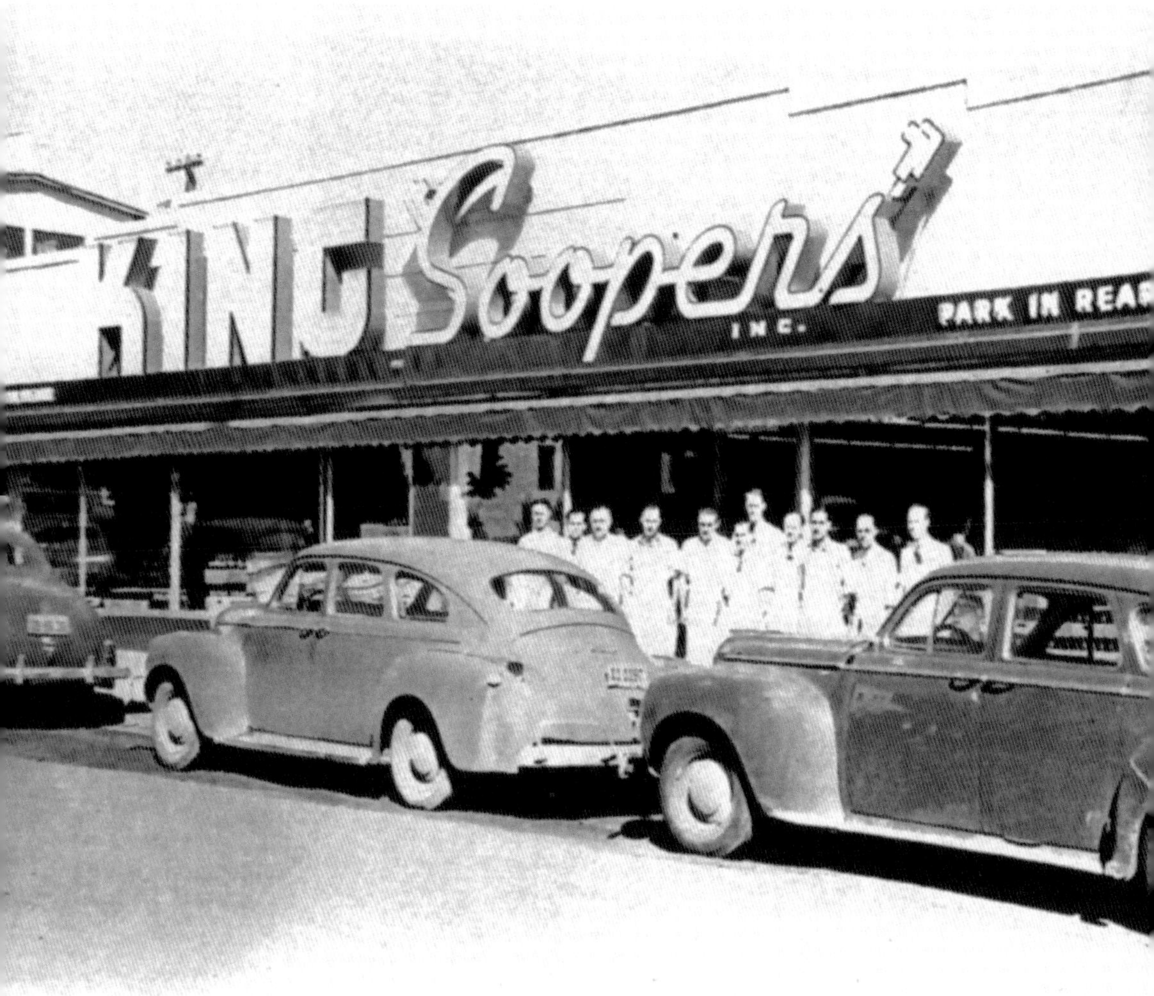

Lloyd King

An innovator in the business of grocery chain stores, Lloyd King started with his first King Soopers in Arvada in 1947.

After returning from naval service during World War II, King purchased a meat market at 7503 West Fifty-seventh Avenue in Arvada. From that meat market evolved the first of over 100 King Soopers stores across the Front Range. An example of some of King's revolutionary marketing ideas include a self-service meat market, an in-store pharmacy with generic products, and an in-store deli and bakery. King served as president of King Soopers until 1972. "He was always concerned about the customer," said Russ Dispense, Kings Soopers vice president of marketing after Lloyd King's death in 1998.

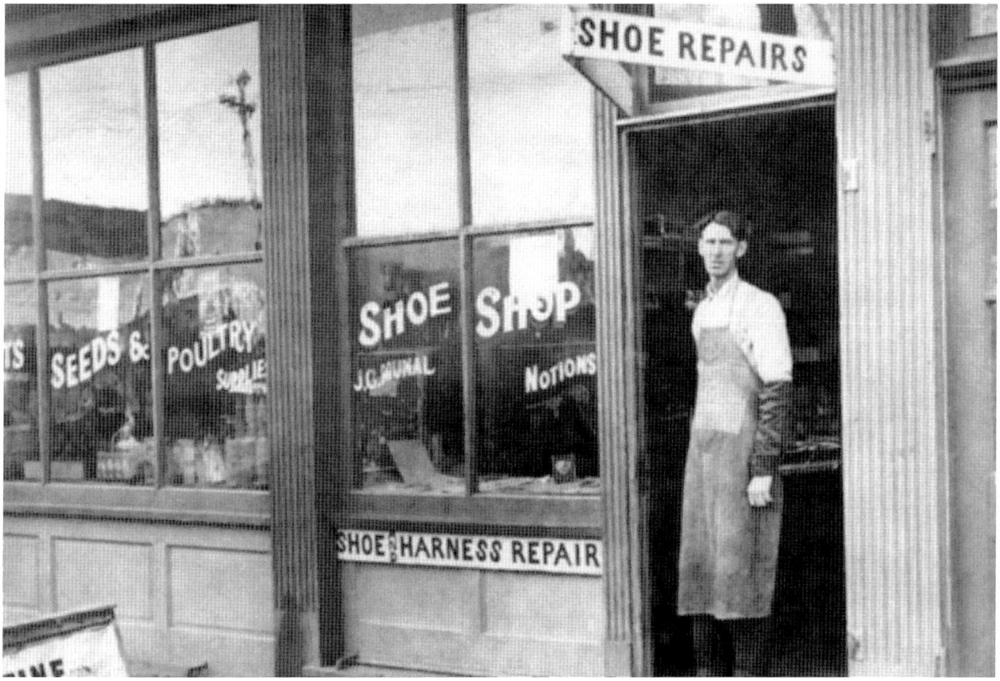

Joseph Munal

The son of a Civil War veteran, Joseph Munal was born in Illinois in July 1868. Migrating to Denver as a young man, Munal ran a farm near Sloan's Lake. In 1908, Joe; his wife, Lily; and their daughter moved to Arvada, where Munal was employed at the A.L. Davis lumber yard. In 1912, Munal opened his shoe repair shop ay 7524 Grandview Avenue, which he operated until his death.

A lifelong lover of music, Joe started the Arvada Band. The band was open to men of all degrees of musical talent, and many times, Joe Munal paid for instruments so that those who could not afford to purchase their own could continue playing with the band. Munal was also active in helping get the Arvada High School building at Ralston Road and Wadsworth Boulevard built in the 1920s.

Joseph Munal passed away on September 10, 1925.

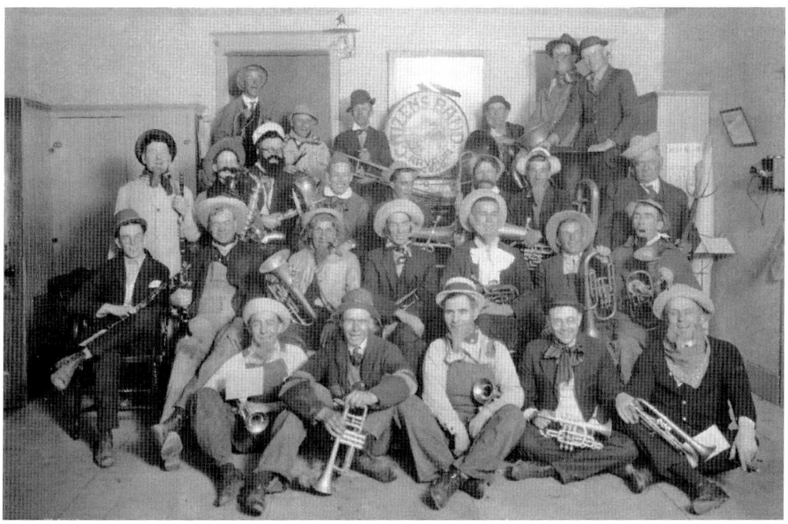

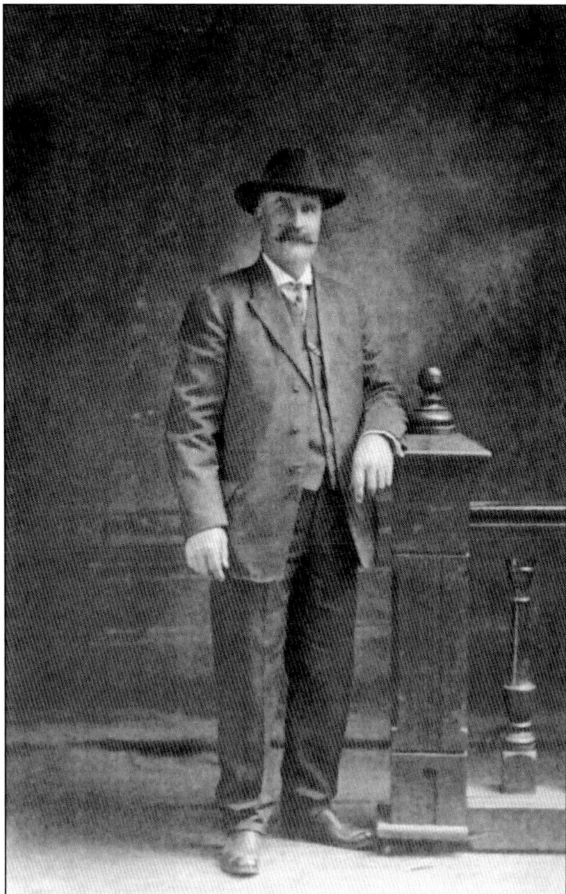

A.L. Davis

One of Arvada's leading businessmen in the first half of the 20th century, Davis left a lasting impact on the community.

Born in Illinois in 1865, Alfred Lee Davis came to Arvada in 1907. Soon after, Davis opened the A.L. Davis lumberyard on the C&S railroad tracks east of town. The lumberyard was destroyed by fire in 1912, and Davis went into the auto dealerships business. Davis also served as Arvada mayor from 1915 to 1917 and also served as a trustee on the town board. A.L. Davis died on December 12, 1950, in Arvada.

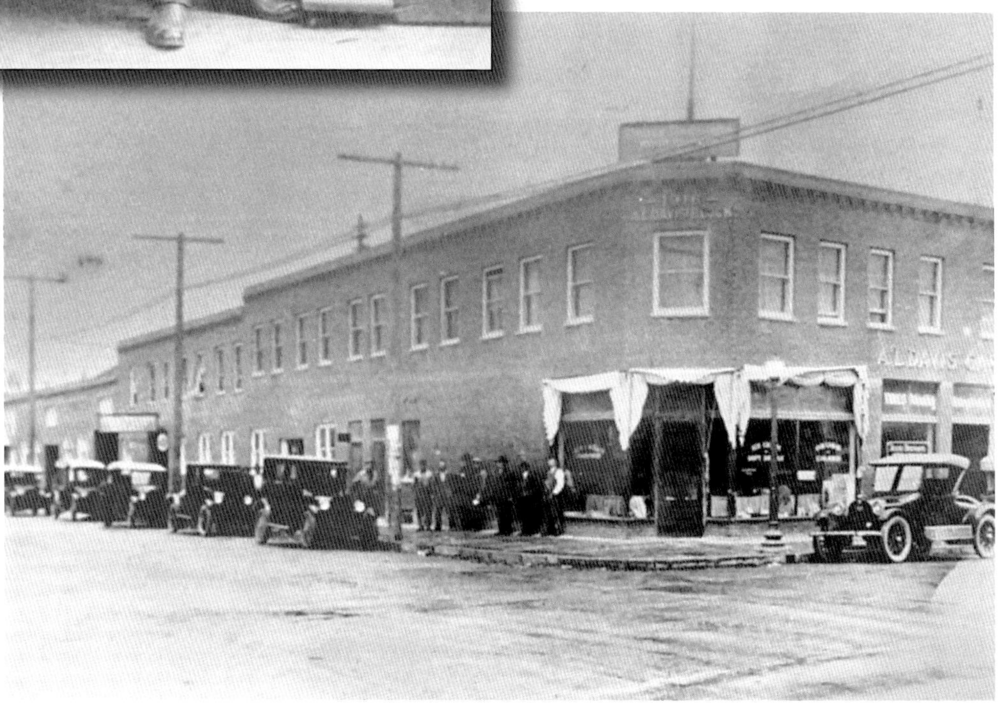

Lloyd Gorrell

As editor and publisher of the *Arvada Enterprise*, Lloyd Gorrell carried on his father's legacy while making one of his own.

Lloyd moved to Arvada with his parents, Russell and Hazel, at the age of two in 1923. Russell had recently purchased the town newspaper and set about to publish the *Enterprise*, which he did until his death in 1940. Upon his father's passing, Lloyd, at the young age of 19, became the editor and publisher. Along with his wife, Leona, Lloyd worked long hours getting the weekly paper out. Lloyd served on the Arvada Volunteer Fire Department for 30 years among many other civic duties. Lloyd was the Arvada Man of the Year in both 1956 and 1970. The *Arvada Enterprise* printed its last edition on April 2, 1970. In 1986, Gorrell was inducted into the Jefferson County Hall of Fame.

Lloyd Gorrell passed away on November 17, 2009.

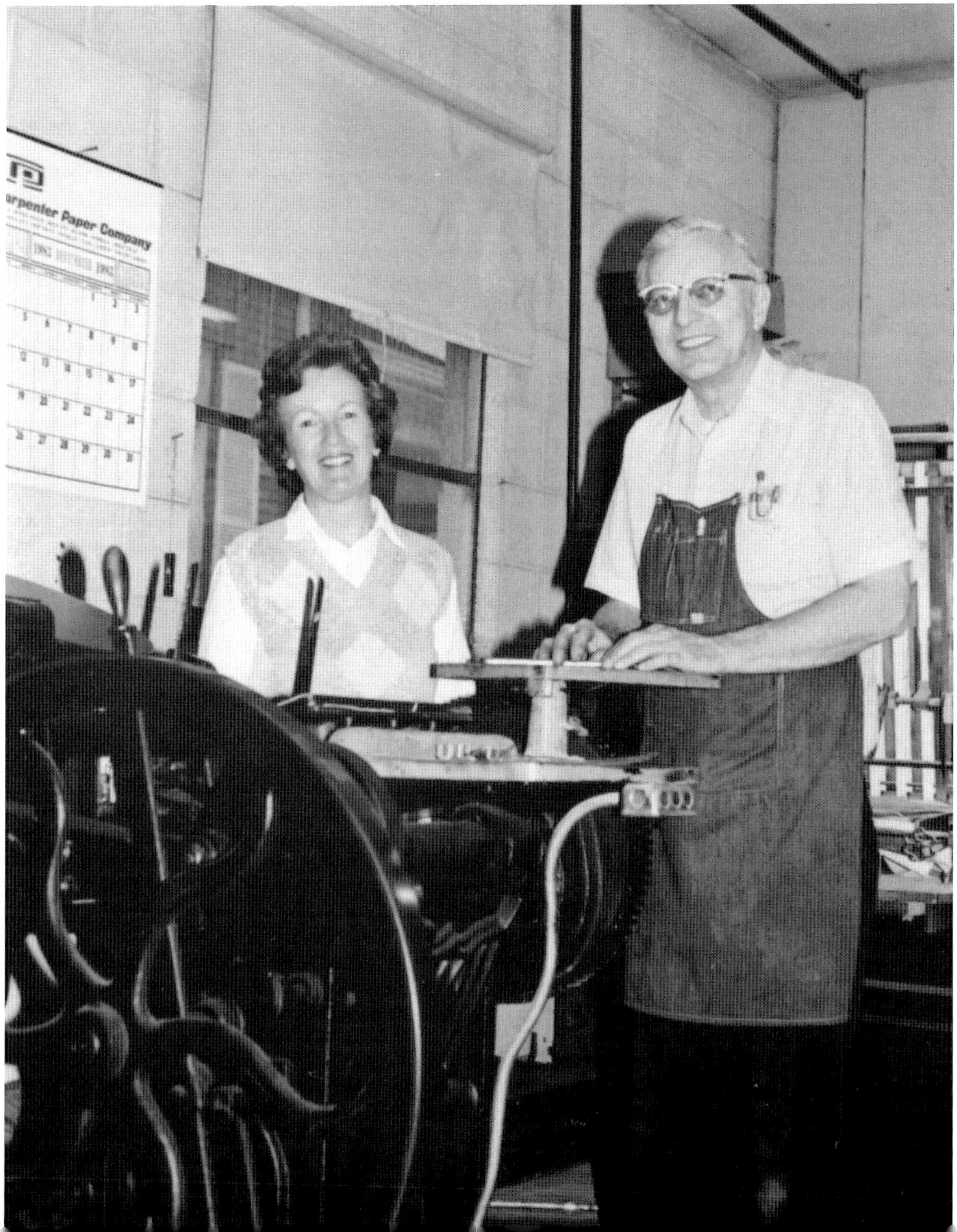

Ralph Ashton

One of Arvada's early auto dealers, Ralph Ashton was a founding member of the Arvada Chamber of Commerce. In 1922, the Ashton Motor Company opened selling Chevrolet cars. In 1933, Ralph Ashton wanted a new home for Ashton Motors and attempted to secure a loan from a bank. When the loan was not attained, Ashton went to a private party and secured gold coins to use for the construction of his building, leading to the building being named the Gold Coin Building.

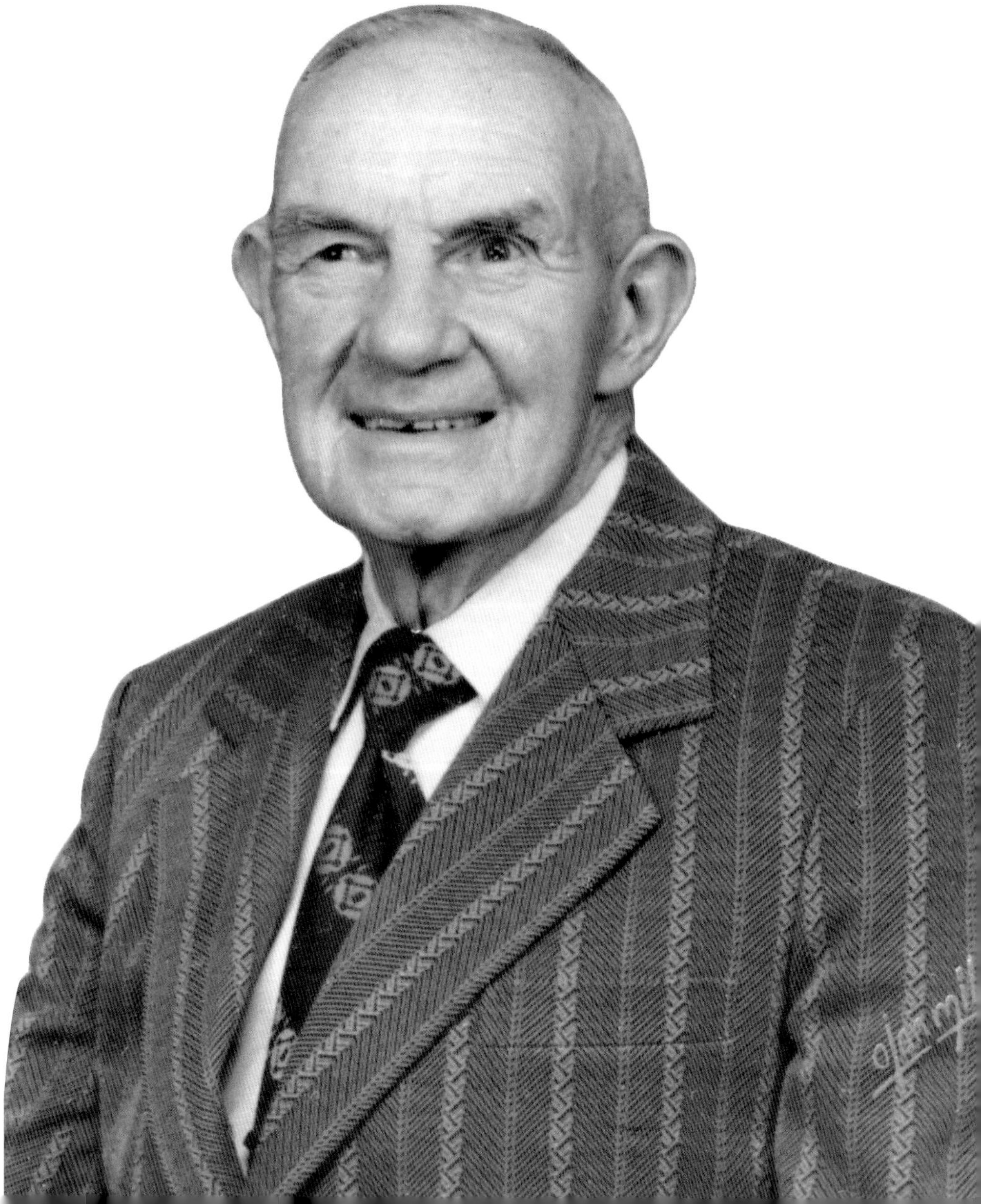

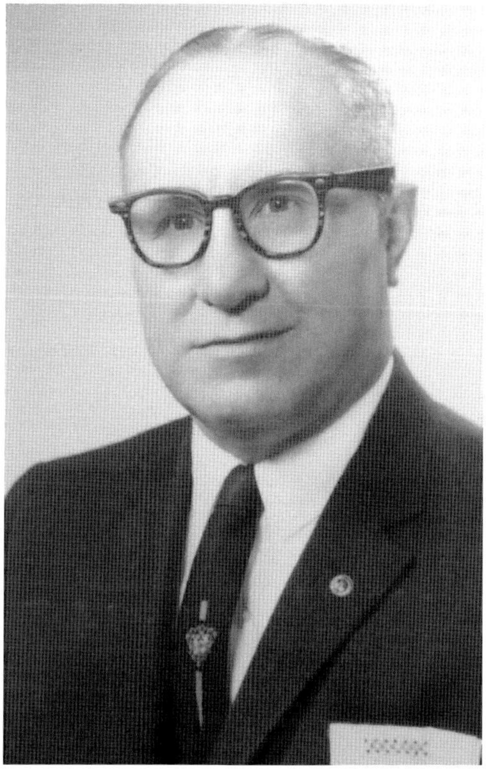

Frank Tiller
Owner of Tiller Cash, Coal and Feed Co., Frank Tiller was Arvada's Man of the Year in 1967.

In 1924, Frank's father, Fred, opened Tiller's Cash, Coal and Feed Co. in Arvada. In 1944, Frank and his partner, Louis G. Schaaf, took over ownership of the Arvada Flour Mill from E.E. Benjamin. On May 24, 1977, Fred Tiller donated the flour mill to the Arvada Historical Society.

Frank Tiller died on June 29, 1970, in Arvada.

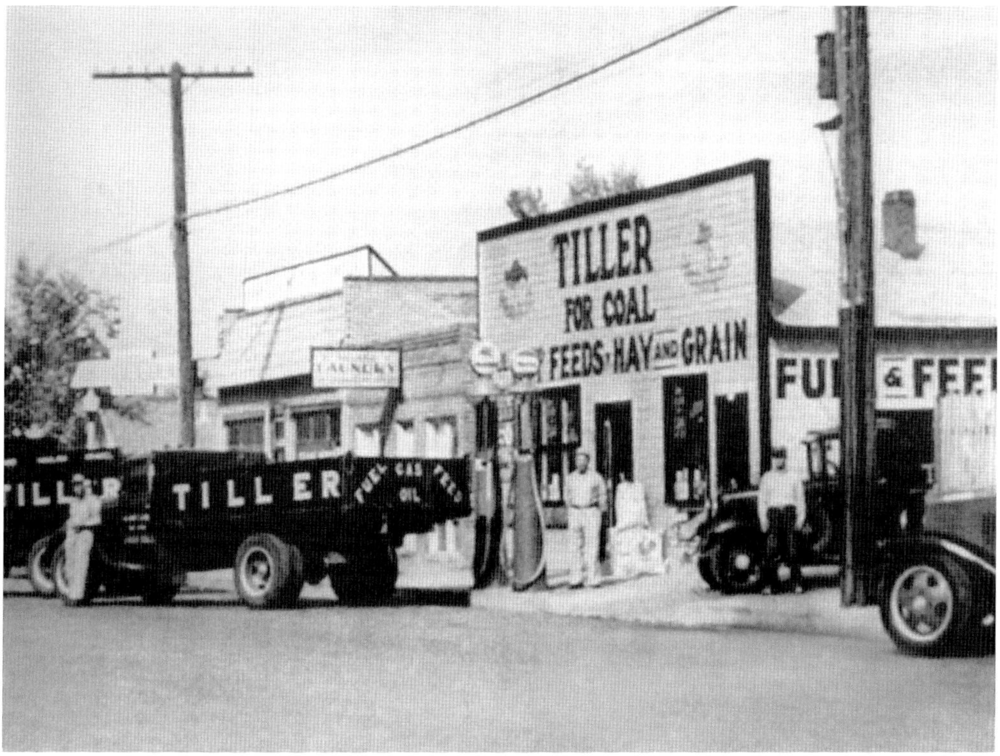

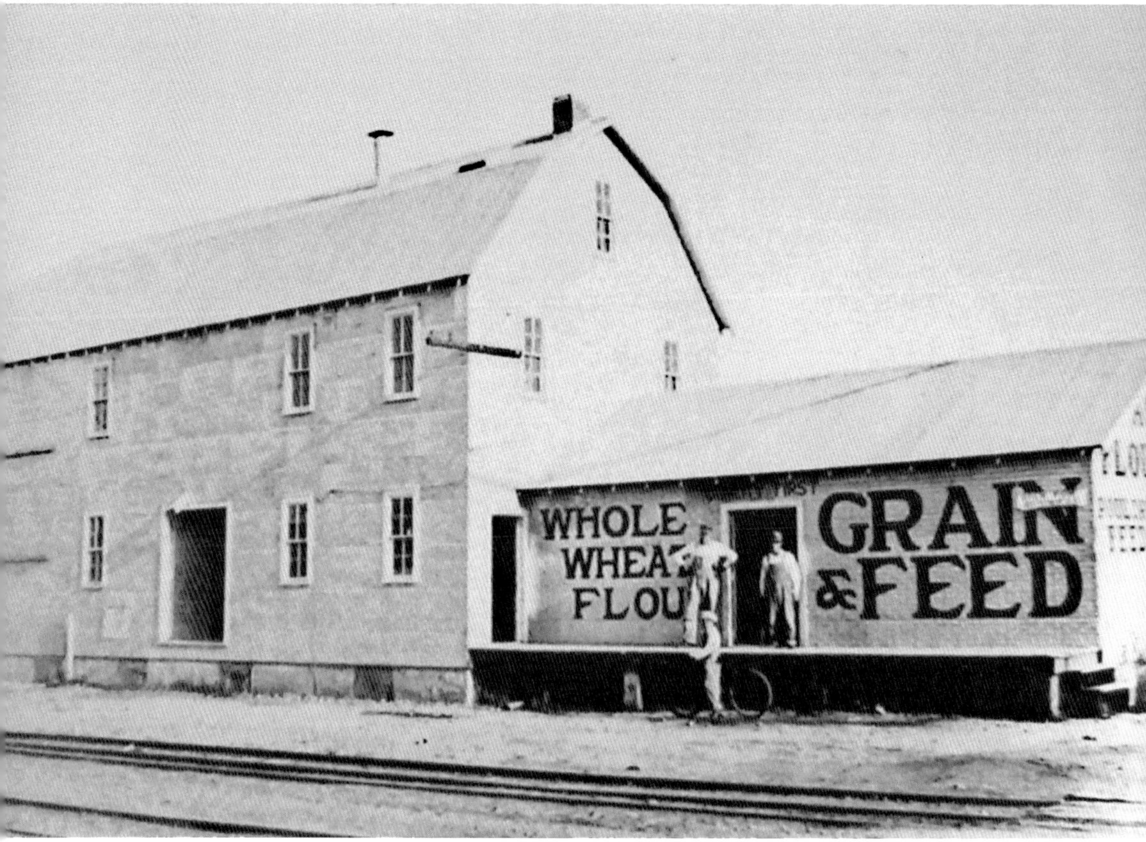

E.E. Benjamin

A lifelong Jefferson County resident, entrepreneur E.E. Benjamin built Arvada's iconic flour mill in 1925.

Born in Golden in 1883, Benjamin worked at various mills throughout his youth. In 1925, Benjamin built the Arvada Flour Mill on the south side of the C&S railroad tracks on Wadsworth. Before the mill opened, a contest was run to pick a brand name for the flour to be produced. Arva-Pride was the winner, and it was that name that was stamped on countless colorful flour sacks over the years.

On May 1, 1944, Benjamin sold the mill to Frank Tiller. Eleven days later, E.E. Benjamin passed away in Arvada.

Luke Heesacker

Business owner and family man Luke Heesacker's love for his community shows in his commitment to various organizations.

Originally from Nebraska, Heesacker moved with his family to Arvada at the age of 15. He attended Arvada West High School and, in 1971, began working at Arvada Rent-Alls. Luke purchased the business in 1986 along with two others. Since then, Heesacker's company has won Arvada Business of the Year, and he has been a member of the Chamber of Commerce and Arvada Economic Development Association. Luke has helped many local schools and churches with his donations of time, money and equipment. In 2011, Heesacker won the Lloyd J. King Entrepreneurial Spirit Award, an award named after another legendary Arvada businessman. Luke was named one of the "100 People Who Most Influenced Arvada" in 2004. Luke and his wife, Karen, reside in Arvada.

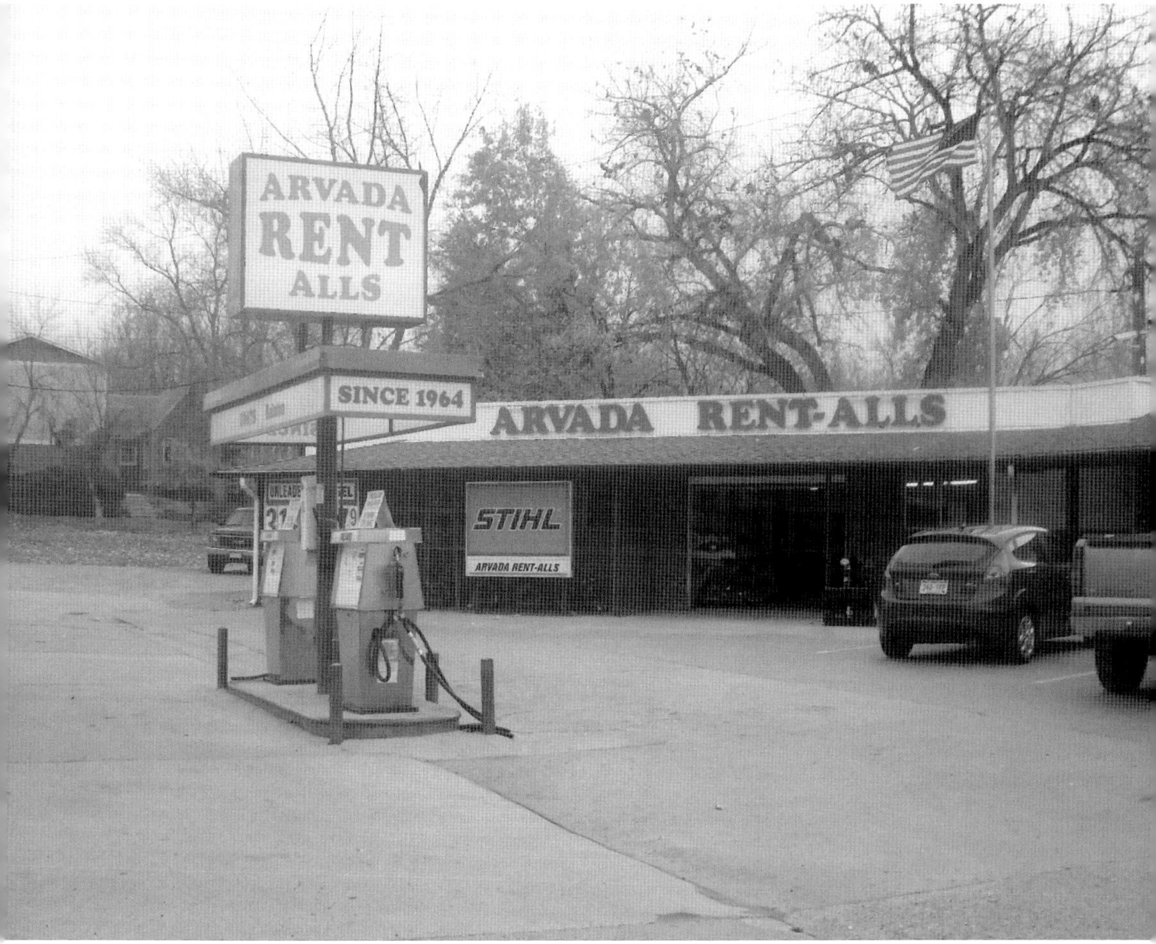

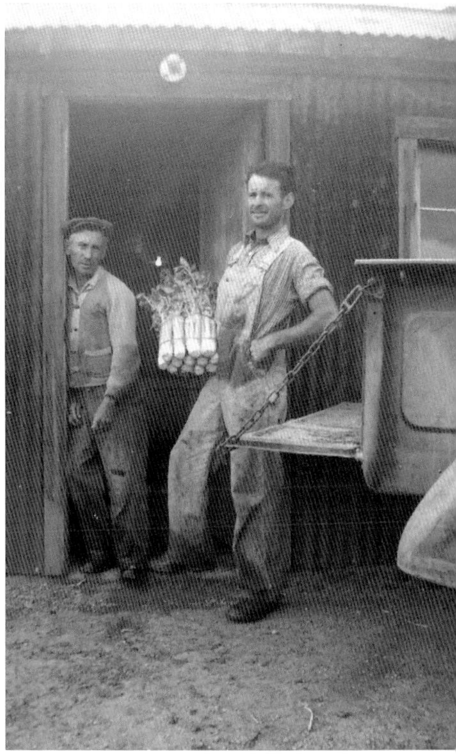

Lotito Family

The Lotito family were known for their Pascal celery. Rocco and Concetta Lotito moved to Arvada in 1932 and purchased 30 acres of land. They soon started raising vegetables. But it was Pascal celery that became their cash crop. A labor-intensive crop, the celery had to be ready for the Thanksgiving/Christmas season. In 1940, Vincent Lotito, won first prize with his celery at the Arvada Harvest Festival.

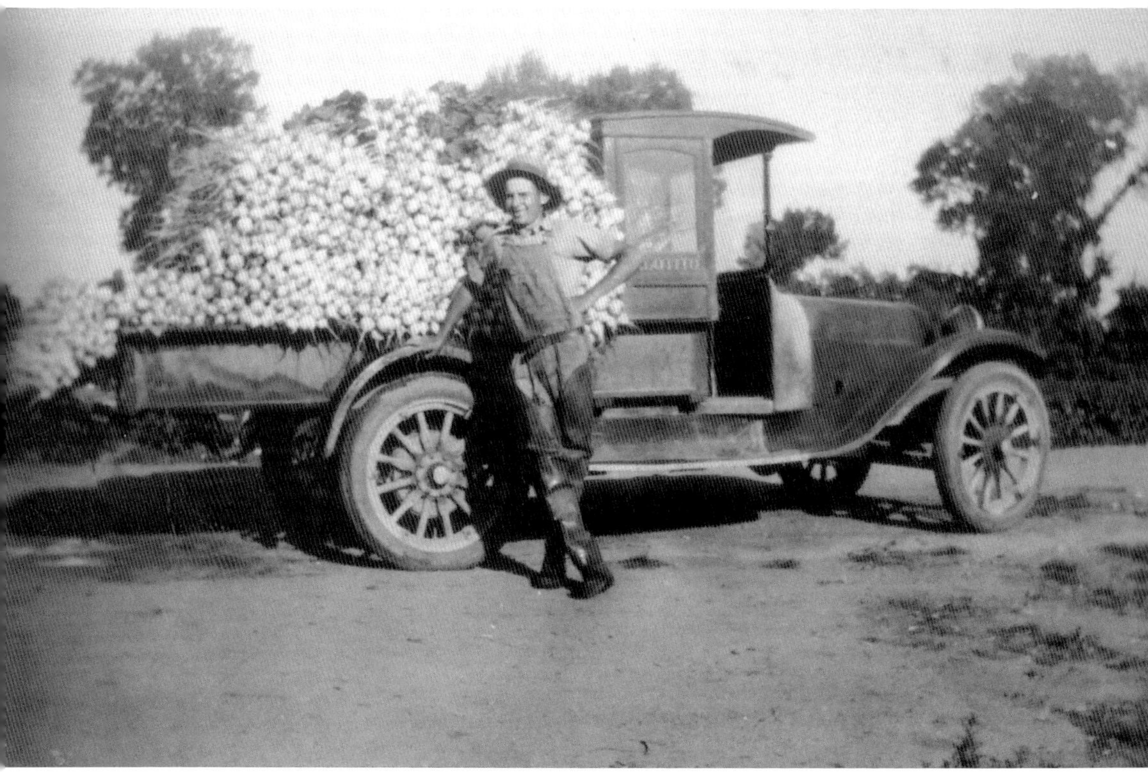

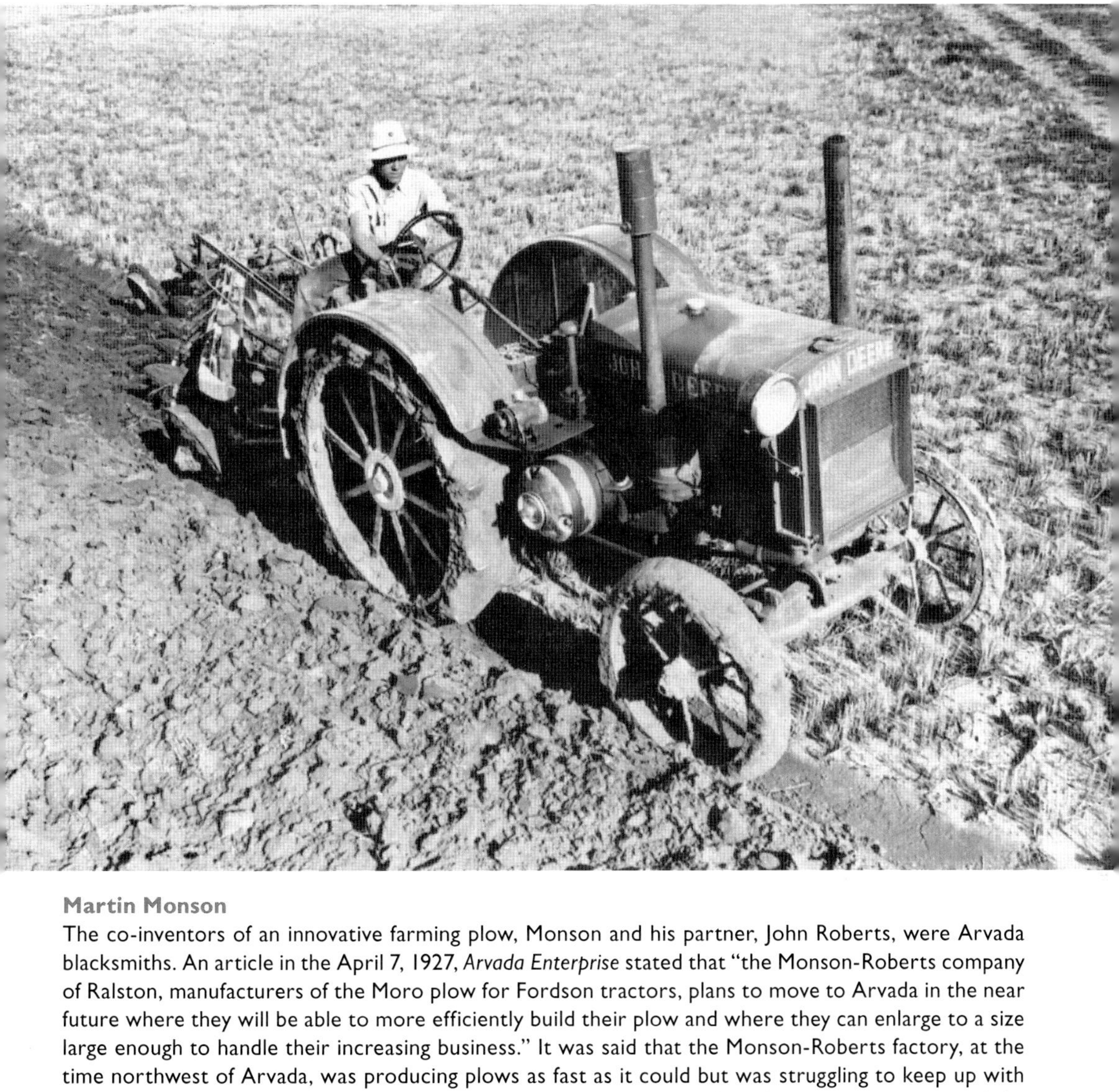

Martin Monson

The co-inventors of an innovative farming plow, Monson and his partner, John Roberts, were Arvada blacksmiths. An article in the April 7, 1927, *Arvada Enterprise* stated that "the Monson-Roberts company of Ralston, manufacturers of the Moro plow for Fordson tractors, plans to move to Arvada in the near future where they will be able to more efficiently build their plow and where they can enlarge to a size large enough to handle their increasing business." It was said that the Monson-Roberts factory, at the time northwest of Arvada, was producing plows as fast as it could but was struggling to keep up with the demand. After the original article, nothing else was mentioned of the factory, so it is assumed the venture never happened.

Lee Beghtol

Owner of several different eating and drinking establishments in Arvada, Beghtol was also the town's first uniformed police officer in 1941.

Lee and his wife, Cora, moved with their children to Arvada in 1920 from Kentucky. Lee worked at the Evans and Bennett Feed and Coal store and then opened the Pig 'N' Bun Restaurant on Grandview Avenue in 1936. Begthtol had served as the night traffic officer for Arvada in 1925 and was day marshal in 1926. Hired in 1941 as Arvada's first uniformed police officer, Beghtol had to pay for the uniform himself. From 1943 to 1944, Lee Beghtol served as Arvada's police chief. He also served on the town board and city council. Beghtol also operated Lee's Tavern, Nick's Inn, and the L&G Grill, all in Arvada.

Lee Beghtol passed away on April 28, 1964, at the age of 76. He is buried in the Arvada Cemetery.

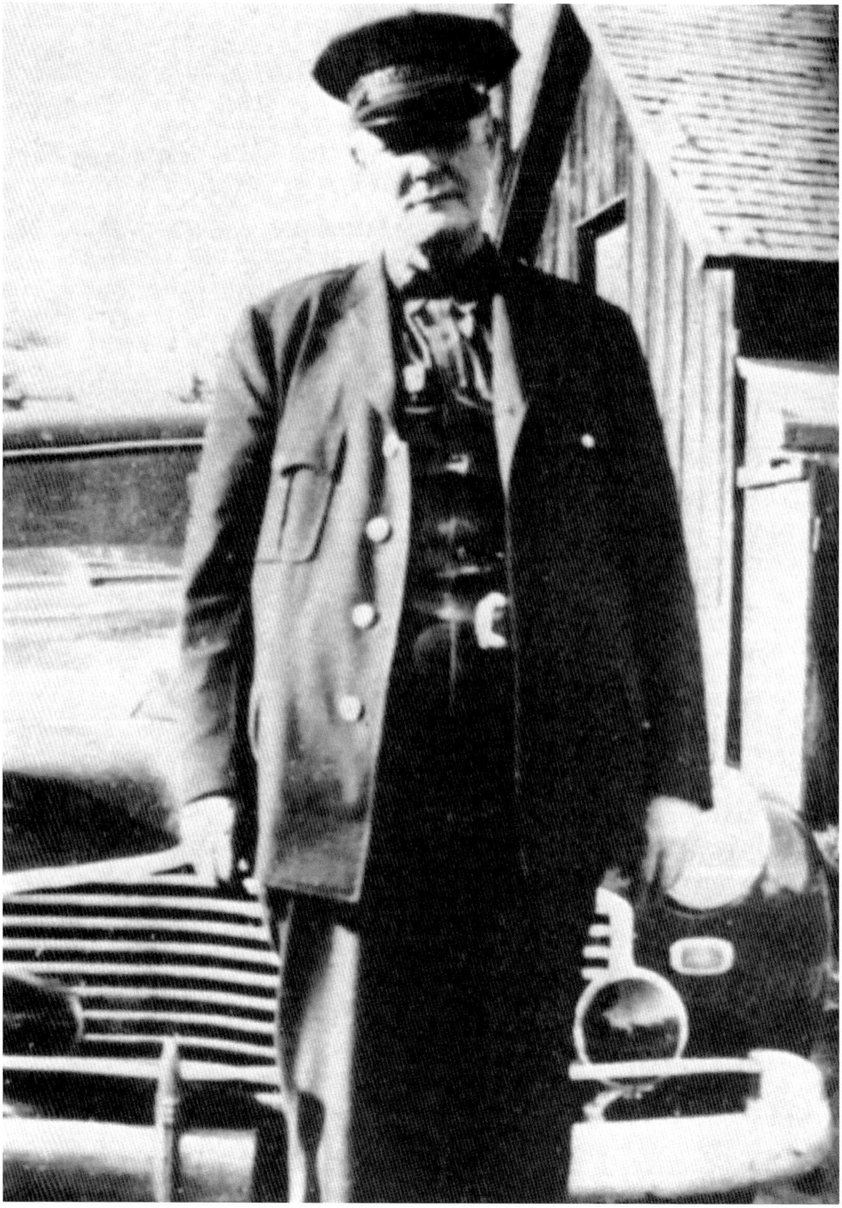

Tom Jacobson

The Arvada Man of the Year for 2010, Tom Jocobson has served the community for over 30 years.

A leader in various Arvada civic and philanthropic organizations, Jocobson is part owner of Sportsline, an Arvada sports equipment store. "He is well-respected because of the way he goes about his life, and he has a sense of ethics that is to be admired," said Duane Youse, a former Arvada Man of the Year of Jacobson in 2011. Tom is a volunteer at the Ralston House, a child advocacy center in Arvada, and is heavily involved in the Arvada Jefferson Kiwanis Club along with the Arvada Community Food Bank.

Sportsline is known for employing teens, and Jacobson—along with his brother Fred—mentors his young employees. "We try to teach them some values," Jacobson said in 2011. (Courtesy Arvada Chamber of Commerce.)

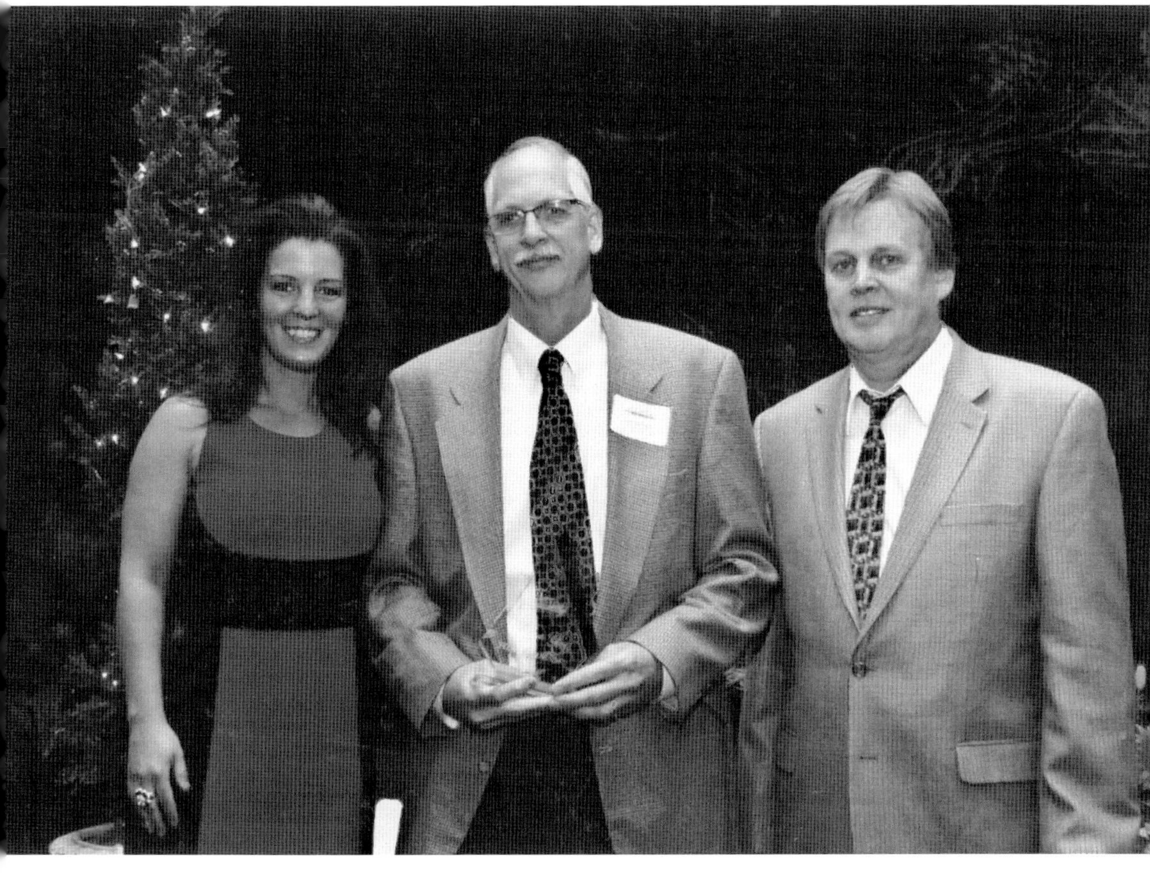

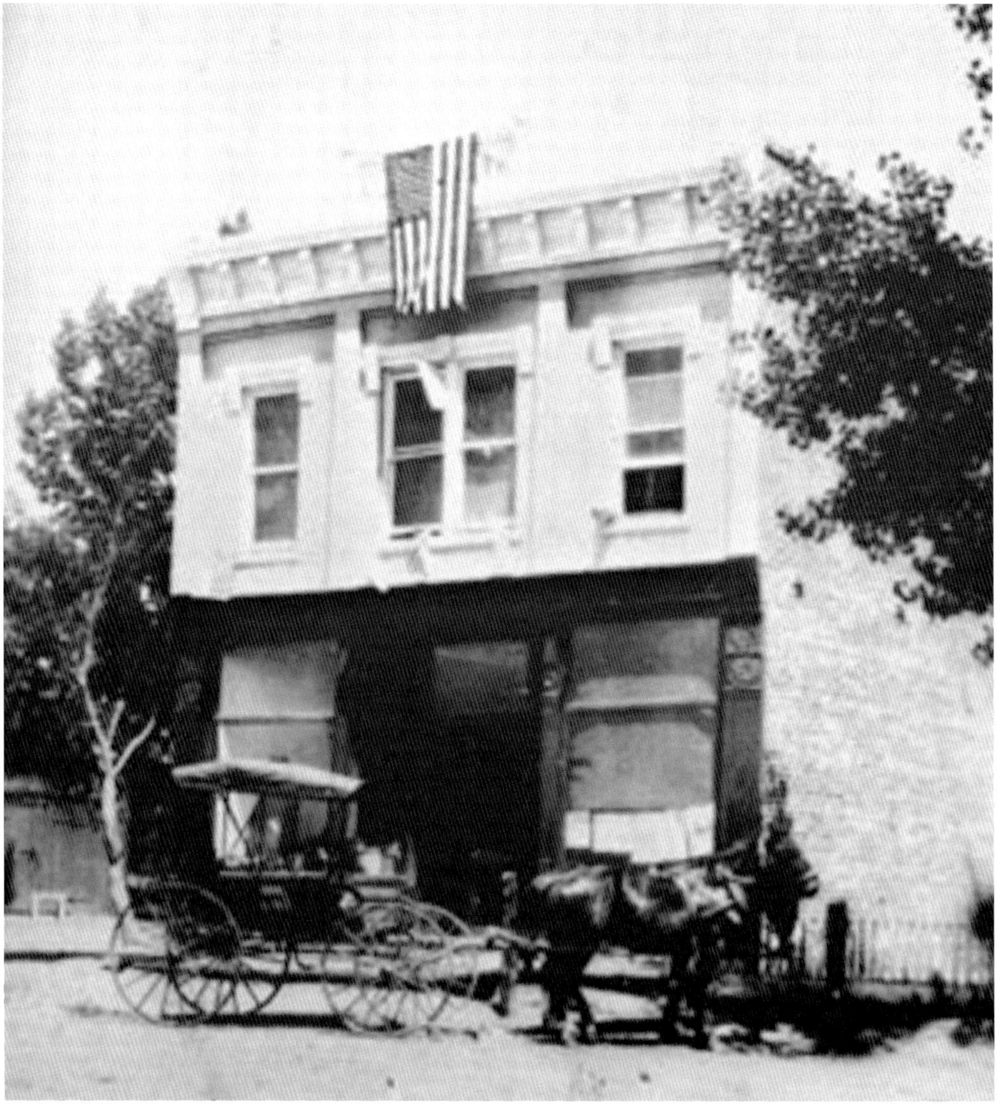

Albert Barth
An influential Arvada businessman in the late 1800s and early 1900s, Barth helped bring many modern conveniences to the town.

A German native, Albert H. Barth immigrated to America with his family as a youth and settled in Kentucky. When Albert was 16, his parents died, leaving the teen to raise his five brothers and sisters. Albert came to Arvada in the 1880s and ran a grocery store for several years. He purchased property on the northeast corner of what are currently Grandview Avenue and Webster Street and built the Barth Building in 1898. The building housed a hardware and grocery store and the large upstairs was used as a community hall.

Albert married Nannie Holmes of Nebraska in 1899. The couple had two children.

It was with Albert Barth's insistence that Arvada got its first telephone in 1904. He was also involved in bringing electric lights and a modern water system to Arvada. On April 3, 1906, Barth was elected Arvada mayor. He later served on the town board.

Albert Barth died in 1921.

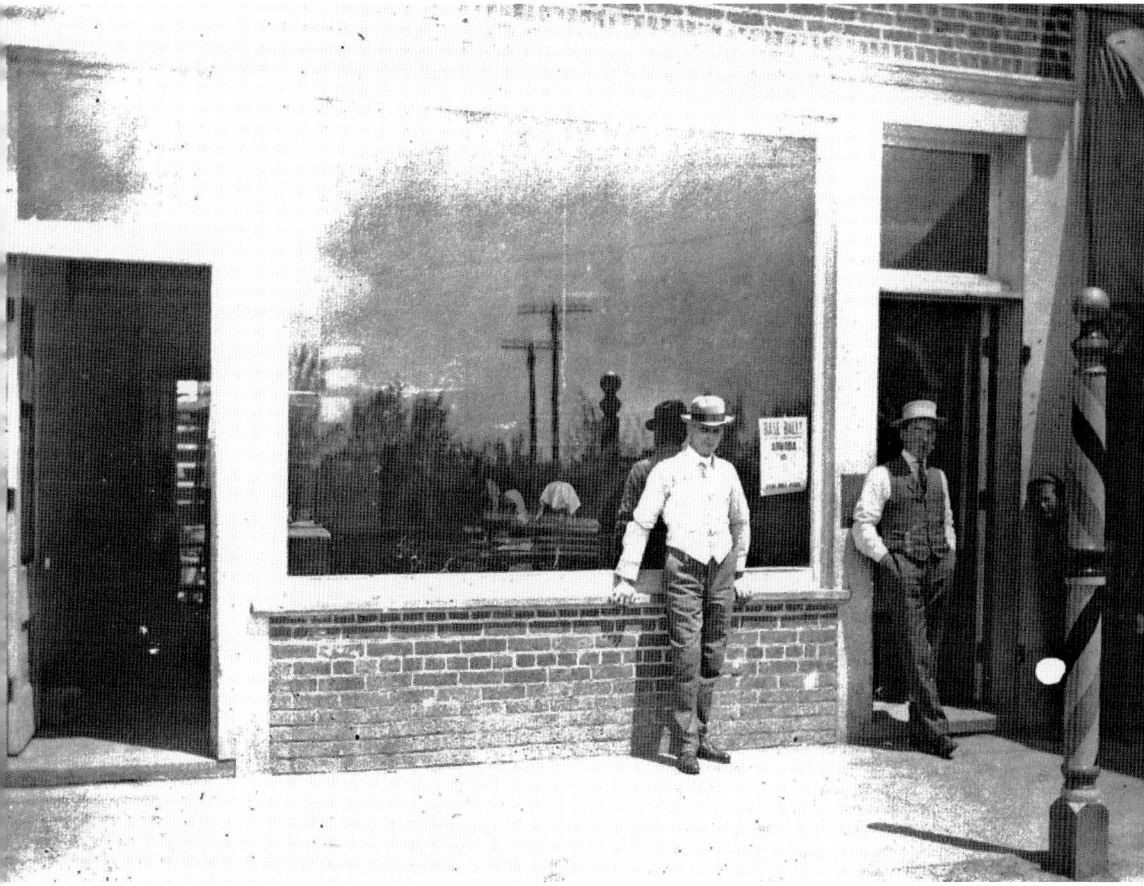

William Peterson
Peterson was a beloved owner of the local pool hall in Arvada whose presence made a lasting impact on a generation.

W.E. "Bill" Peterson came to Arvada in 1908. His first business was a barbershop–pool hall in 1914. Later, in 1921, he moved to 7509 Grandview Avenue. One of the rules of Peterson's establishment was no swearing. If a young woman walked into the pool hall, Peterson would let out with a loud whistle to warn the young boys to be on their best behavior. Bill raised his three daughters after the death of his wife, Mary Ellen, in 1930.

While Bill was a devoted father to his girls, he also was a mentor to thousands of boys and young men who frequented the pool hall. In 1966, while recalling the young men who came into his life over the years, Bill said, "They were all special. They were my pals. We played baseball and football together." In the 1950s, Bill's daughter Gladys and her husband, Bob Henderson, took over the pool hall. In 1972, Peterson's Pool Hall closed.

Bill Peterson passed away on March 7, 1974.

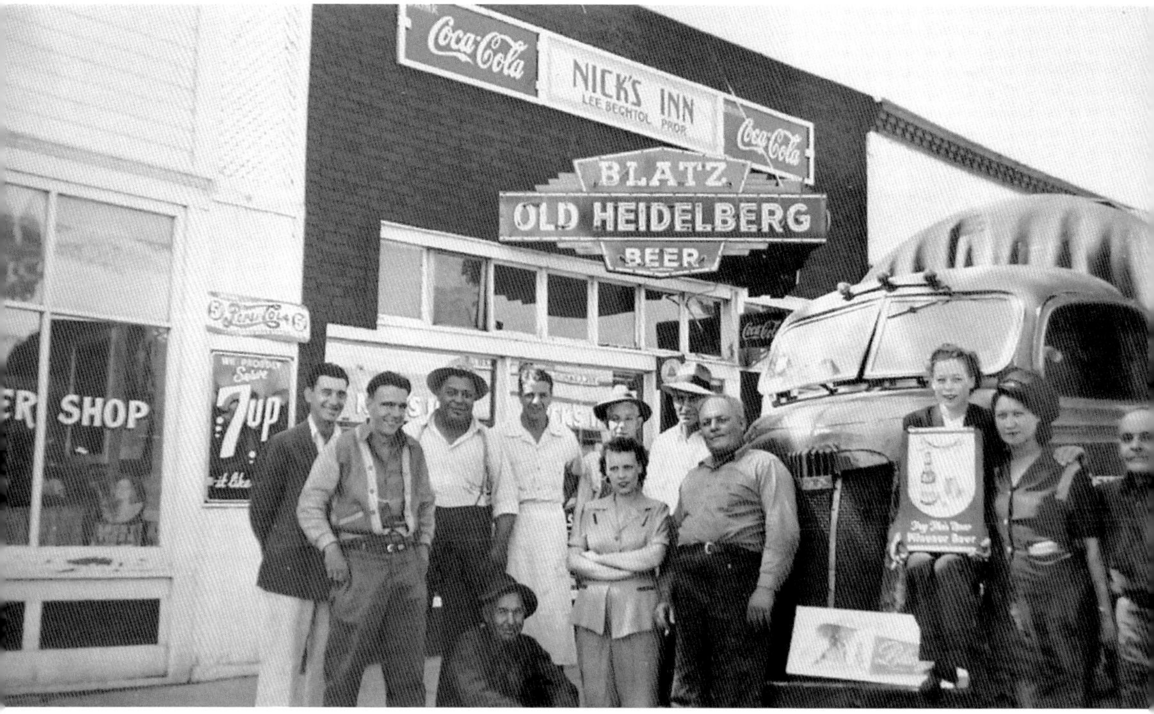

Skinner Family

For over 100 years, the Skinner family has called Arvada home. In that century, the family has owned and operated many businesses.

Benjamin Skinner came to Arvada in 1905 and liked what he saw enough to send for his wife, Lillie, and their three children back in Louisville, Kentucky. Benjamin and Lillie opened a store at Griffith Station near present-day Carr Street and Fiftieth Avenue. It was at their home at that location that the couple welcomed five more children, including Nick, who was born in 1907. Benjamin found time amid running his business, being a part of his growing family, and farming to serve as justice of the peace and was a charter member of the Arvada Masonic Lodge.

In 1927, Nick joined the Marines and served in China. Upon his return to Colorado, he met and married Bernadine Bement of Denver, a professional dancer with a touring troupe. The couple's only child, Nick Jr., was born on September 20, 1932, in Denver. In 1938, Nick Skinner began his career with the Arvada Volunteer Fire Department. That year, he also opened a service station at the corner of Yukon Street and Grandview Avenue. Two years later, he purchased the Columbine Inn and reopened it as Nick's Inn on Grandview. After a stint in the Navy during World War II, Nick came home to Arvada and opened Wadsworth Liquors at 5713 Wadsworth Boulevard in 1947. In addition to running his business, Nick continued to volunteer with the fire department and served on the Arvada Fire Protection District Board of Directors. Nick retired from the fire department in 1961. He passed away on July 6, 1999.

Nick Skinner Jr. served in the Navy in the early 1950s, was an airplane mechanic for Frontier Airlines, and worked as a stationary engineer for Coors. He is still active at the age of 82, volunteering with the Arvada Historical Society.

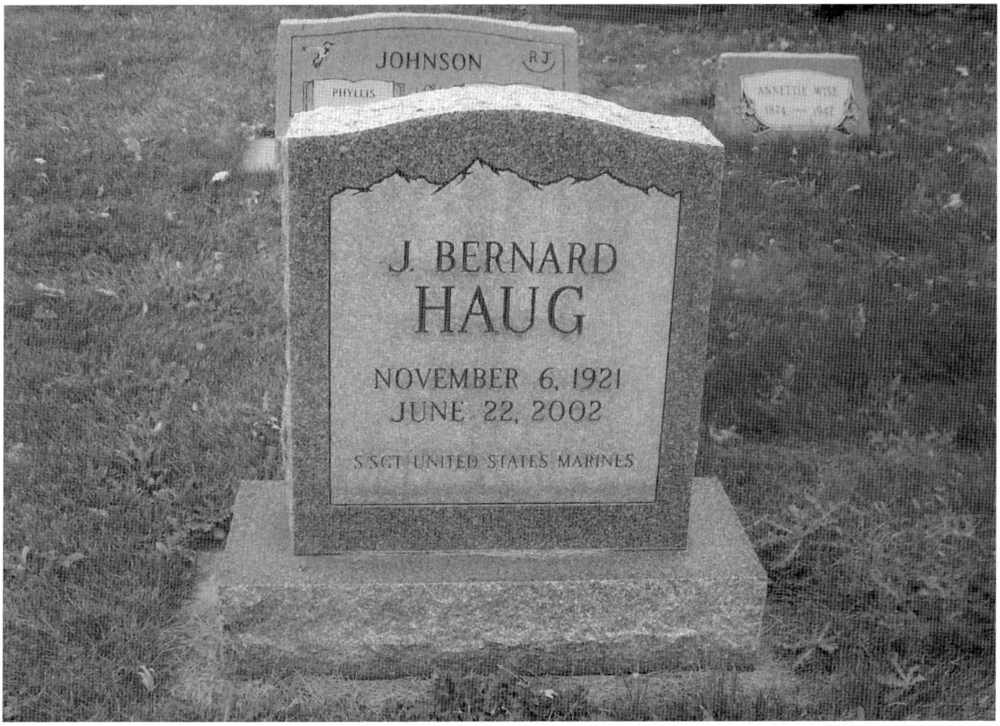

Bernard Haug

The owner of Bernard's Restaurant for over 30 years, Haug was Arvada's Man of the Year in 1981.

Born in Limon, Colorado, in 1921, Bernard Haug came to Arvada after his high school graduation looking for work. In 1942, Bernie joined the Marines. It was while in the service that Bernie served as a cook, even serving food to Bob Hope and his troupe on two occasions, according to Bernie's brother, Max. After the war, Bernie attended the University of Denver for a degree in hotel and restaurant management. In 1952, Bernie and Max rented Ralph's Café in Arvada. After leaving that business, Bernie worked other jobs in Kansas City, California, and Honolulu. In 1964, on a trip back to Arvada to visit family, Bernie decided to give the restaurant business another try, and Bernard's Restaurant was born. When Haug was named Arvada Man of the Year in 1981, it was estimated that the restaurant served around 1,000 people a day. Bernard's was famous for its home cooking and served no food product that was not prepared and cooked at the restaurant. Another memorable feature of the restaurant was the thousands of whiskey decanters that graced the walls. Over 30-plus years, Bernard's of Arvada became a local institution. Hundreds of banquets for local churches, athletic teams, and civic organization were held at the restaurant over the years, and Bernard sponsored many youth programs in the area. An avid traveler, Bernard enjoyed talking to his customers of his adventures. In 1989, Bernard's of Arvada closed.

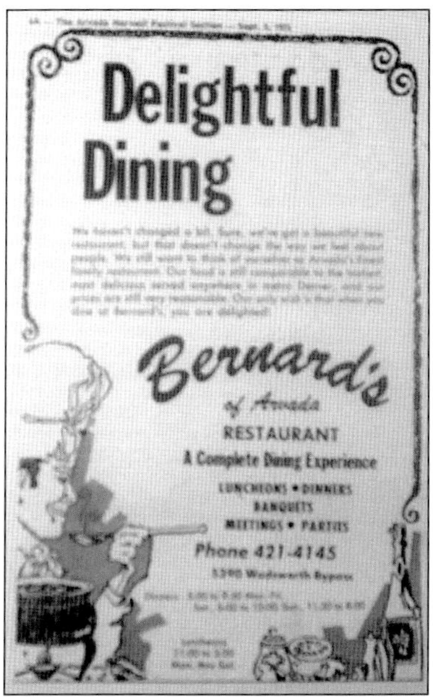

Bernard Haug died on June 22, 2002. He is buried at the Arvada Cemetery.

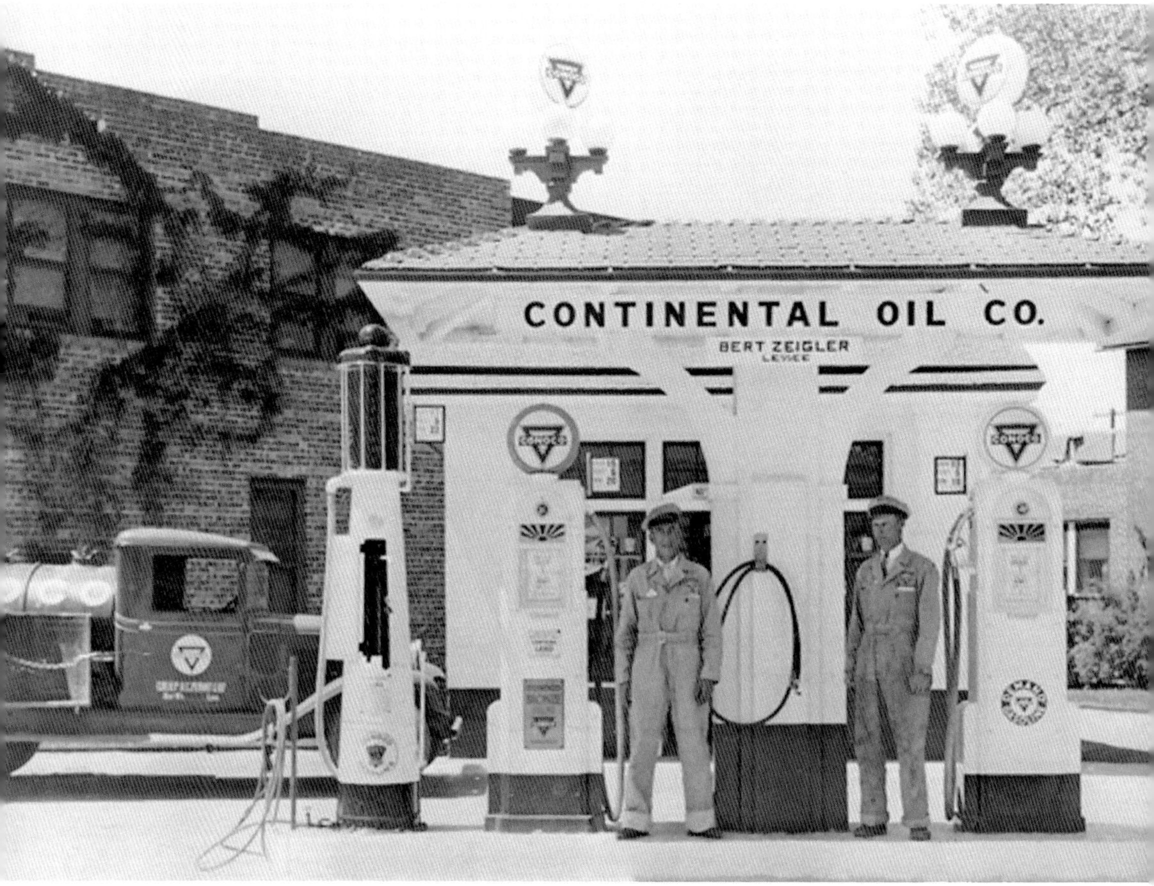

John Kahler Exline

A longtime Arvada resident, Exline owned various businesses in the area.

Born in Canton, Ohio, on September 29, 1900, Kahler and his family moved to Oklahoma in 1908 by covered wagon. The family settled in Seiling, Oklahoma, where they rented farmland and occasionally hauled freight. Kahler graduated from high school in Seiling in 1918, and he wed his first wife soon after. He worked at many jobs as the couple's family grew to include two children. In 1931, Kahler moved to Arvada, where Oklahoma friends of his had settled. He would spend the next 61 years there. After his divorce from his first wife, Kahler married Amie Reese. He managed the Pig 'N' Bun restaurant in Arvada for a time and, in 1936, began as manager of the Conoco station at the corner of Grandview Avenue and Wadsworth Boulevard. He stayed on as manager until 1959. After the station closed, Kahler and Amie built and opened Clear Creek Liquors at 5070 Wadsworth Street by the Wadsworth Drive-In. The Exlines sold the store in 1970 and retired. Amie passed away in 1986, and Kahler provided care for his sister-in-law, Arvada chiropractor Viva Mahorney, until her death.

John Kalher Exline passed away on September 22, 1992.

John Banks

The station agent for the Arvada Depot for 33 years, John Malden Banks, was born in Missouri in 1875. He came to Arvada in 1913 when he was named the station agent for Arvada's Colorado & Southern Railroad on Grandview Avenue. A tall man with a great sense of humor, Banks was active in many town activities. John M. Banks died on January 29, 1959.

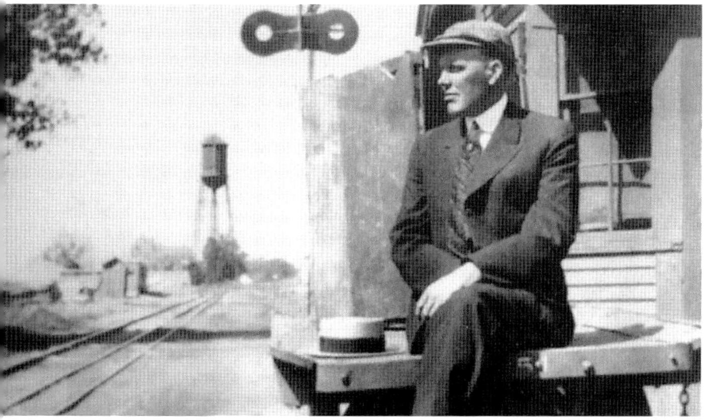

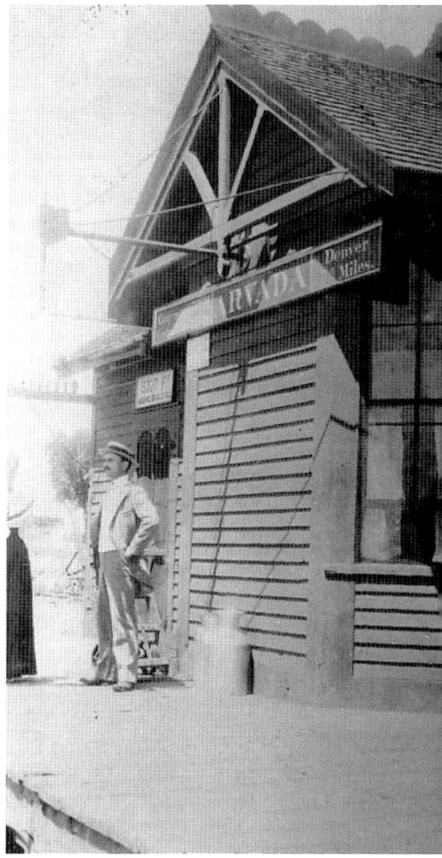

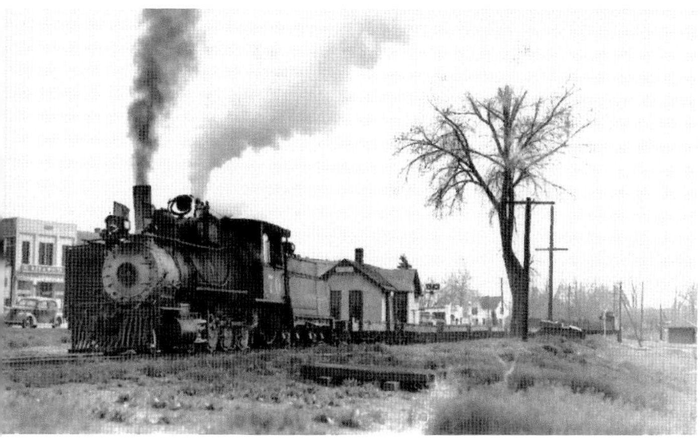

John White Shannon

Shannon ran the Hackberry Ranch north of Arvada from 1924 to 1936.

Moving with his wife, Elizabeth, and their first three children to Arvada in December 1924, John Shannon took over as farmer of the Hackberry Ranch for Judge Robert Strong of Denver. A huge wheat harvest in 1926 helped Shannon become known as one of the area's most prolific farmers. Milk from the ranch was shipped to Coors Brewery in Golden to go in Coors Malted Milk. On 60 acres, Shannon raised corn and wheat. Livestock included cattle and horses. The family raised chickens and ducks, too. The Shannons also raised a family of eight children—four boys and four girls.

Years later, Ruth Shannon Robertson recalled that when she was a child in the early 1930s, an Indian in full regalia showed up at the farm looking for food. Mrs. Shannon, afraid for her children's safety, gave the man a loaf of freshly baked bread and sent him on his way. From then on, on baking day, Elizabeth Shannon always baked an extra loaf of bread in case the Indian ever came back.

The family enjoyed picnics in the mountains and pulled together with their neighbors at harvest time, going from farm to farm to bring in all the crops.

John Shannon died either by accident or suicide on July 24, 1936. Unable to keep up with the mortgage payments, Mrs. Shannon and the children moved back to Greeley. (Author's collection.)

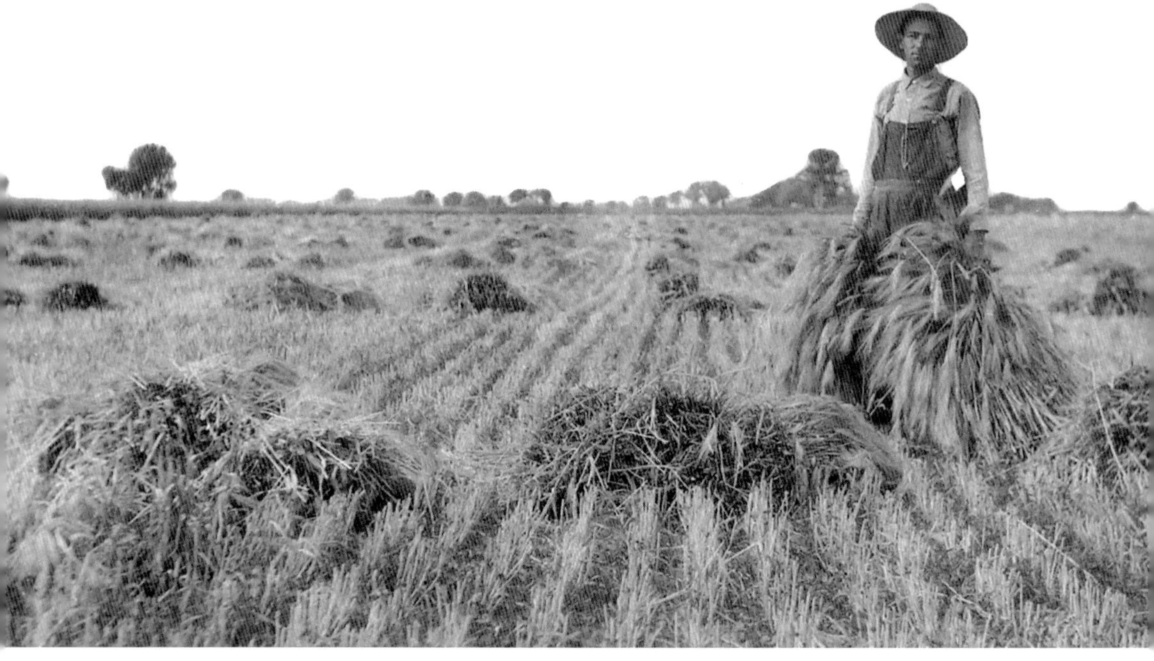

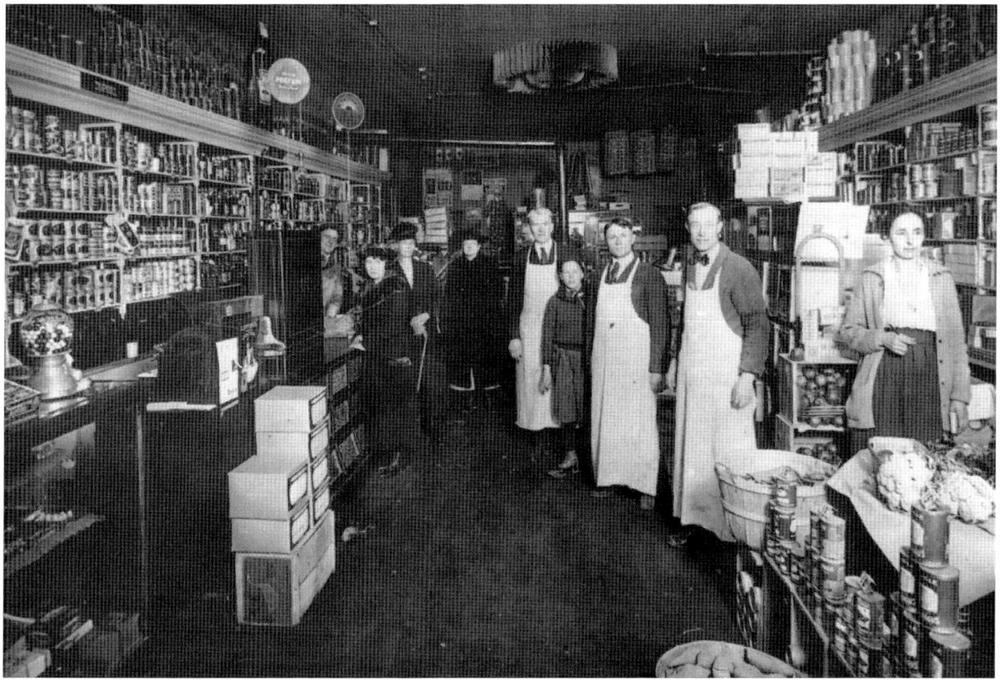

J.T. Kennedy
The well-known grocer was very active in Arvada in the early 1900s.

Not much is known of Kennedy's early life. He married Alice Secrest in Arvada on October 22, 1901. It is reported he ran a grocery store in Arvada as early as 1905. In 1912, Kennedy served a mayor pro-tem for Arvada. In 1914, he opened his grocery store on Grandview Avenue. Kennedy helped organize Arvada's second bank, the First State Bank of Arvada, in 1913 and served on the bank's board of directors. Before the Arvada Chamber of Commerce, the town had many other business organizations, such as the Arvada Commercial Club, of which Kennedy was a member. In 1930, Kennedy opened a store on the Davis Block that he ran until 1937.

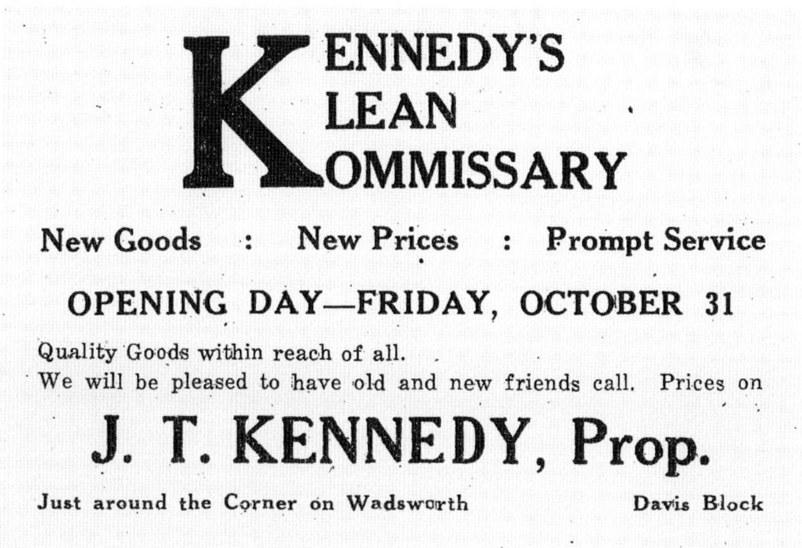

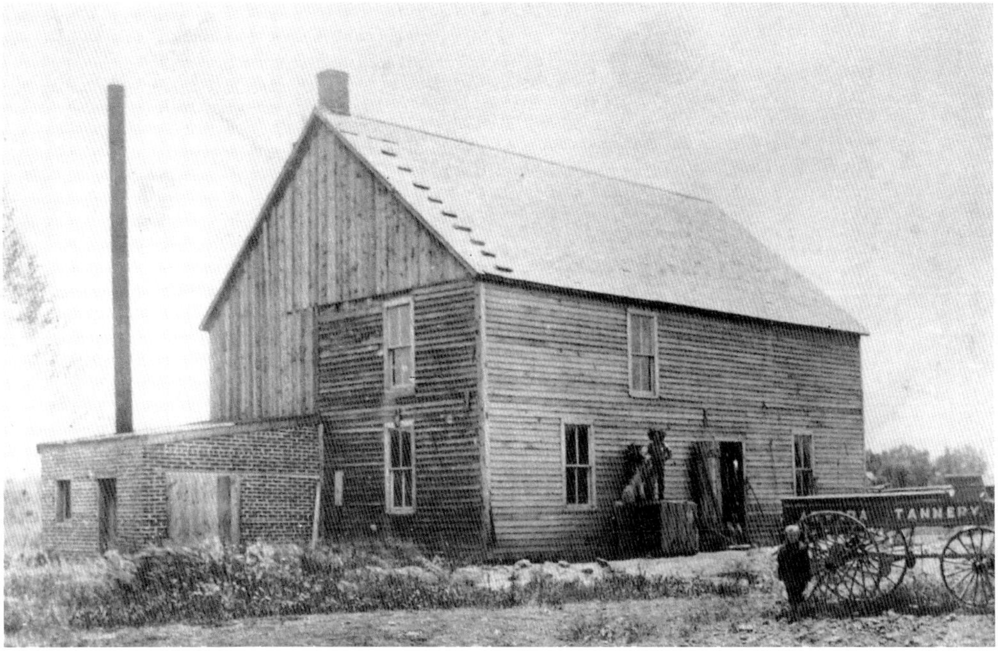

Louis Klumker

Along with William Grobels, Louis Klumker ran the Arvada Tannery.

In 1888, the Arvada tannery was opened. Both men had learned the trade in their native Germany.

They ran a prosperous tannery. Klumker and Grobels tanned all kinds of different hides at their Arvada business, including coyote, cow, and even bear. It is said they tanned hides sent back to America from Teddy Roosevelt's 1909 African safari.

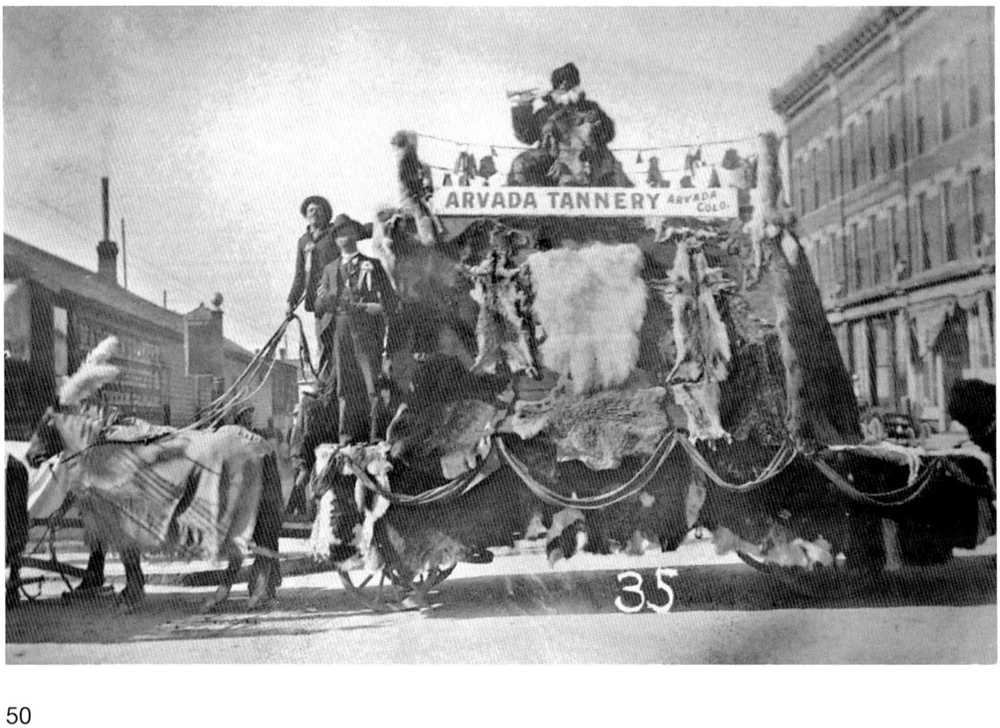

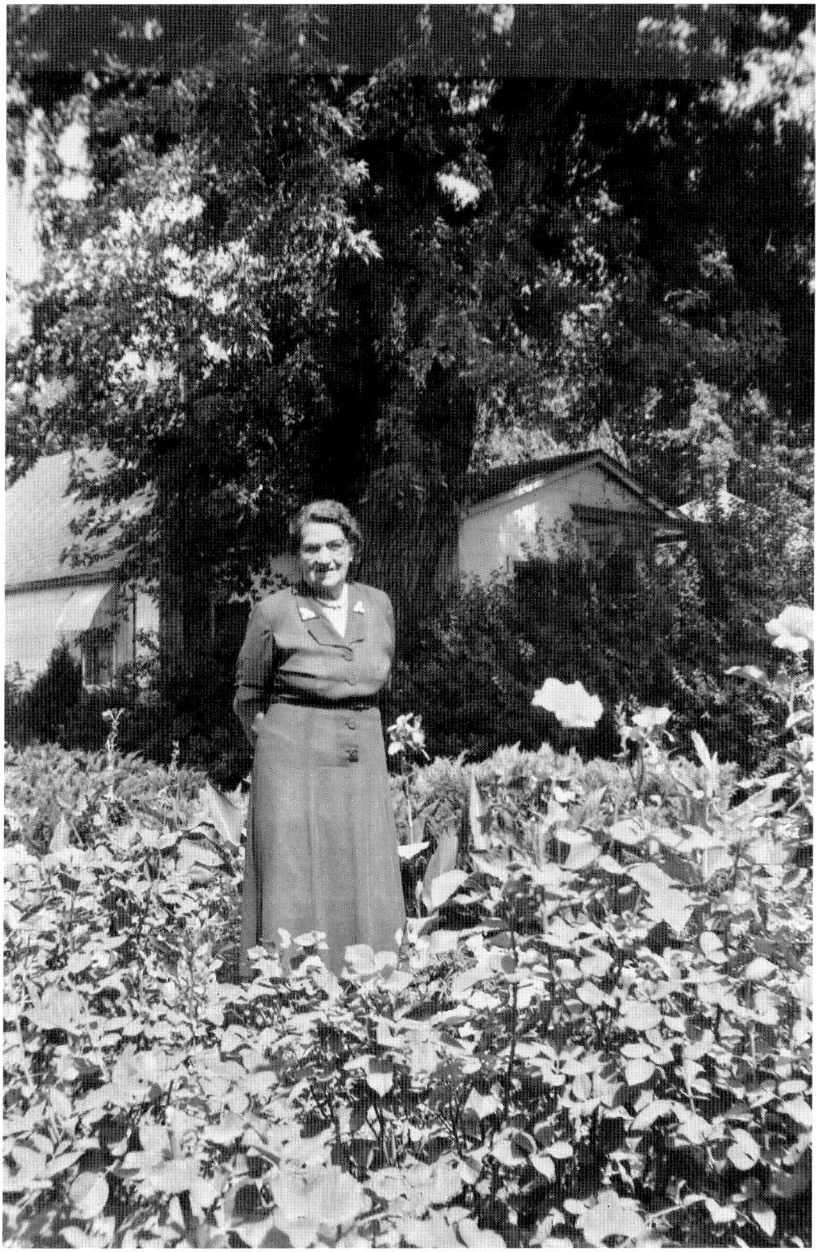

Fred and Olive Vetting

The couple's love of horticulture was evident in Arvada's landscape for many years.

Fred and Olive Vetting came to Arvada in 1906. Before coming to Colorado, Fred, along with a brother-in-law, ran a seed business in Wisconsin. In 1912, Fred opened a seed store on Grandview Avenue. In 1920, the Rocky Mountain Seed Company was established by Vetting in Denver. The store was open until 2011.

Olive Vetting was named Arvada Woman of the Year for her efforts to beautify the town. Olive planted flowers on Marshall Street, donated trees to many projects and was a member of the Arvada Garden Club.

George Wendt

Wendt ran the Arvada Pharmacy for 21 years.

Born in Arvada on April 2, 1907, George Wendt's first job as a child was folding newspapers for the *Arvada Enterprise*. He also worked at various stores in town. While a teen, George worked at the F.A. Mahannah pharmacy at the corner of present-day Grandview Avenue and Webster Street. It was at this job that George chose being a pharmacist as a career. He attended Capitol College of Pharmacy and Barnes Business College. After three years working in Fort Collins, Wendt returned to Arvada in 1935 and opened the Arvada Pharmacy. Remembered as a friendly, caring man, George mentored many youngsters in his years owning the pharmacy, which came to be a popular hangout for adolescents in town.

George served as a member of the Arvada Fire Department, was on the city council, and was a member of the Arvada Masonic Lodge and various other organizations. In 1964, George and his wife, Vivian, moved to San Diego, California, where George died on April 6, 1992.

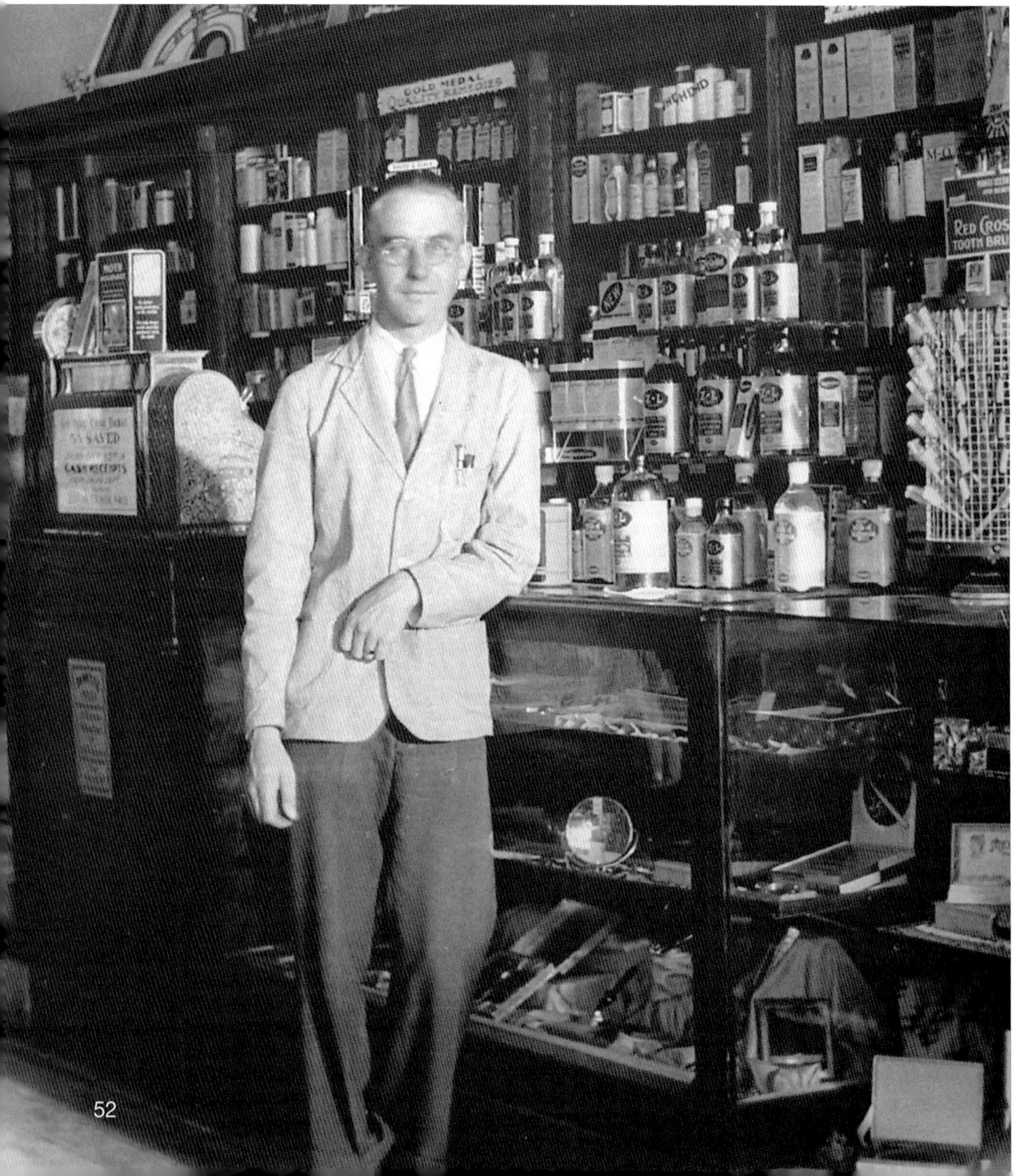

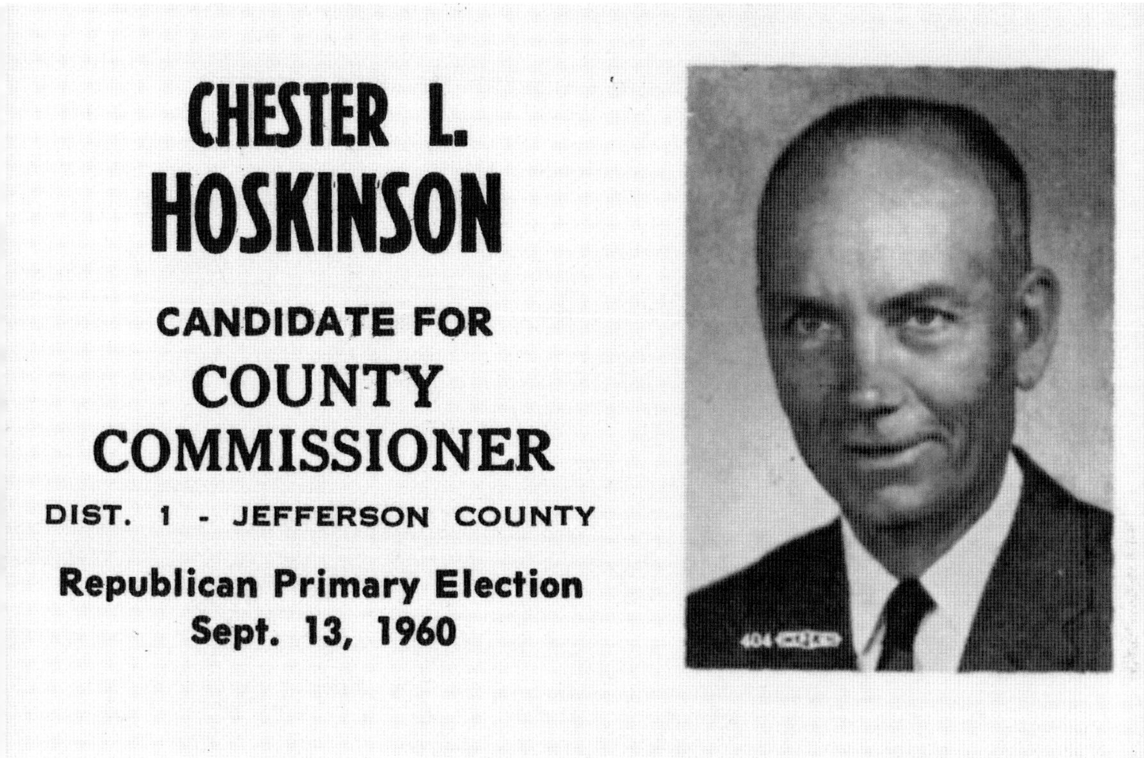

Chester Hoskinson
Hoskinson was a prolific home builder in post–World War II Arvada.

Chester Hoskinson was born in Kansas in 1905. He settled in Colorado in 1941. During World War II, Hoskinson served at Lowry Field and Buckley Naval Air Base. He went on to work at Fort Logan and on the Alaskan Highway. Hoskinson began buying land lots and building homes on the land. He soon became one of the first contractors in the area. It is said that by 1952, Hoskinson had built 97 percent of the homes in Arvada since the end of the war.

Chester Hoskinson was named Arvada Man of the Year in 1951. He also served on the Arvada Town Board and was Jefferson County commissioner. He helped build the Arvada Masonic Lodge that was demolished in 2014, assisted in forming Arvada Saving and Loan, and constructed the building for the business at Fifty-seventh Avenue and Yukon Street.

Chester Hoskinson passed away December 4, 1996.

Riess Stenger

Arvada banker Stenger kept the Arvada First National Bank afloat during the Great Depression.

Riess Stenger was born in Omaha, Nebraska, on February 14, 1896. His father, Ernest, was at one time president of the Denver Tramway Company. Riess was employed as a cashier at the First National Bank in Delores, Colorado, and at the First National Bank in Fort Morgan, Colorado, before coming to Arvada in 1927. He became a cashier at the Arvada First National bank in March 1928, and in August of that year, he bought an interest in the bank and became its president. In 1930, Riess served as treasurer of the Arvada Chamber of Commerce.

After the National Bank Holiday in 1933, the Arvada First National Bank was one of 4,407 banks allowed to open nationwide. Upon reopening, no large sums of money were allowed to be withdrawn, but a deposit of $2,500 in gold was made. Stenger served as chairman of the bank board from 1970 until 1984. In 1985, a 30-acre farm owned by Stenger at Fifty-eighth Avenue and Oak Street in Arvada was dedicated as Stenger Soccer Complex.

Riess Stenger passed away in Denver on February 18, 1986.

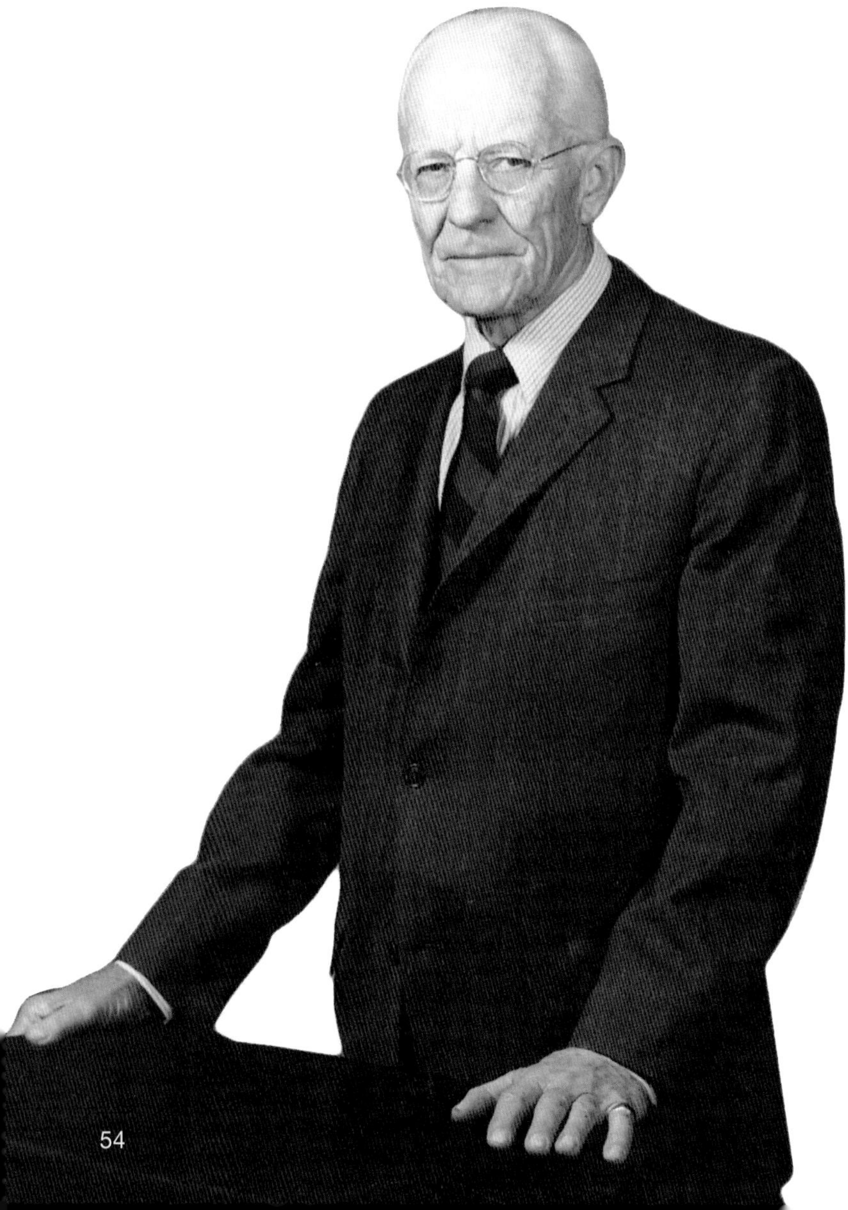

J. Harold Holliway

This insurance agent was the Arvada Man of the Year in 1974.

Born in Sitka, Kansas, on February 25, 1927, Harold Holliway served in the US Marine Corps after his high school graduation. Holliway graduated from the University of Denver in 1950 and came to Arvada in 1953. He joined the Jefferson County Finance Co. and was influential in getting the company into insurance. In 1966, he started Holliway Insurance on Ralston Road. Being active in the community was very important to Harold. In 2004, he said, "I've always believed that if you make a living in your community, if your community provides your livelihood, then you should live there and be active. I've raised my family here, done business here and stayed here for my life." It was Holliway's love for Arvada that led him to get involved in the 1960s and 1970s in the city's economic growth. In 1966, Holliway served in the Arvada Home Rule Committee and Citizens' Committee. In 1976 and 1977, he was the chairman for the Downtown Turnaround committee that was involved in revitalizing the rundown Olde Town Arvada. Holliway was president of the Arvada Chamber of Commerce in 1981. He also served as director for the North Jeffco Foundation.

Continuing his involvement in the community, Harold was a member of the Arvada Jaycees, the Arvada Elks Club, and the Lions Club. Harold and his wife, Ruthie, belonged to the Arvada Methodist Church, and Holliway Insurance sponsored many high school band and athletic events.

Harold Holliway died on October 22, 2006.

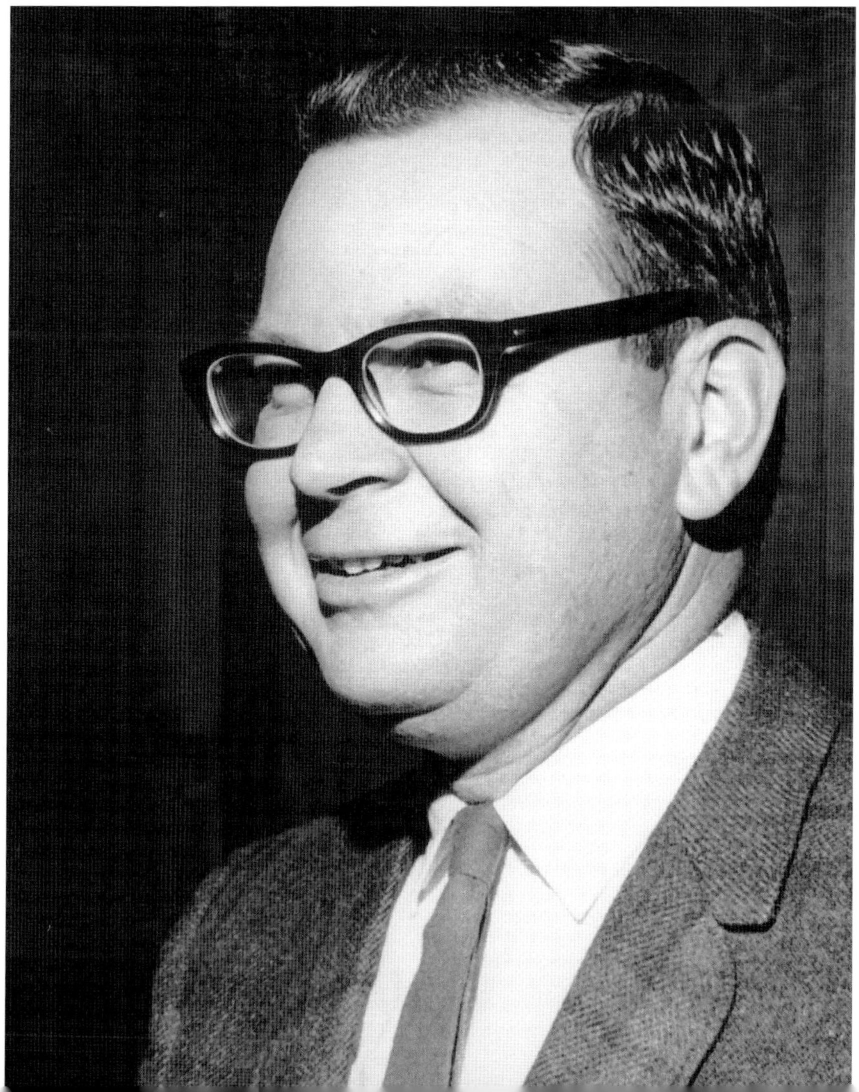

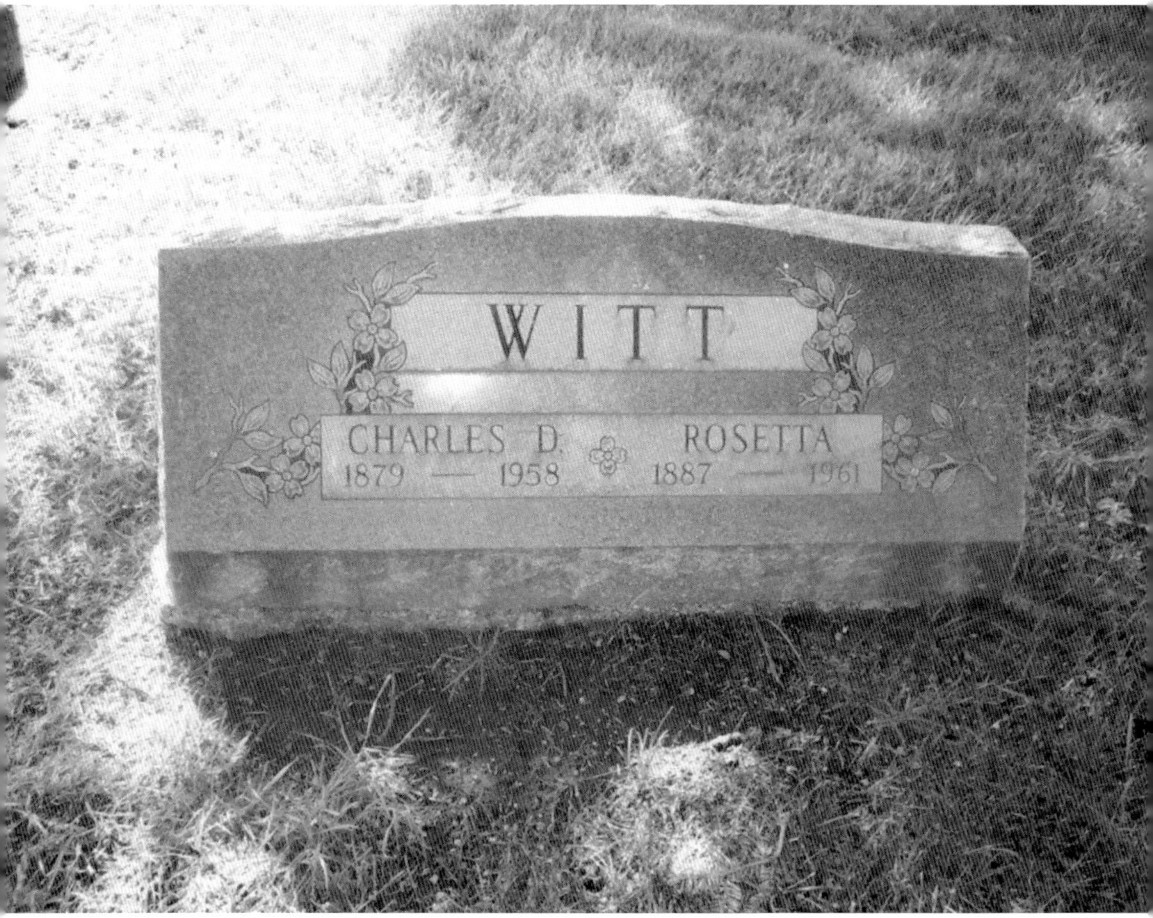

Rosetta Witt

This well-known and well-respected store owner was the victim of an unsolved murder.

Rosetta Shafer was born in Red Willow County, Nebraska, on March 6, 1887. Rosetta and her brother were orphaned when they were young, and the two were raised by their paternal grandparents. At an early age, Rosetta displayed a talent for sewing and quilting, activities she would enjoy all her life. In 1900, Rosetta met Charles Witt when both were performing in a theatrical company. The couple wed on September 11, 1904. Two children came out of this union: Lester, born in 1905, and Erma, born in November 1915.

Charles was diagnosed with tuberculosis, and in May 1918 the Witts came to Colorado. They settled in Arvada in the fall of that year. Charles worked at the A.L. Davis garage. The Witts were members of the First Baptist Church of Arvada, where Rosetta sang in the choir and played piano. She was also involved in the Ladies' Aid, which did quilting. In 1937, Charles and Rosetta bought a grocery store at present day Fiftieth Avenue and Carr Street. The store was south of the Griffith Station tramway stop. Rosetta was active in the Griffith Lane Sewing Club, which made beautifully colorful quilts.

On Monday, October 2, 1961, Rosetta was at the store alone when an unidentified man entered the business. During the robbery that followed, Rosetta Witt was shot to death.

The tragic murder of Rosetta Witt remains unsolved 53 years later.

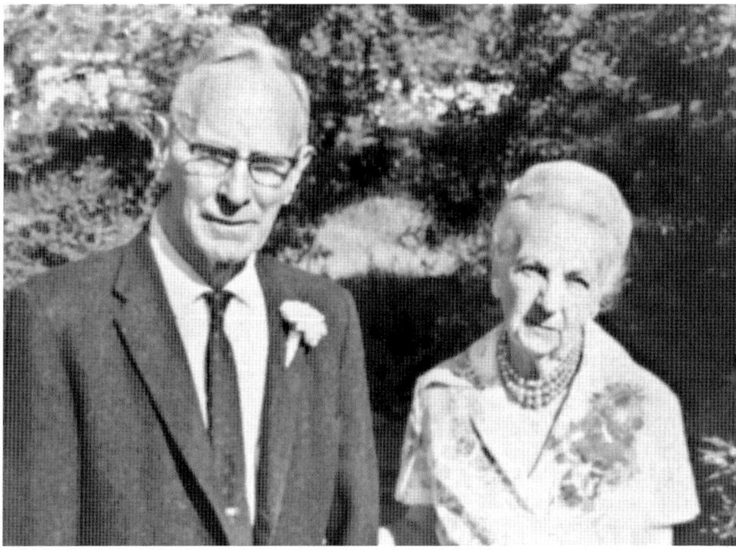

Marquis Johnson

A dedicated businessman and community leader, Johnson was active in the first half of the 20th century. Born in Iowa on April 25, 1881, as a child Johnson moved with his family to Kansas. Marquis studied at Kansas Wesleyan College before transferring to the University of Denver. Marquis married Inez Walker on June 5, 1904. The Johnsons moved to Arvada in 1916. Johnson was employed at the Ford garage in Arvada. In 1921, Marquis was elected for a two-year term as town trustee. The next year, Johnson bought the Arvada Hardware Store from Madeline Flaherty Pratte. Three years later, Johnson sold the hardware store and opened his own insurance company. Johnson also sold real estate through his business.

In 1924, the Arvada Chamber of Commerce was formed, and Marquis Johnson was a charter member. He served as chamber secretary and treasurer for many years. Johnson was a big supporter of the Arvada Harvest Festival, which was started in 1925. During World War II, Johnson served as the Arvada representative for the county rent control board. In 1945, Johnson served on a committee to hold clothing drives for those in war-torn Europe and the Philippines. Arvada's quota was 10,000 pounds of clothing and bedding, and 11,800 pounds were raised. Marquis Johnson died on October 2, 1970.

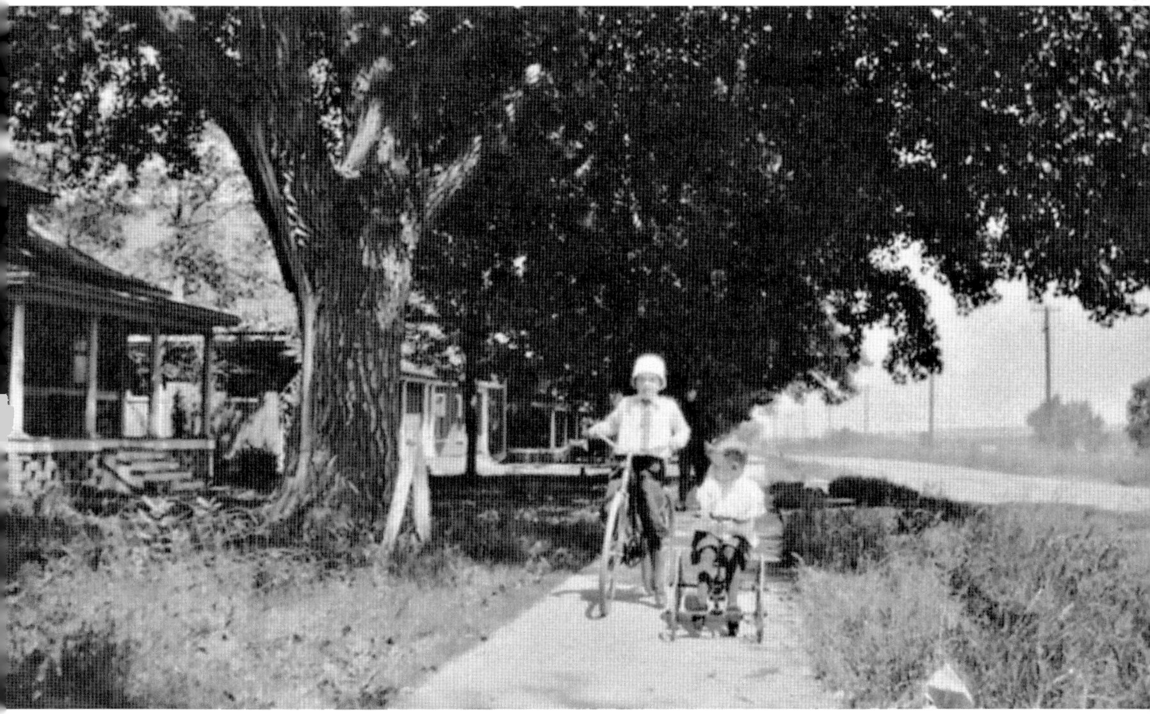

Duane Youse

Youse was the Arvada Man of the Year for 1988.

Born in Clay Center, Kansas, on July 6, 1934, Duane Youse came to Arvada in 1961. In 1968, he opened Duane's Men's Clothier, which was in business for 22 years in Arvada. In 1969, he was elected to the Arvada Chamber of Commerce board, on which he served for many years. After closing his menswear shop in 1990, Youse became involved at the Arvada Community Food Bank. He was codirector of the bank with Jim Scharfenberg from 2000 to 2002. In 2003, Youse became the director of the food bank. Active in the Arvada Jefferson Kiwanis Club, Youse was also the leader of the North Jeffco District Foundation. Duane enjoys travel and mountain climbing. His passion for serving others was evident in a 2006 interview: "Society needs advocates that champion causes. I fall into that area because food is the number one, without food you are not going to exist." (Author's collection.)

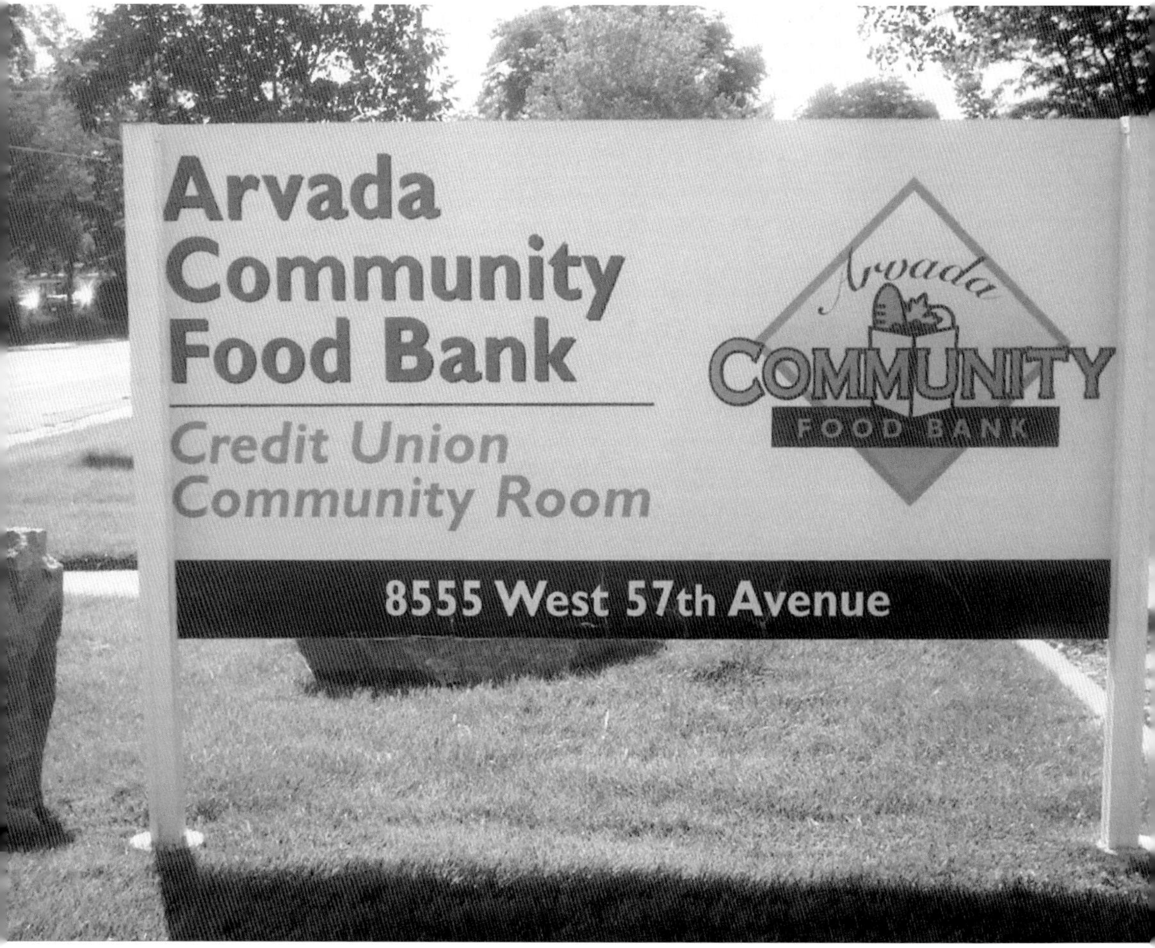

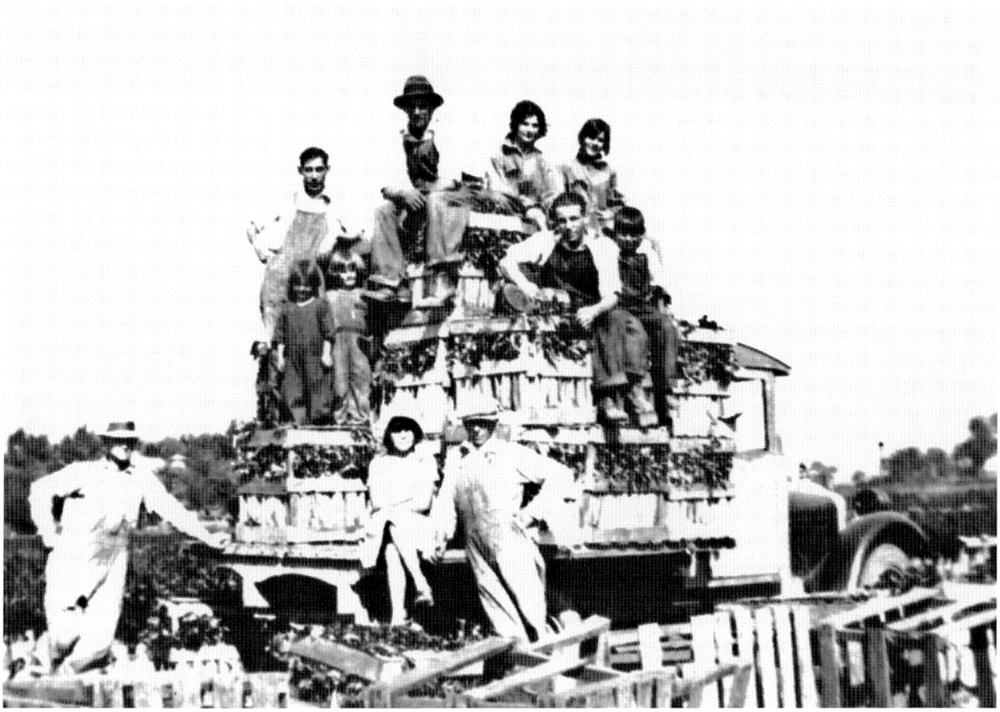

The Spano Family

Known for their delicious Pascal celery, the Spano family were award-winning fruit and vegetable farmers. The Spano family were truck farmers who owned land in Arvada at current Fifty-second Avenue and Marshall Street. In the 1935 Harvest Festival, Joe Spano won first-, second-, and third-place ribbons for his vegetables and flowers.

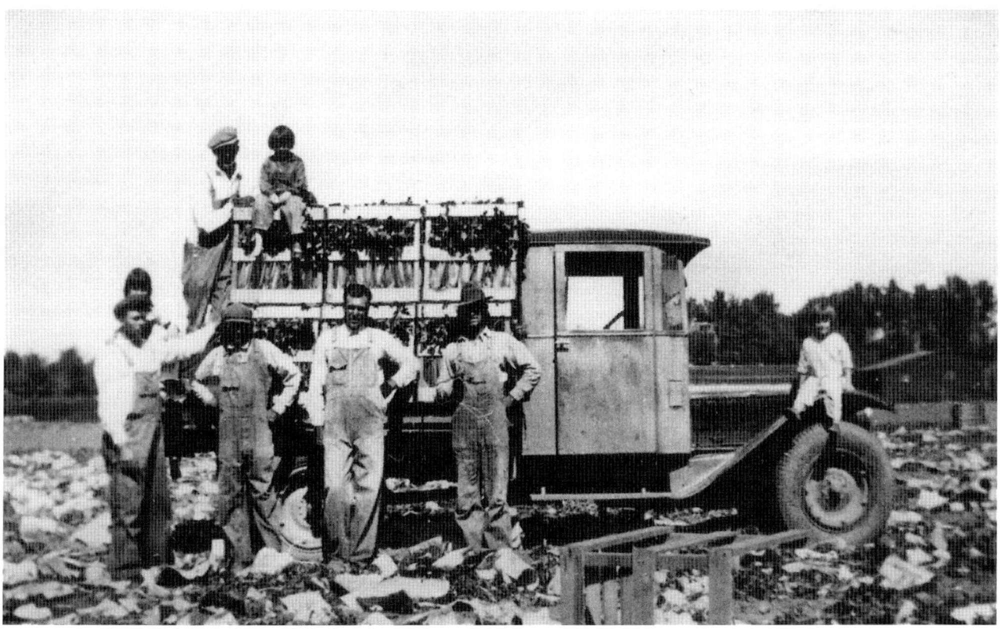

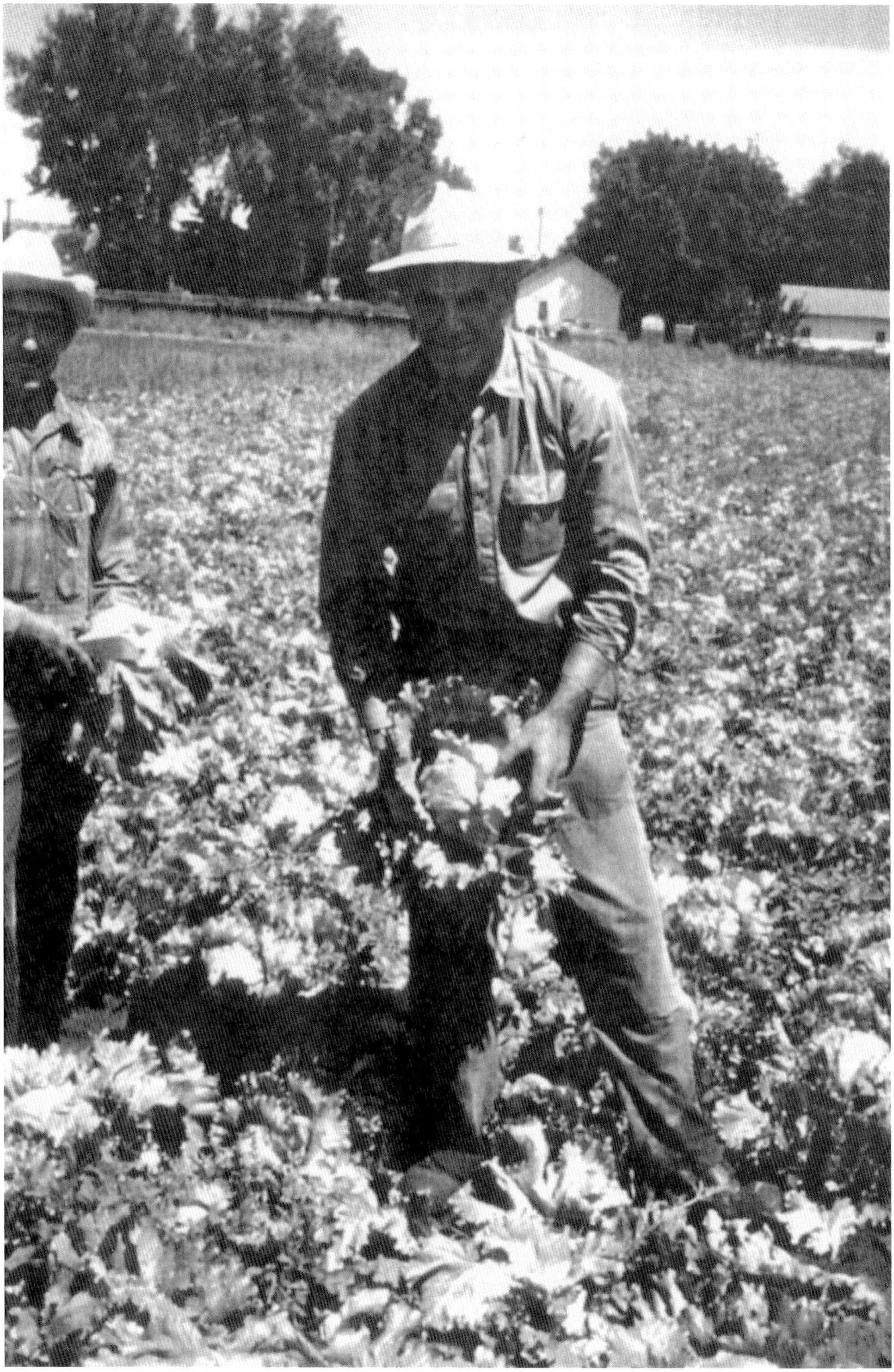

CHAPTER THREE

Hometown Heroes

Firefighters, educators, police officers, doctors, and community leaders have all made an indelible mark on Arvada history.

Dr. Edwin Foster assisted in over 1,000 births in his half a century career. Thomas Vanderhoof, Helen Lawrence, Olive Swanson, and O.B. Drake all taught countless children in their teaching careers, and each has been honored with Arvada schools named after them. In 1927, William Benson was named Arvada night marshal. Following in his footsteps have been hundreds of law enforcement officers, most notably "Smitty" Smith, Arvada's first police chief; Ed McCarthy, the "Lollipop Cop"; and Regina Jo Gailus, the city's first female patrol officer. Clinton Reed and Ozzie Lutz brought spiritual guidance to Arvadans from the pulpit of the Arvada Presbyterian Church.

George Klumker, Harry Hill, and Kennith Mayne answered their country's call to arms with dedication and sacrifice. Of two Arvada legends, the Water Tower and the Arvada Redskin mascot, only one remains, but the other is still fiercely and fondly remembered.

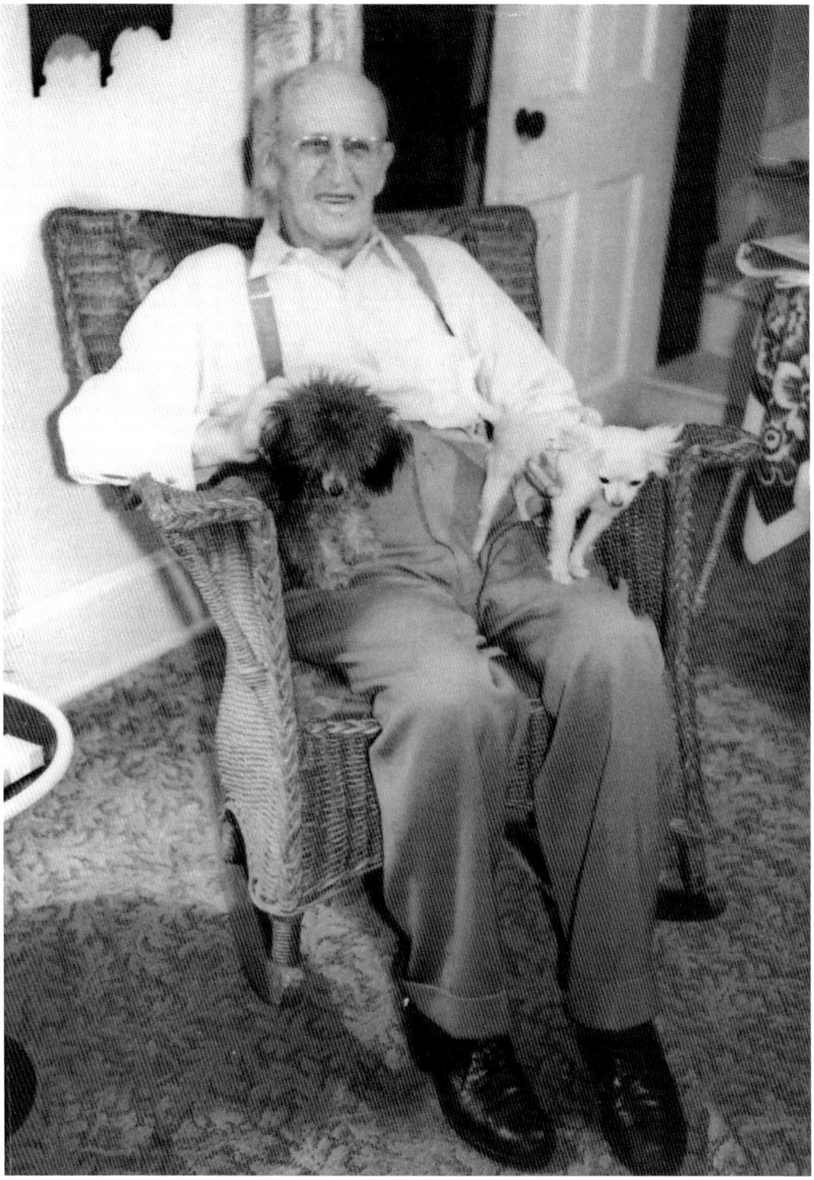

William Benson

A legendary Arvada lawman, William "Billy" Benson was involved and wounded in three shootings in his 26-year career.

William Benson was born on September 18, 1869, in Marshall County, Kansas. In 1904, William and Hettie Benson settled in Arvada. Active in numerous organizations, the Bensons, who never had children, were called Uncle Billy and Aunt Het. In 1927, Benson became Arvada's night marshal. Along with his trusted German shepherd watchdog, Benson patrolled the streets of the still small town. In 1932 and 1934, Benson was shot by burglars at two different locations in town. On October 12, 1940, Benson was with Jefferson County undersheriff C.B. Fugate in Arvada attempting to arrest a bar owner named Carleton. Carleton fatally wounded Fugate and shot Benson in the hand. William Benson retired from his night marshal job in 1953. One month shy of his 100th birthday, William Benson died on August 19, 1969.

Helen Lawrence

An Arvada education pioneer, Helen Lawrence taught generations of students.

Helen Lawrence arrived in Colorado in 1901 from her native Ohio. A tuberculosis patient, Helen, like thousands of others, came to the Rocky Mountains seeking health benefits. Helen's first teaching job was near Bergen Park in Jefferson County. Helen came to Arvada in 1904 and began her 35-year teaching career at the Arvada Grade School. Lawrence retired in the 1930s and passed away in February 1941. In 1954, the Arvada Grade School was renamed Helen Lawrence Elementary School in honor of the dedicated, beloved educator.

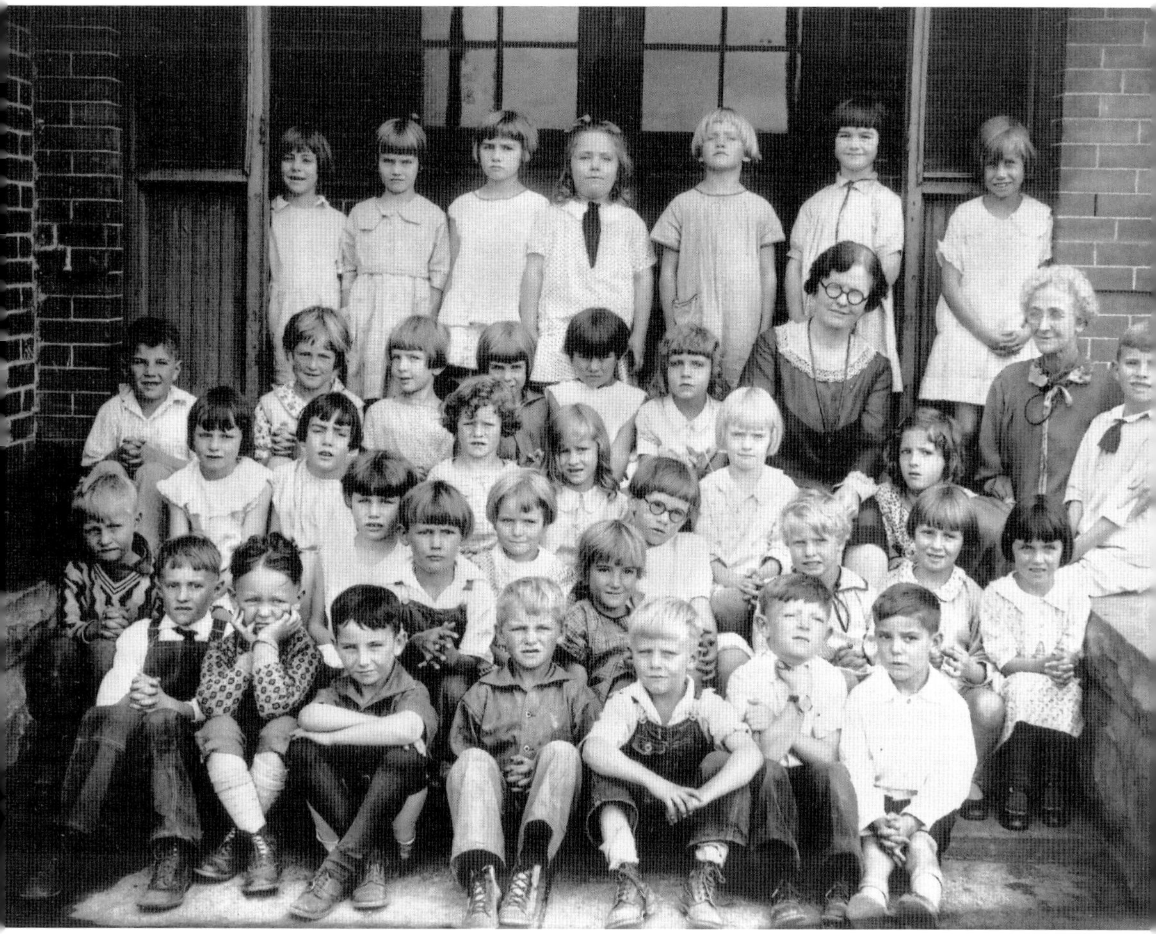

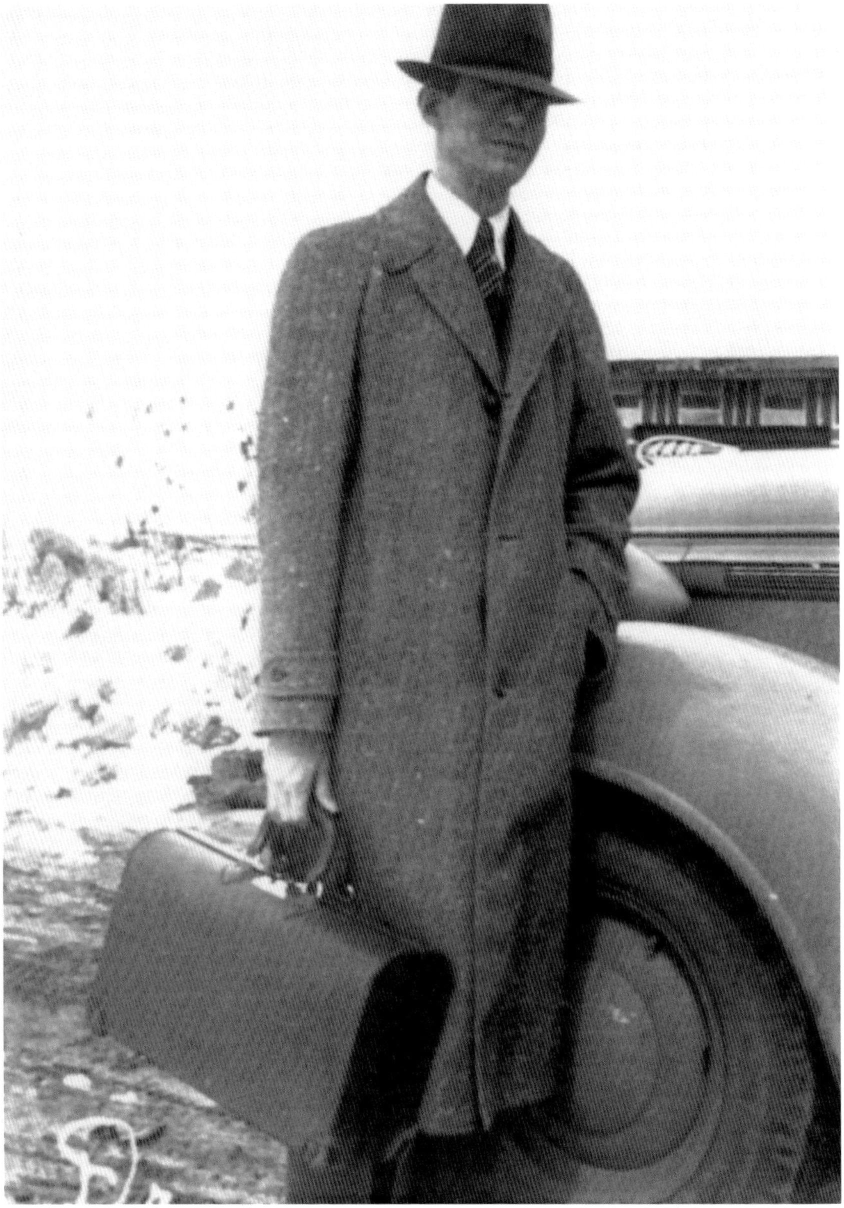

Dr. Thomas Thorn
Throughout his 45-year medical career, Dr. Thorn treated generations of Arvadans.

Thomas Roy Thorn graduated in 1927 from Missouri College of Medicine and Science. That same year, he came to Colorado. Wanting to practice his profession in a small community, Thorn—along with his wife, Alice, and their first child—settled in Arvada in May 1931. Besides his practice in Arvada, Dr. Thorn also served on the staffs at both St. Anthony's and Lutheran Hospitals. Known for giving free examinations to schoolchildren, Dr. Thorn was also the doctor for Leyden Mine for many years.

During World War II, Thorn served as the Jefferson County examining officer for the draft. Over the years, Thorn earned degrees in medicine from five different hospitals.

Dr. Thomas Thorn passed away on April 16, 1976.

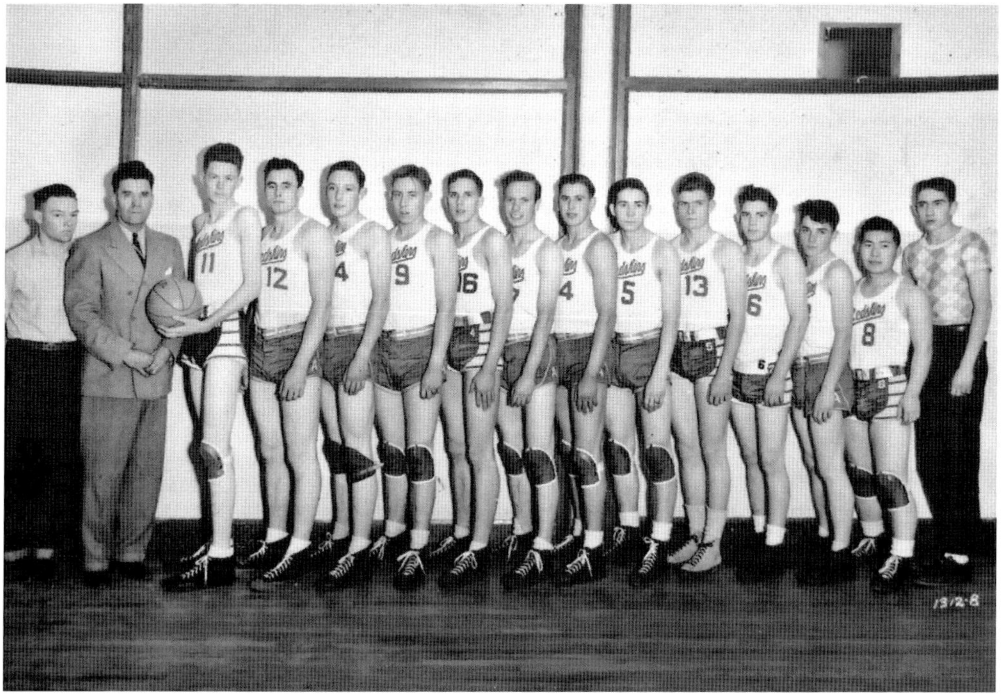

Redskins

According to legend, Arvada High School acquired its mascot from red football jersey that bled red dye onto the players skin. Coach Thomas Vanderhoof called his players "redskins," and the name stuck. From 1924 to 1993, the Arvada Redskins served as a beloved hometown mascot. In 1993, upon charges that the name was offensive, the name was changed—a move that to this day is not without controversy.

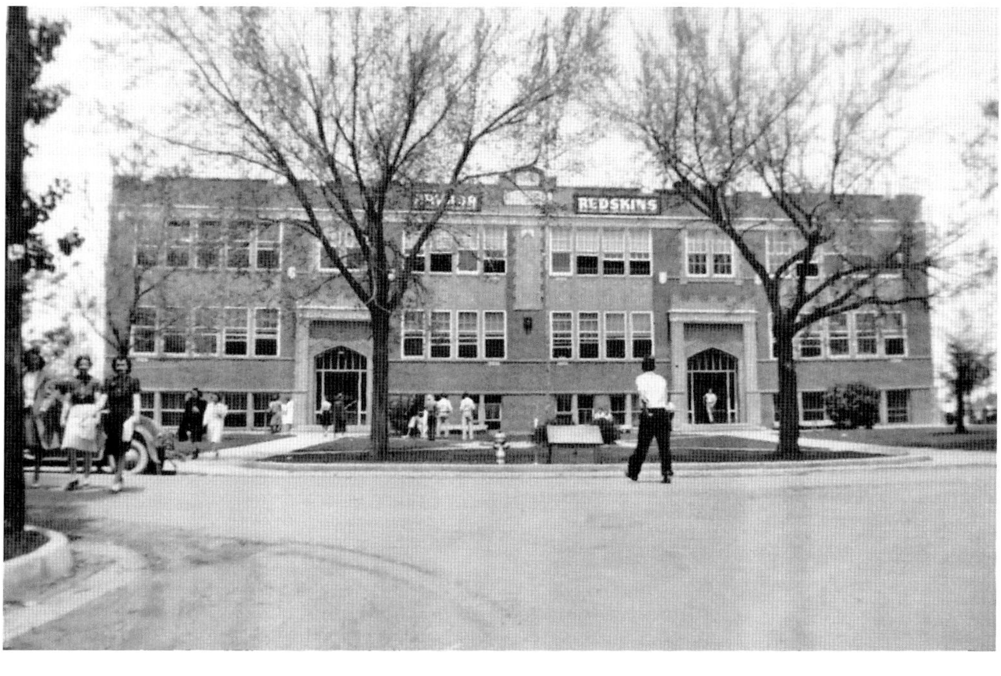

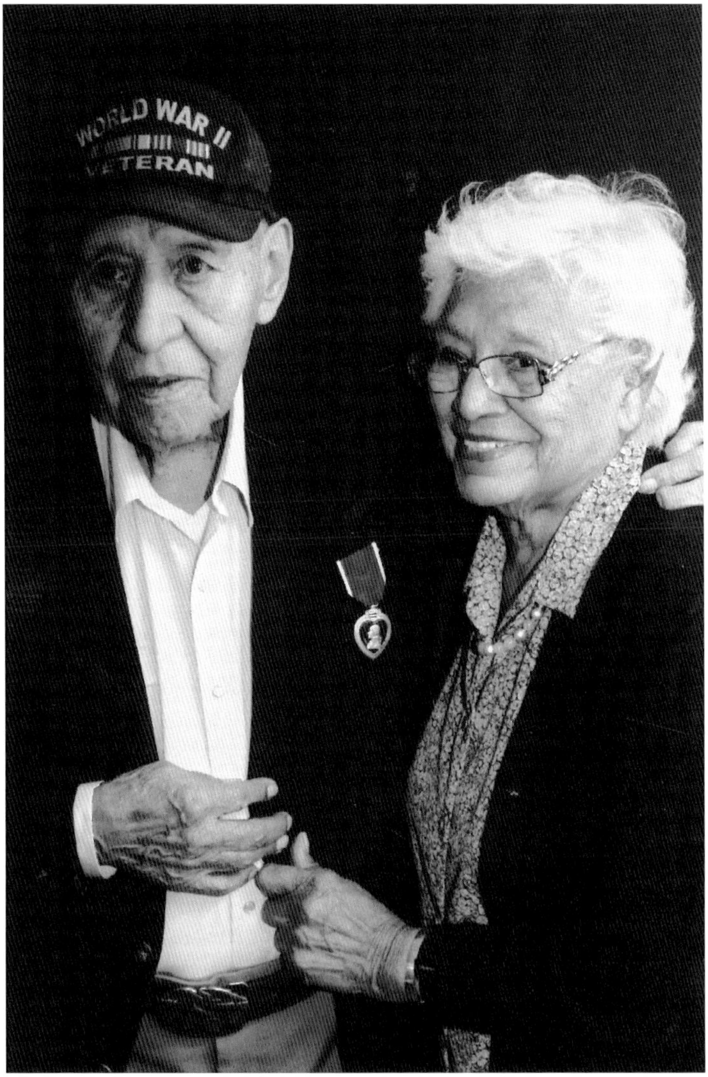

Emil and Irene Gimeno

The legacy of Emil and Irene Gimeno is evident not only in their large family but also in the mark the couple left on Arvada, their hometown since 1948.

Wed in 1942, Emil enlisted in the Navy in 1944. Serving aboard the aircraft carrier USS *Yorktown*, Emil saw action in the Pacific. While her husband was away at war, Irene worked at the Rocky Mountain Arsenal helping build bombs. Upon returning home, Emil started his own construction business. "I started a construction company so my children could go to college," Emil stated in 2013. Education had always been a big part of the Gimeno family. Emil attended night school, and Irene earned an associate's degree in art at the age of 63. Irene had been active in the YMCA, League of Women Voters, Women of the League of United Latin American Citizens, the Arvada Art Guild, and many more organizations.

Emil was involved in the reconstruction of Bent's Fort and, in 2004, wrote the book *The Adobe Castle of the Santa Fe Trail: The History and Reconstruction of Bent's Old Fort.*

Emil and Irene celebrated their 71st wedding anniversary in June 2013. They still reside in the Arvada home Emil built 30 years ago. The couple has 9 children, 21 grandchildren, and 27 great-grandchildren.

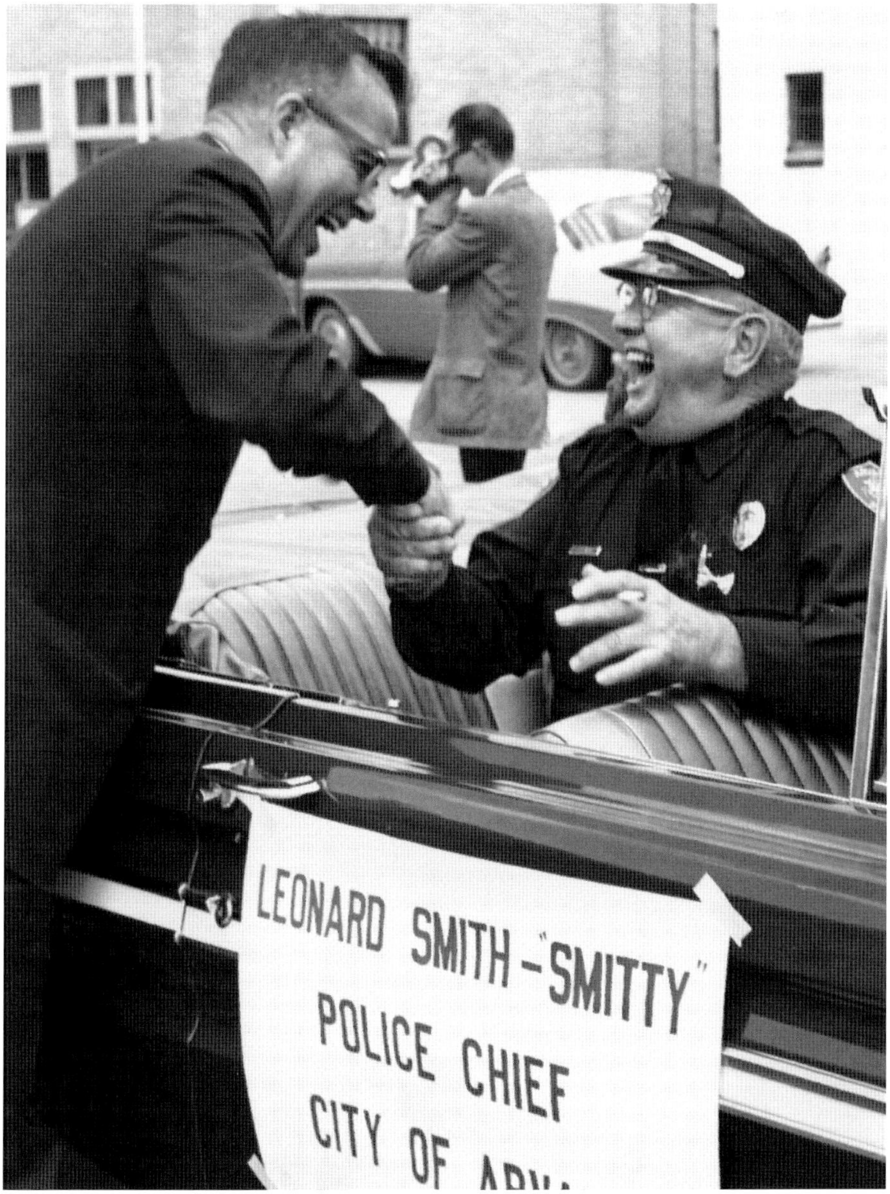

Leonard "Smitty" Smith

A 20-year veteran of the Arvada Police Department, Smitty—as he was affectionately called—was a beloved Arvada officer.

Born in Arvada on the first day of 1906, Smith attended school in Arvada, graduating in 1925. Beginning in 1935, Smith served for several years in the Colorado State Patrol. In 1944, Smitty was appointed Arvada's first chief of police. In addition to his law enforcement duties, Smith was in charge of reading the town's water meters, street maintenance, and town water repairs. During Smith's years in office, Arvada acquired its first patrol car, built a new jail, and instated the force's first radio communications system. Leonard Smith retired from police work in 1966 and went on to serve on city council from 1967 to 1969. He enjoyed gardening and fishing and was active in the Arvada Lions Club.

Leonard "Smitty" Smith passed away on April 15, 1984.

Max Haug

One of Arvada's most active residents for over 60 years, Max Haug has served Arvada well.

The Haug family moved from Limon, Colorado, to Arvada in 1941. Max graduated from Arvada High School and entered the Navy. After his service was over, Max returned to Arvada. He opened his real estate business in 1959. A charter member of the Arvada Elks Club, Max also served as president of the Arvada Historical Society and the Arvada Olde Town Association. His biggest achievement was the founding of the Arvada Community Resources Association (ACRA) in 1968. The group has helped needy families in Arvada. Of all his endeavors, Max said in 2004 that ACRA was the outreach he was most proud of. At the time, Haug stated, "I imagine over the years the group has probably served 10,000 families, at least."

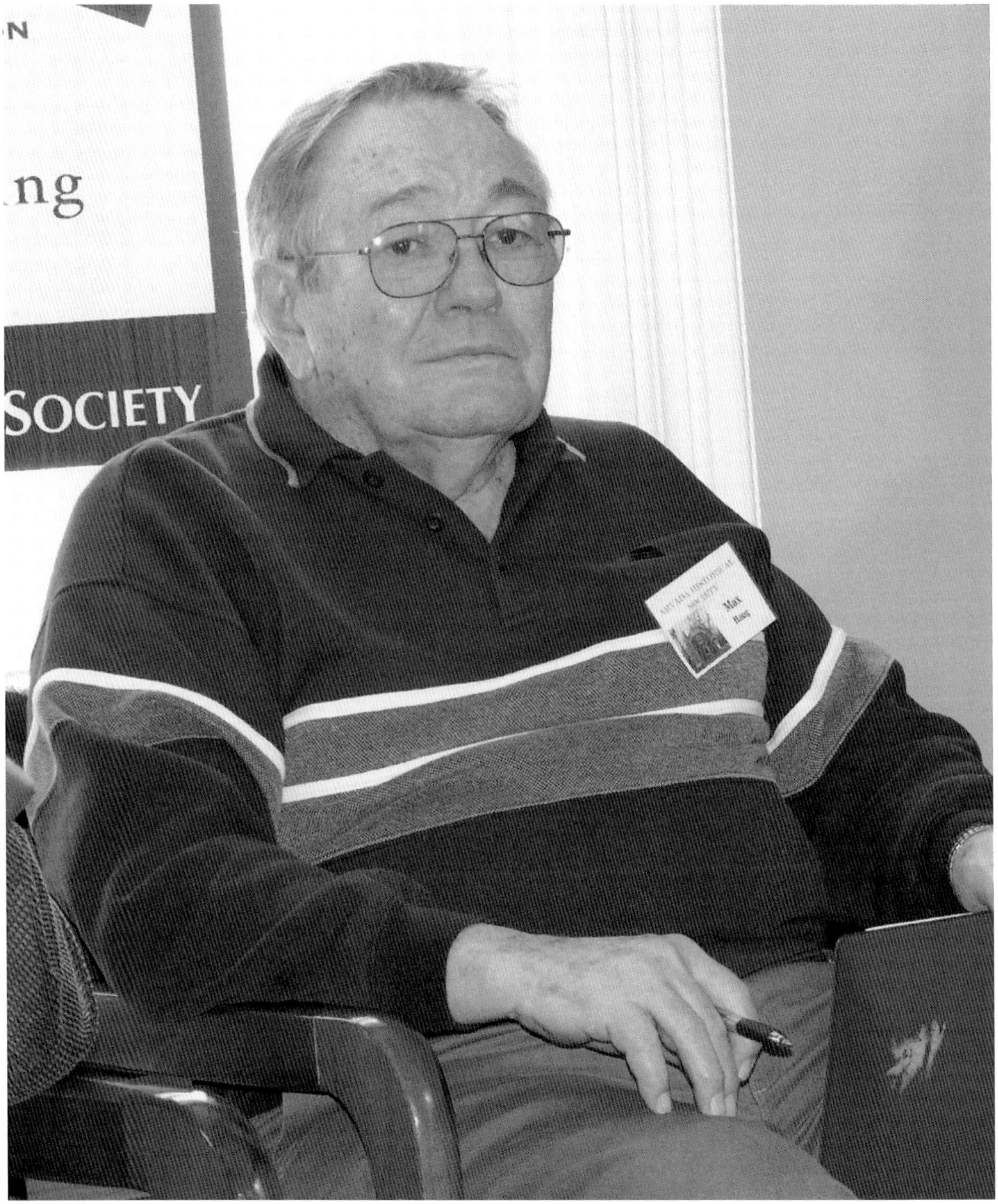

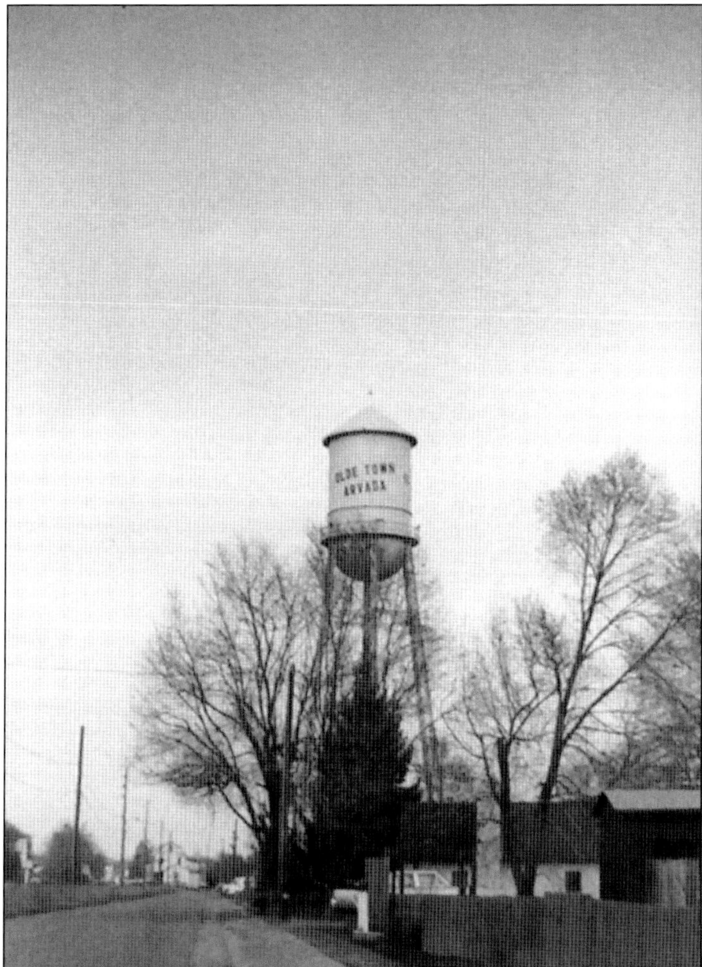

Water Tower

Arvada's most well-known landmark, the Arvada Water Tower, still stands tall after 104 years.

In 1909, a safe water source for the city had become a paramount need due to various outbreaks of waterborne illnesses. That year, voters approved a $40,000-bond issue and work began on the artesian well. On October 12, 1910, Arvada held a Celebration Day to usher in the new well. The highlight of the day was when crowds lined the streets to watch a firefight between the Arvada Volunteer Fire Department and another local band of firemen. The contest was to demonstrate the high water power that surged through the hoses, powered by the new gravity-fed system. The hometown firemen easily won, sending a four-foot ball across their opponents' line.

The tower was used to provide the city's water until 1975.

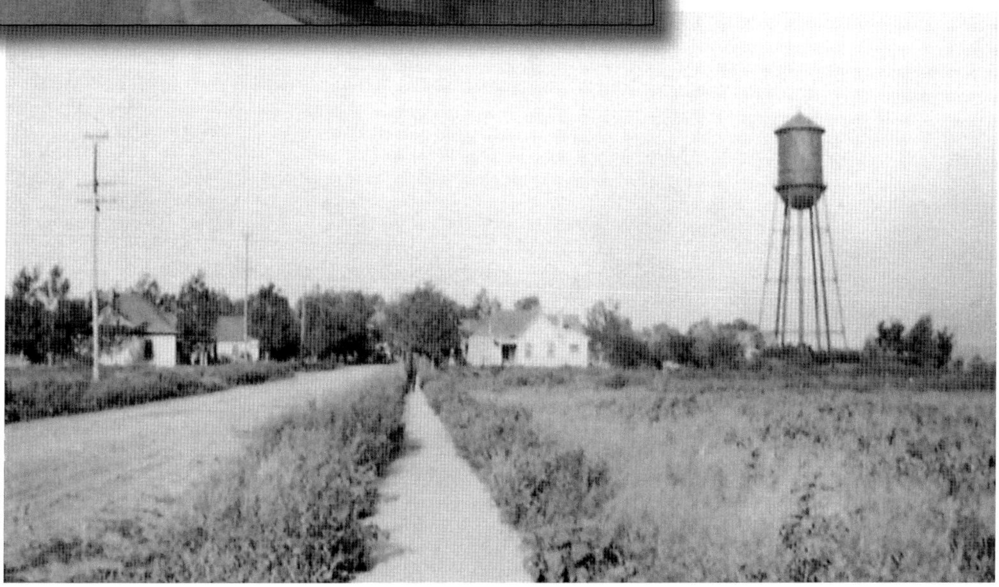

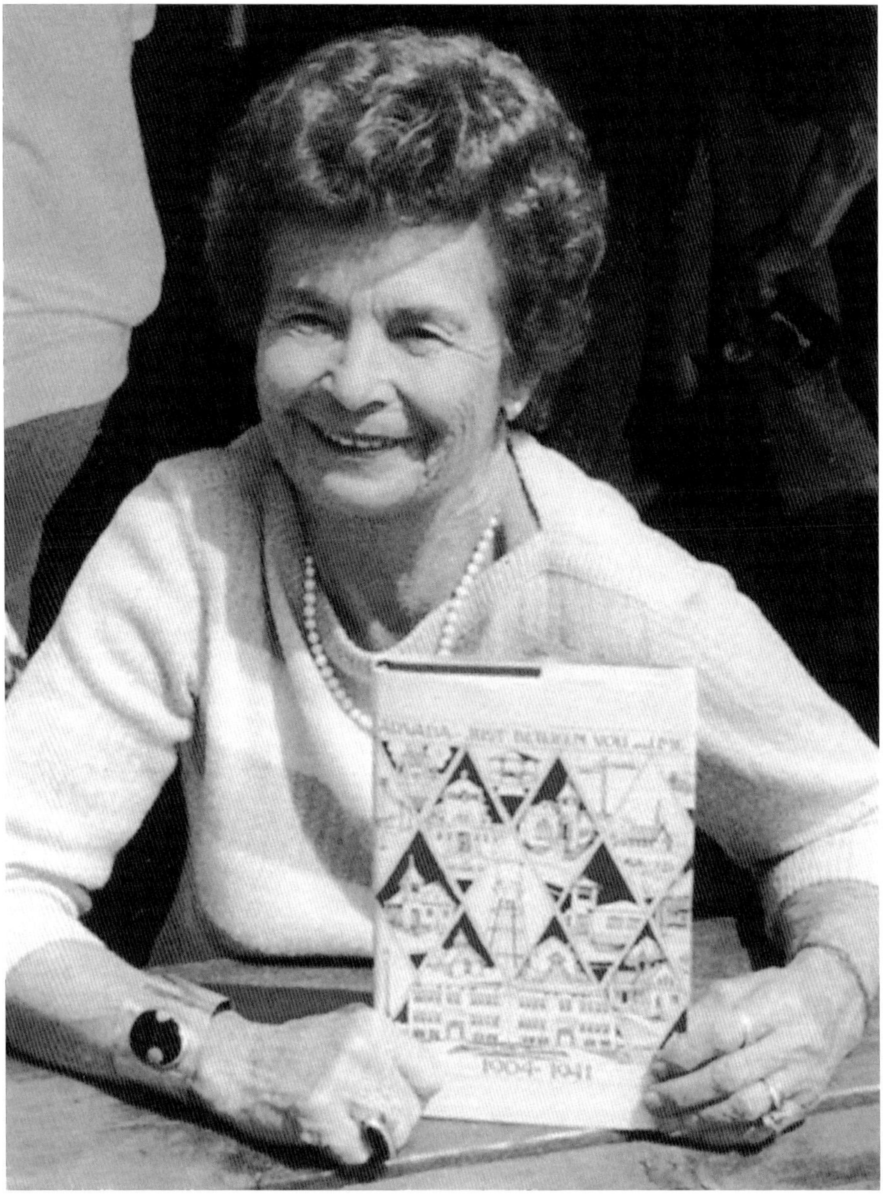

Marcetta Lutz

A charter member of the Arvada Historical Society, Marcetta Rhodes Lutz was passionate about preserving and sharing Arvada history.

Born in 1920 in Panama to an Army communication expert and his wife, Marcetta moved to Arvada in 1936. She graduated from Arvada High School and then attended the University of Denver, where she met Harold Lutz. The couple wed in 1943, and while Harold served in World War II, Marcetta worked for the Army's Code Department. After the war, the couple settled in Arvada. Marcetta became a teacher. In her years with the Arvada Historical Society, Marcetta served as archivist, president, and newsletter editor. She also coauthored many of the society's books. Marcetta was named Arvada Woman of the Year in 1987.

Marcetta R. Lutz passed away in December 2008.

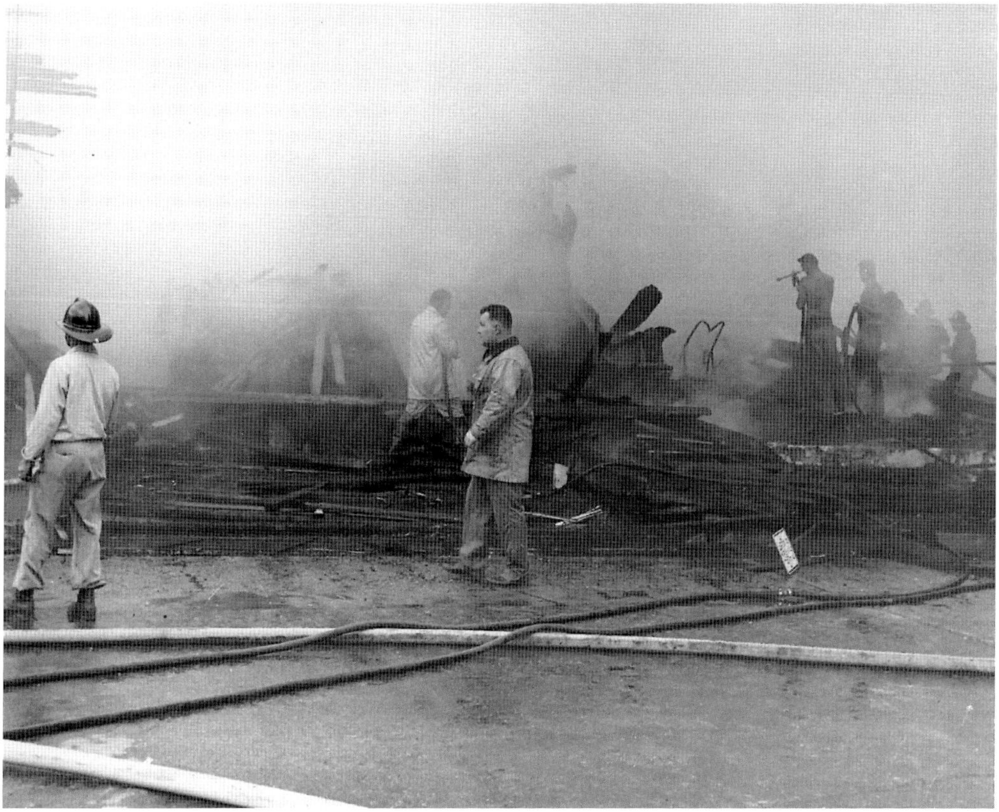

Fred "Fritz" Sedlmayr

Arvada's fire chief for 16 years, Sedlmayr led the fight against Arvada's most infamous fire in 1960.

Born in Denver on May 26, 1917, Fred "Fritz" Sedlmayr graduated from Denver's North High School in 1936. He married Arvadan Catherine Pavelka. The couple had four children: Fred Jr., Pat, Sandy, and Marilyn. A big man at six feet, four inches, and more than 300 pounds, his family affectionately called Fred "big, grumbly bear."

Sedlmayr joined the Arvada Volunteer Fire Department in 1949. He became chief in 1951. Firefighting was a family activity for the Sedlmayrs, with Catherine answering calls and sounding fire alarms for the department. Fred believed in giving credit to his fellow firemen and police officers and was not one to boast of his own accomplishments. In 1958, Sedlmayr was voted Arvada's Man of the Year. His strong work ethic made a big impression on his son Fred Jr., who said in 2001, "Dad was a man who wouldn't sit still—he always had to be working. I think he picked up that during the Depression—he was just unstoppable." Fred worked at Coors for 32 years, retiring in 1977.

On Saturday May 14, 1960, a blaze started by an arsonist broke out at the Metz Lumber Company at the corner of Fifty-seventh Avenue and Wadsworth Boulevard in Arvada. With Fred Sedlmayr's leadership, the Arvada Volunteer Fire Department, along with other local departments, had the blaze under control in 90 minutes. The lumberyard was destroyed, and damages were estimated at $200,000. Fred Sedlmayr retired from the Arvada Fire Department in 1967. At that time, Lloyd Gorrell, publisher of the *Arvada Enterprise*, wrote that Sedlmayr was "one of Arvada's most dedicated public officials."

Involved in both the Arvada and Lakewood Elks Clubs, Fred also served as a counselor for the Denver Area Council of the Boy Scouts of America, helping Scouts earn their Fireman Merit Badges.

Fred Sedlmayr passed away on June 11, 2001, at the age of 84. (Courtesy Sedlmayr family.)

Dr. Edwin Foster

Dr. Foster delivered thousands of babies in his over 50-year career in Arvada and was one of the town's most prolific physicians.

Foster and his family came to Arvada in 1908, purchasing the home of Dr. Richard Russell at 7401 Grandview Avenue and took over Russell's practice. At that time, Foster made all house calls in a horse and buggy. In 1911, the doctor bought an auto from the Arvada Motor Co. It came in handy for Foster served the people of not only Arvada but also Ralston Valley, North Denver, Golden, and Morrison. He was also the official physician for the Denver Tramway System, the Leyden Coal Mine, and the Colorado & Southern Railroad.

Generosity was one of the keys to Foster's endearment to his patients. Many times if a child needed glasses, braces, or other treatments and the family could not pay, Foster made sure the youngster was provided for. "Don't send them a bill—just another thing for them to worry about. They'll pay when they can," the doctor would say.

Besides his medical practice, Foster found time to serve on the Arvada District No. 2 School Board and was on the Arvada Town Board as the health officer. At the age of 88, Edwin Foster continued to keep up his practice, with his wife, Hortense, assisting her husband as she had done throughout his career. In 1953, he was named Arvada's Man of the Year. The following year, E.L. Foster Elementary School was named after him.

Dr. Edwin Lincoln Foster passed away in January 1960.

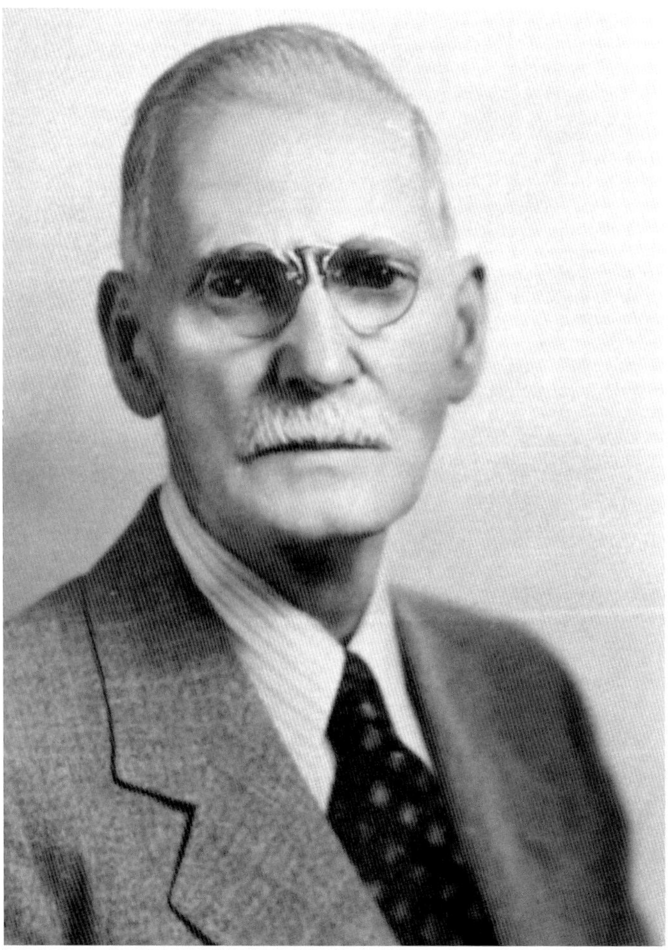

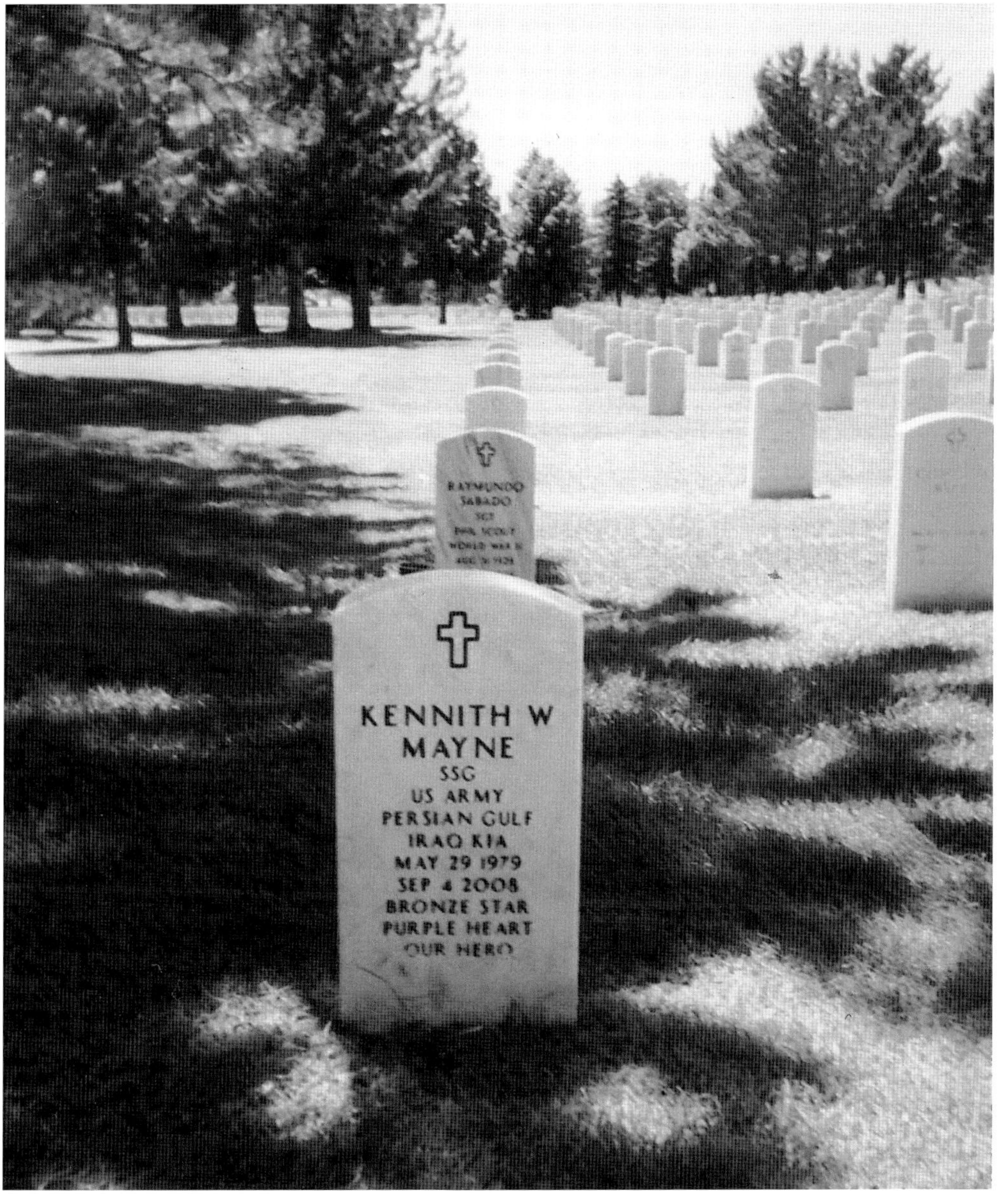

Kennith Mayne

Sergeant Mayne was an Arvadan who was killed in Iraq in 2008.

Born in Bellflower, California, Mayne moved to Arvada at the age of two. After graduation from Arvada West High School in 1997, he joined the Army. His first deployment in Iraq was in 2003 with the 101st Airborne. In 2008, Sergeant Mayne again went to Iraq. His mother, Michelle Benavidez, sent him toys, candy, and food, which he enjoyed sharing with the Iraqi children. On September 4, 2008, Mayne along with Pfc. Bryan Thomas of Michigan were killed when the Humvee they were in hit a roadside bomb outside Baghdad.

"He was a hero," Mayne's mother, Michelle, said in 2008. "He believed what he was doing over there."

Sgt. Kennith Mayne is buried at Fort Logan National Cemetery. (Author's collection.)

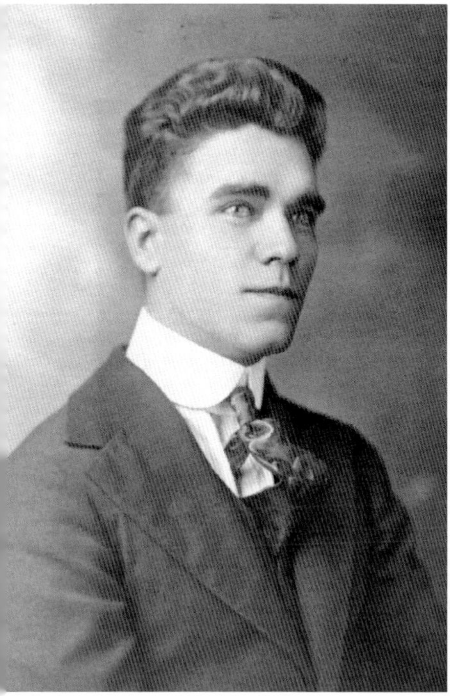

Thomas Vanderhoof

In 1922, Thomas Vanderhoof began his teaching career at Arvada High School. For the next quarter century, "Coach Vandy" influenced countless athletes and students.

As the school's agriculture teacher, Vanderhoof established the first Colorado chapter of Future Farmers of America. He also inaugurated the high school's first football team in 1923, and it was Vanderhoof who christened the team the Redskins.

"Play to win—fight hard and clean—but win or lose, play the game well," was Coach Vanderhoof's motto to his players. Thomas and his wife, Marjorie, raised four children: Mary Lee, Rose, Sue, and Dennis. Aside from his teaching and coaching duties, Vanderhoof served on the town board for 12 years, was active in the Arvada Chamber of Commerce, and sat on the Jefferson County School Board. In their later years, Thomas and Marjorie ran a flower shop in Lakewood and a bowling alley in Westminster. In 1970, Thomas Vanderhoof was inducted into the Colorado Coaches Hall of Fame. In 1969, Vanderhoof Elementary School opened at Fifty-eighth Avenue and Simms Street.

Thomas Vanderhoof passed away at the age of 86 in 1985.

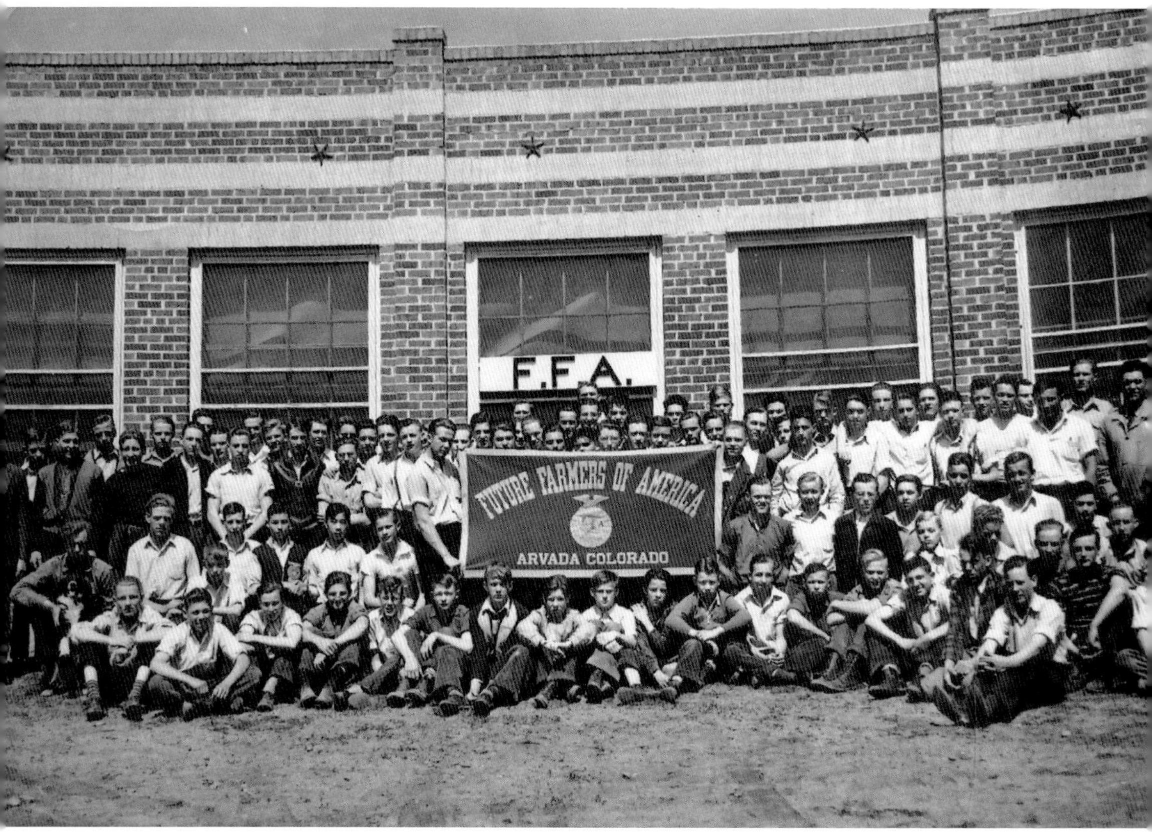

George Klumker

George Klumker was an Arvada native, and a Disabled Veterans Chapter was named after him in 1946. The son of Mr. and Mrs. Martin Klumker, George was a 1937 graduate of Arvada High School. Soon after his graduation, George joined the Navy and became a pharmacist mate. He was serving on the Philippine Islands when the Japanese attacked Cavite on December 10, 1941. Klumker was taken prisoner by the Japanese and forced to take part in the Bataan Death March in April 1942. The Klumkers knew nothing of their son's fate until they received a message naming him a prisoner of war near Manila. On October 24, 1944, the unmarked Japanese freighter on which Klumker and others were being transported to Japan was torpedoed. On June 28, 1945, the Klumker family received the heartbreaking news.

The George G. Klumker Disabled Veteran's Chapter 22 at 4901 Marshall Street in Arvada is a memorial to Arvada's first known war casualty. (Courtesy Stan Stewart.)

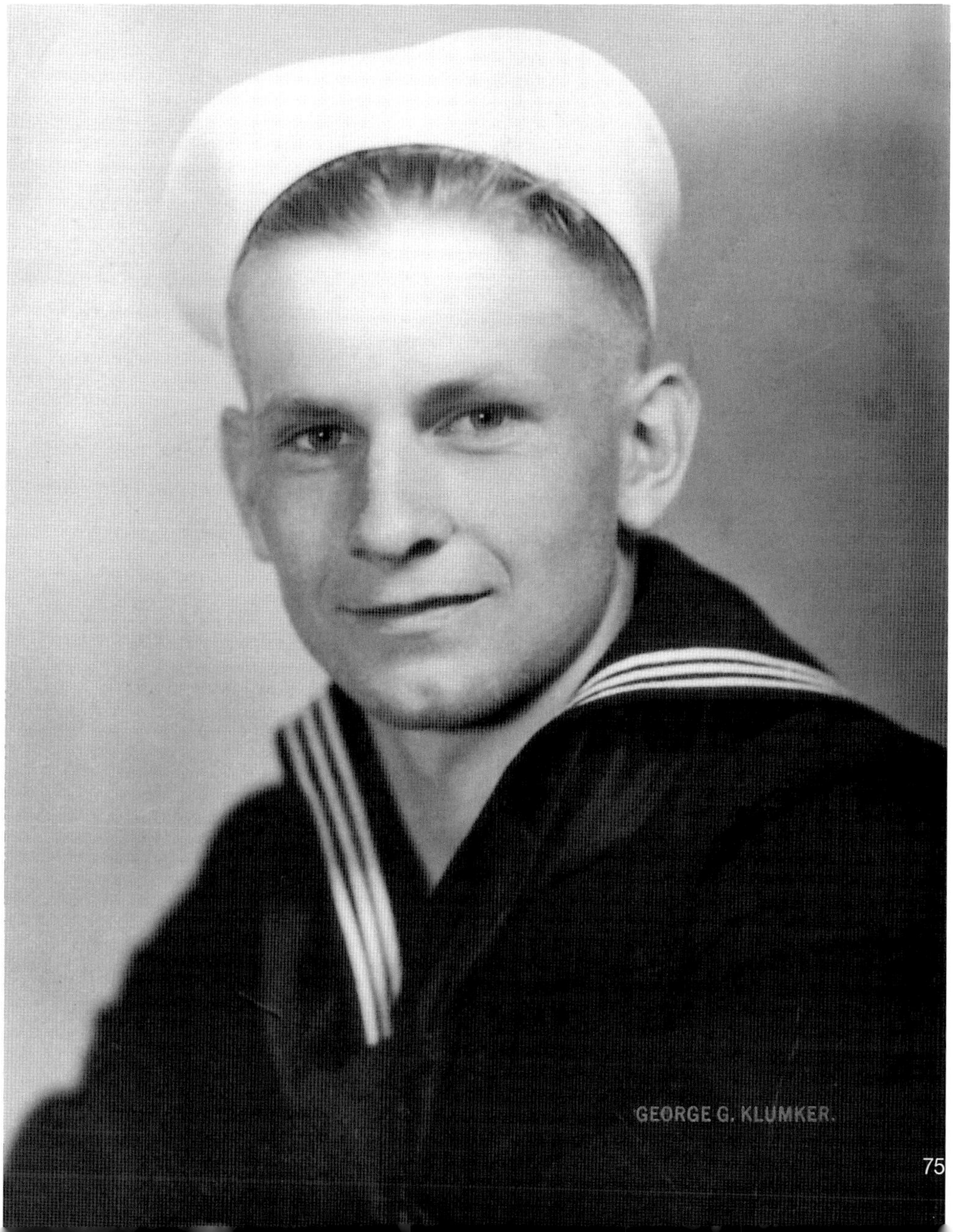

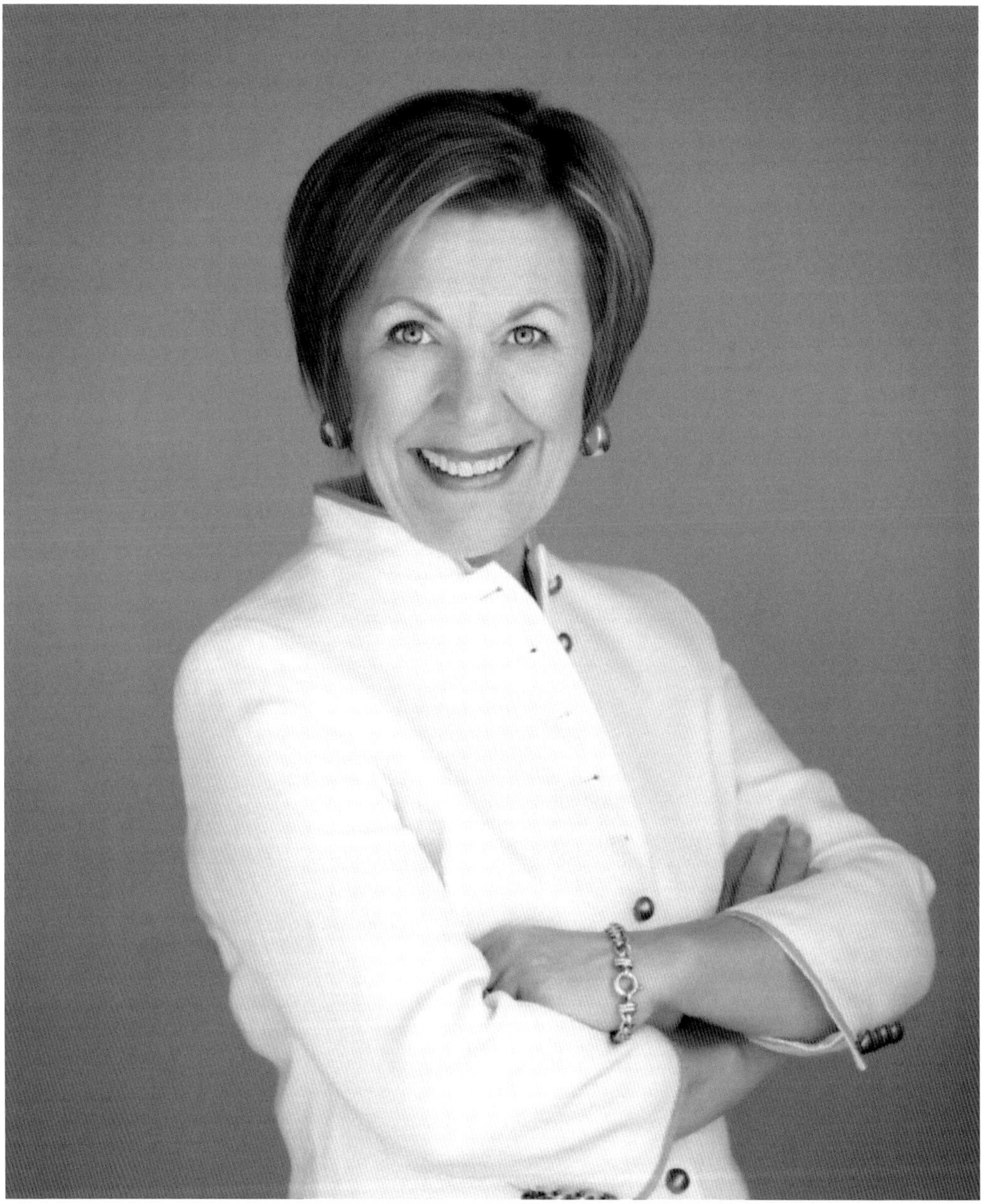

Ereka O'Hara
O'Hara was Arvada's 2010 Woman of the Year.

An Arvada resident since 1972, Ereka O'Hara has volunteered at the Arvada Center for the Arts and Humanities, as well as served on the council there. Ereka also works with the Arvada Chamber of Commerce, an organization she was selected to be chairman of the board for in 2010.

Along with her husband, Arvada City Council member Bob Dyer, Ereka volunteers for various organizations, including the Kiwanis club.

Ereka is a real estate agent. In 2011, upon receiving the Arvada Woman of the Year award, a title that is voted on by past winners, O'Hara said, "I don't do something unless I have a passion for it and feel that I can make a difference." (Courtesy Ereka O'Hara.)

Ed McCarthy

The Lollipop Cop—along with his Volkswagen bug, Siren Says—became a legend to a generation of Arvada youngsters.

Born in Boston in 1921, Ed McCarthy first had dreams of baseball stardom. He played minor-league ball for the New York Yankees until he joined the Marines during World War II. In the 1950s, Ed and his family moved to Arvada in 1959. Over his 25-year career with the Arvada Police Department, Ed started the city's first crossing guard program, drove children with learning disabilities to church every Sunday, and also served as a fireman. In the early 1970s, inspired by the movie *The Love Bug*, McCarthy transformed a VW Bug into Siren Says. The auto was adorned with big red lips, and the headlights became eyes with long eyelashes. Kids love it. Ed's penchant for handing out Jolly Rancher candies to kids earned him his nickname, the Lollipop Cop.

In 1982, McCarthy was named National Police Officer of the Year and, in 1984, was Arvada Man of the Year. Ed McCarthy retired in 1984. "I had a wonderful career and I just want everyone to be as happy as I am. I hope I made Arvada a little better place to live in," McCarthy said in 2004.

Edward McCarthy passed away on February 8, 2006, in Westminster, Colorado. (Courtesy City of Arvada.)

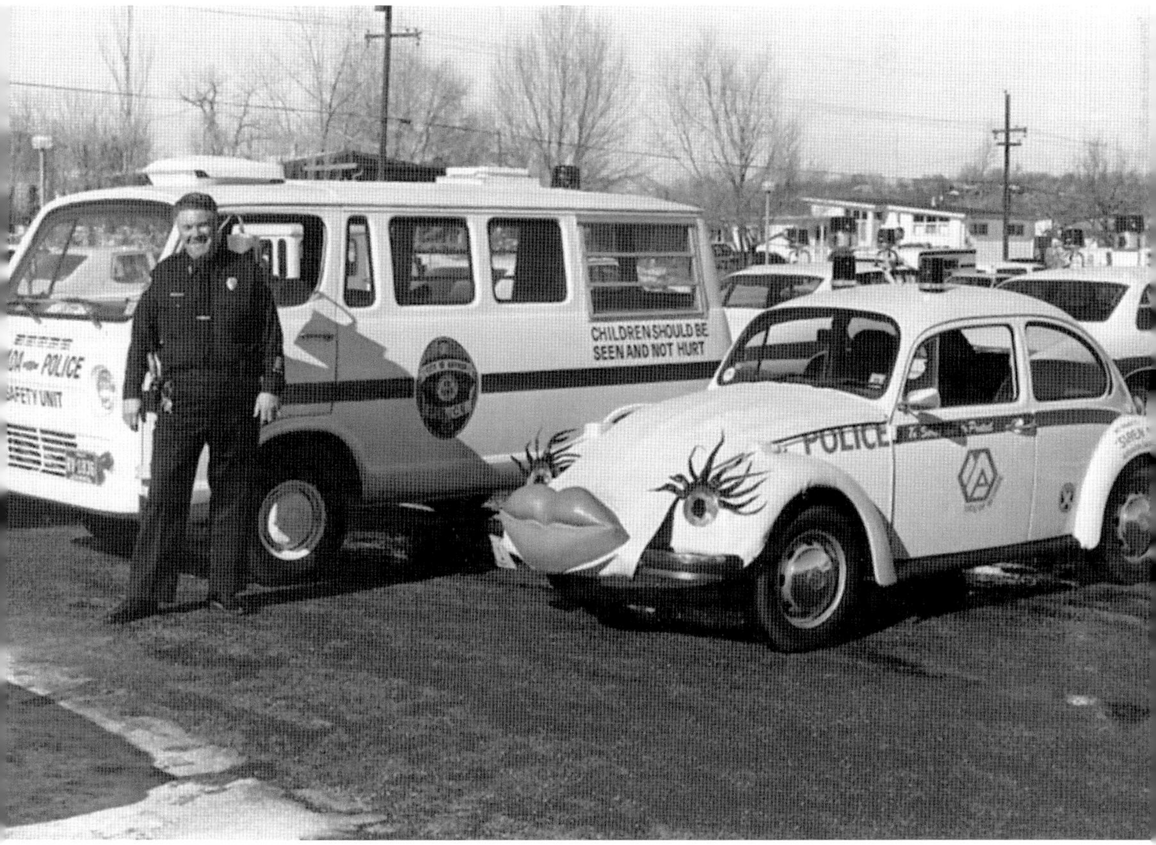

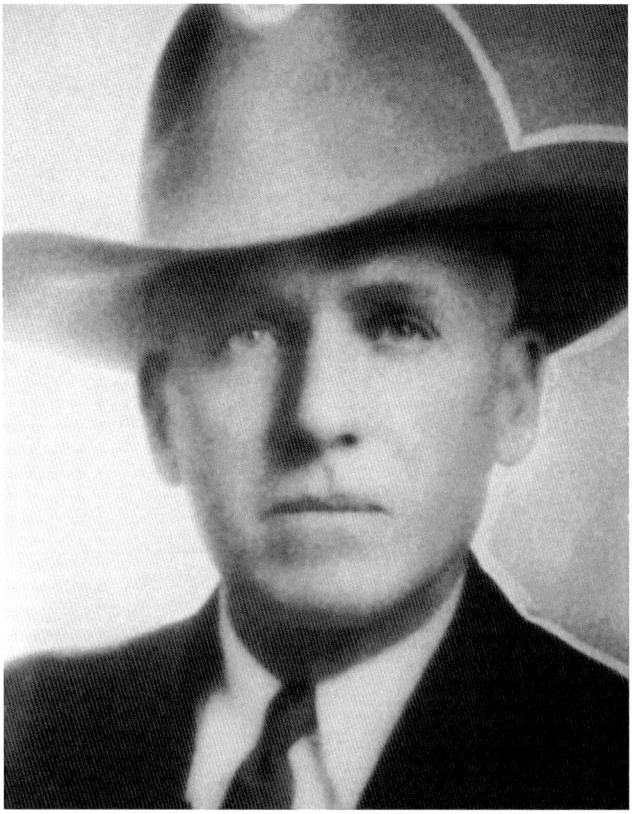

Clarence "C.B." Fugate

Although not an Arvada resident, it is Fugate's tragic death in the town in 1940 that makes the local lawman a legend.

Clarence Bunch Fugate was born on July 19, 1887, in Lead Hill, Arkansas. Arriving in Colorado in 1915, C.B. settled in Lamar. The next year, Fugate joined the Colorado National Guard and went to the Mexican border to battle Emilio Zapata and Pancho Villa during the Mexican Revolution. He also served in the Colorado 157th Infantry during World War I, taking part in three major battles of that conflict. Upon returning to Colorado, C.B. settled in Pleasant View. Stories of Fugate paying for groceries for needy families and providing coal for neighbor during the Depression added to his popularity. From 1930 to 1934, C.B. served as Jefferson County deputy sheriff. In 1936, he became the county undersheriff. On July 4, 1940, Bunch announced his campaign for the office of county sheriff. An extremely popular candidate, Fugate looked like a shoo-in for office.

In the early morning hours of October 12, 1940, Fugate was called to Arvada to aid in a shooting situation at a local tavern. Jack Carleton, owner of the Columbine Inn; his wife, Marjorie; and former bartender Art Marcum were involved in a love triangle. While the trio sat drinking, according to published reports of the time, Marcum told Jack Carleton that he, Marcum, was taking Marjorie Carleton away. Carleton, angered, got his gun and shot Marcum three times. Arvada night watchman Bill Benson called for help. C.B. Fugate arrived a while later. Entering the café, Fugate asked Carleton where is weapon was. "In the kitchen," Carleton replied. As Fugate entered the kitchen, Carleton asked if he was going to be arrested. "Yes," Fugate replied. With that Carleton leveled his weapon and fired at Fugate, mortally wounding the officer. After a gun battle with Benson and Deputy Anthony Muench, Carleton fled the tavern and was soon captured. Art Marcum survived his wounds; Jack Carleton was given a life sentence to Canon City prison where he died in 1961. Clarence Bunch's funeral was one of the largest ever in Jefferson County history. He is interred at Crown Hill Cemetery in Wheat Ridge.

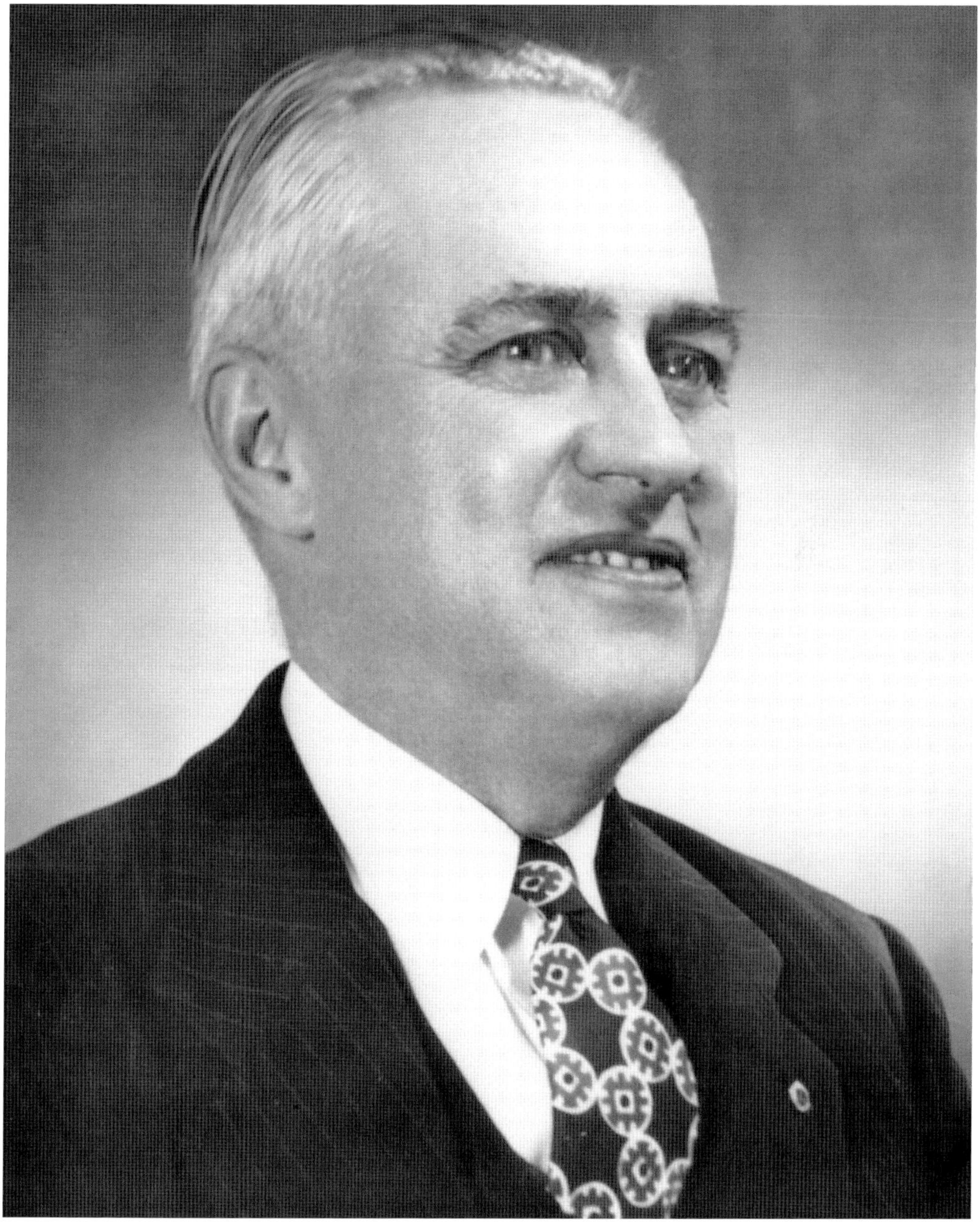

Thomas Mills

One of Arvada's first dentists, Mill was active in many facets of town politics.

Born in Illinois in 1895, Mills spent time in Montana from 1913 to 1918 working on farms and teaching school. He attended Denver University Dental School and graduated in 1923. That same year, Mills came to Arvada and opened his dental practice in the Davis Block. Serving on the town board from 1932 to 1940, Mills also served two terms as town mayor.

In 1942, while mayor, Mills organized a civil defense council for Arvada during the early days of World War II. He also served as the general chairman for the council.

Thomas Mills retired from his dental practice in 1970. He passed away on September 22, 1976.

Homer "Doc" Webber

Two-time Arvada Man of the Year, "Doc" Webber helped establish much of the city's government structure. Born in Virginia Dale, Colorado, in 1912, Webber and his wife came to Arvada in 1943. Webber was hired in 1955 as a temporary bookkeeper for the City of Arvada. One of Webber's first causes as a city employee was to call for a better water supply and sewage waste disposal system. After much hard work, the Denver Metropolitan Sewer District was established. Webber also served as Arvada financial director and treasurer from 1955 to 1972 and was assistant city manager. Webber was selected Arvada Man of the Year in both 1965 and 1972.

Homer "Doc" Webber died on November 7, 1983.

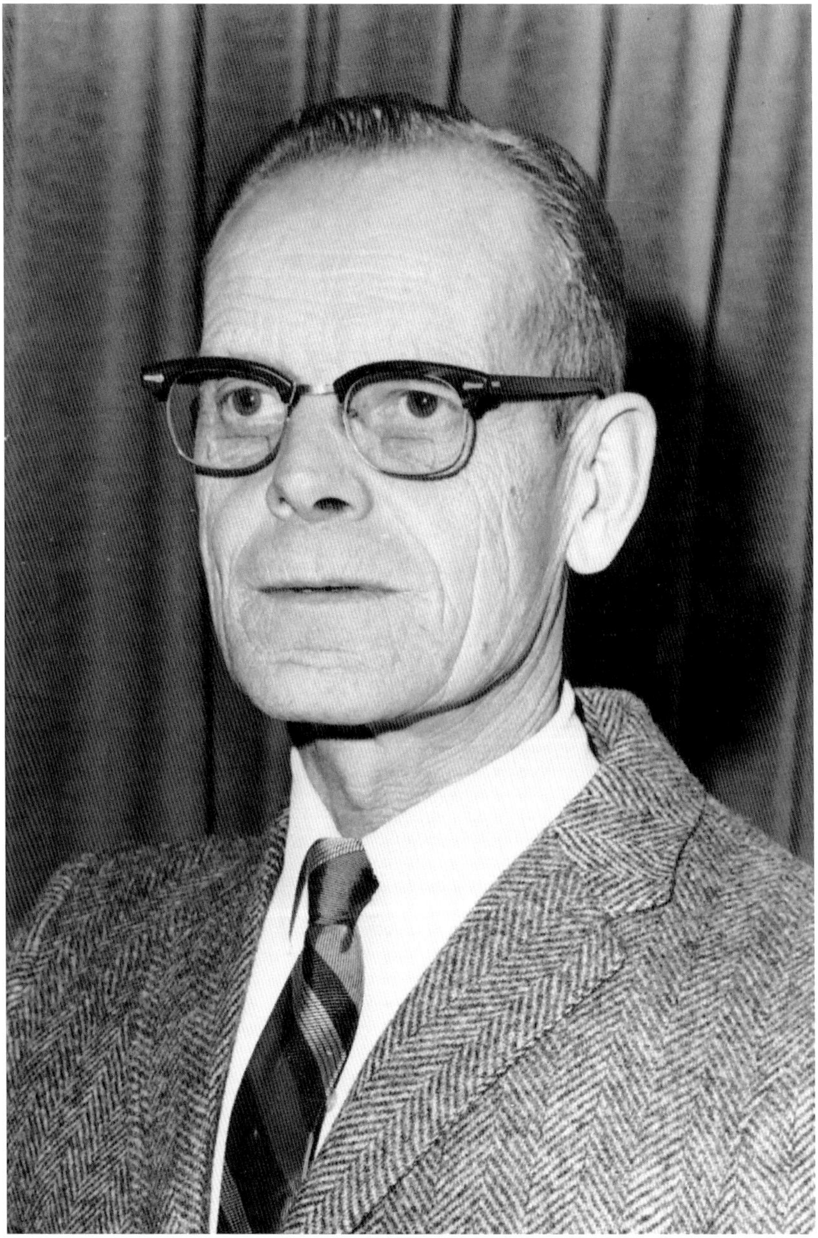

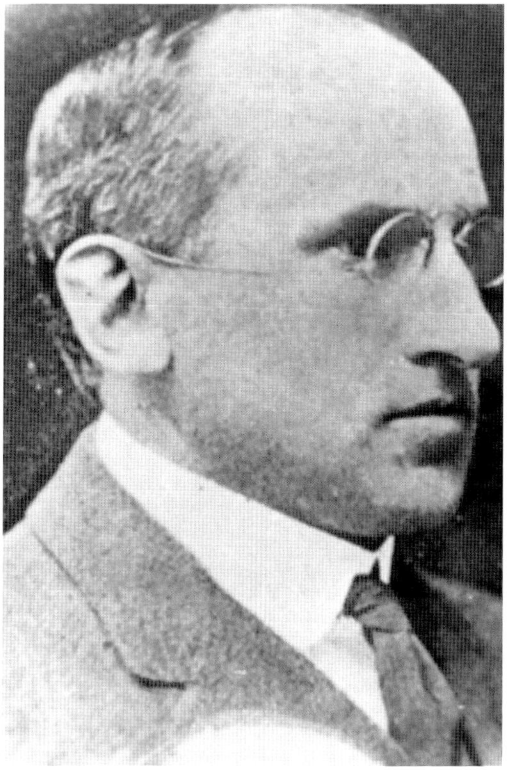

O.B. Drake

O.B Drake was one of Arvada's most respected educators of the early 1900s.

Drake was elected principal of the Arvada School on June 12, 1903. That year, there were nine high school students, and Angie Bates became the first graduate of the school in 1904. In 1915, he helped form the Arvada Library along with the PTA. Drake also called for the building of a new high school building in 1916. O.B. resigned as school superintendent in 1919.

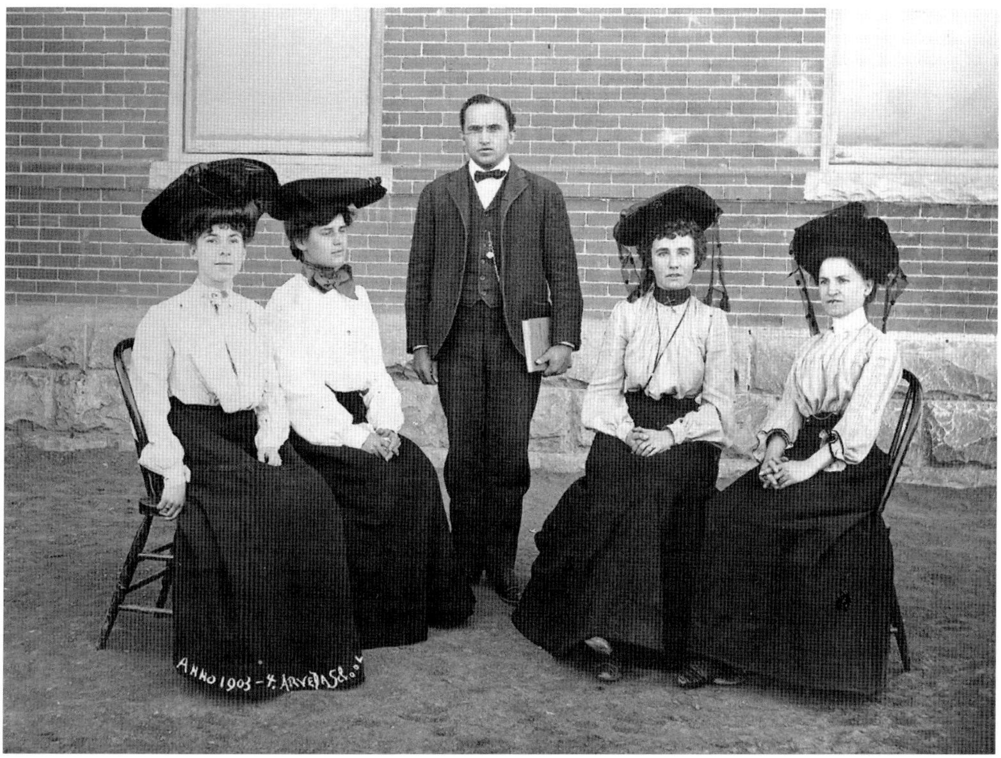

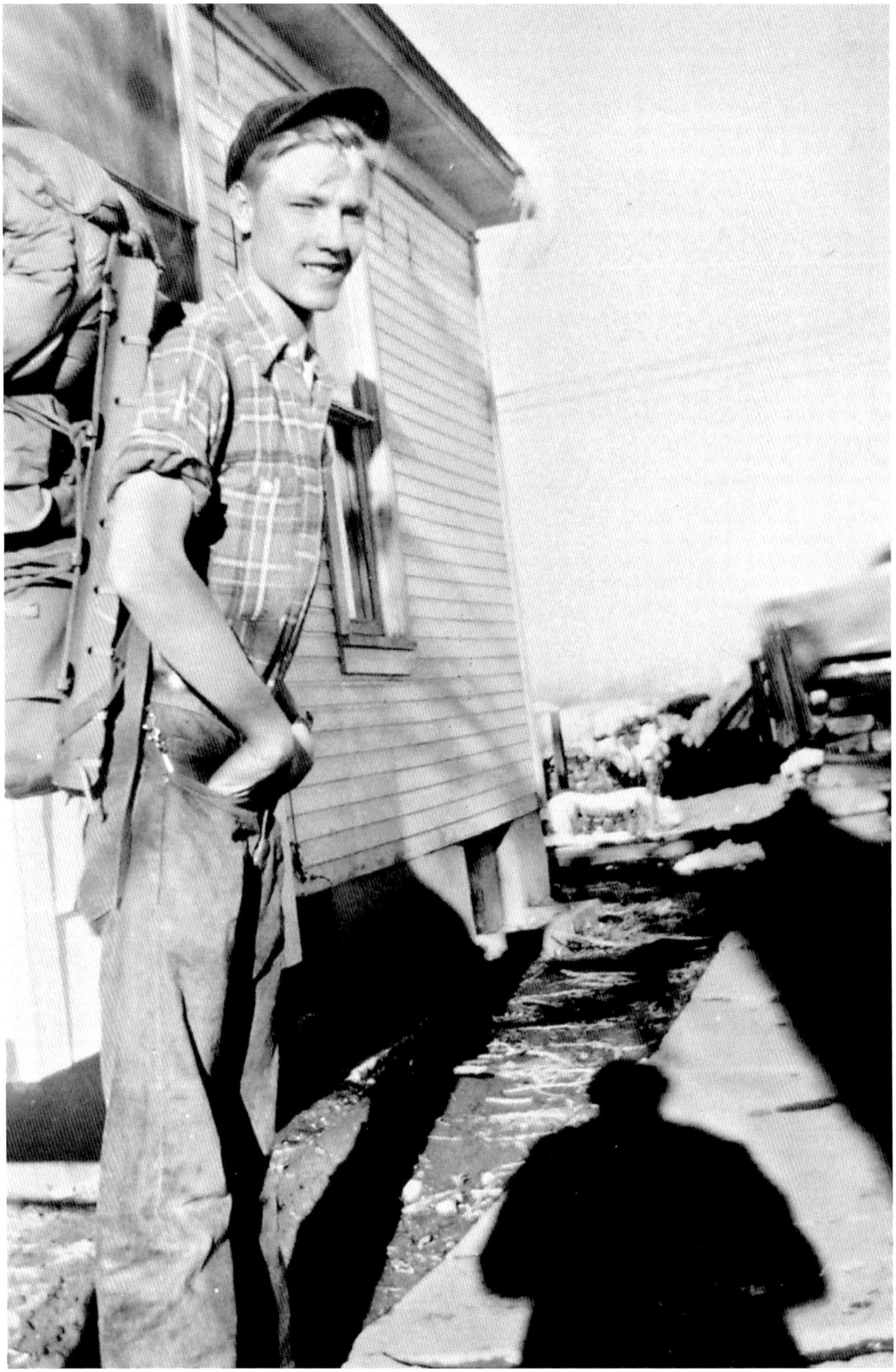

Gordon Williams

A lifelong Arvada resident, Williams served as past president of the Arvada Historical Society.

Born on August 14, 1930, in Arvada, Gordon was the nephew of Jefferson County sherriff James Biggins Jr. He attended school in Arvada, and during his high school years, Gordon worked at the George Wendt and Evans Pharmacies in town as a soda jerk. After graduating from Arvada High School in 1948, Gordon became a lineman for the Arvada Electric Company. In 1950, Williams joined the air force, where he served until 1954. He married Dolores Roberts in 1955, and the couple had two children, Debbie and Gordon. Gordon Williams worked for Public Service Co. of Colorado for 38 years.

Williams volunteered with the Arvada Fire Department for ten years and served as president of the Arvada Historical Society from 1993 to 1995. He loved volunteering at the Arvada Flour Mill museum, giving tours to school groups. Gordon Williams passed away on March 18, 2011, in Wheat Ridge.

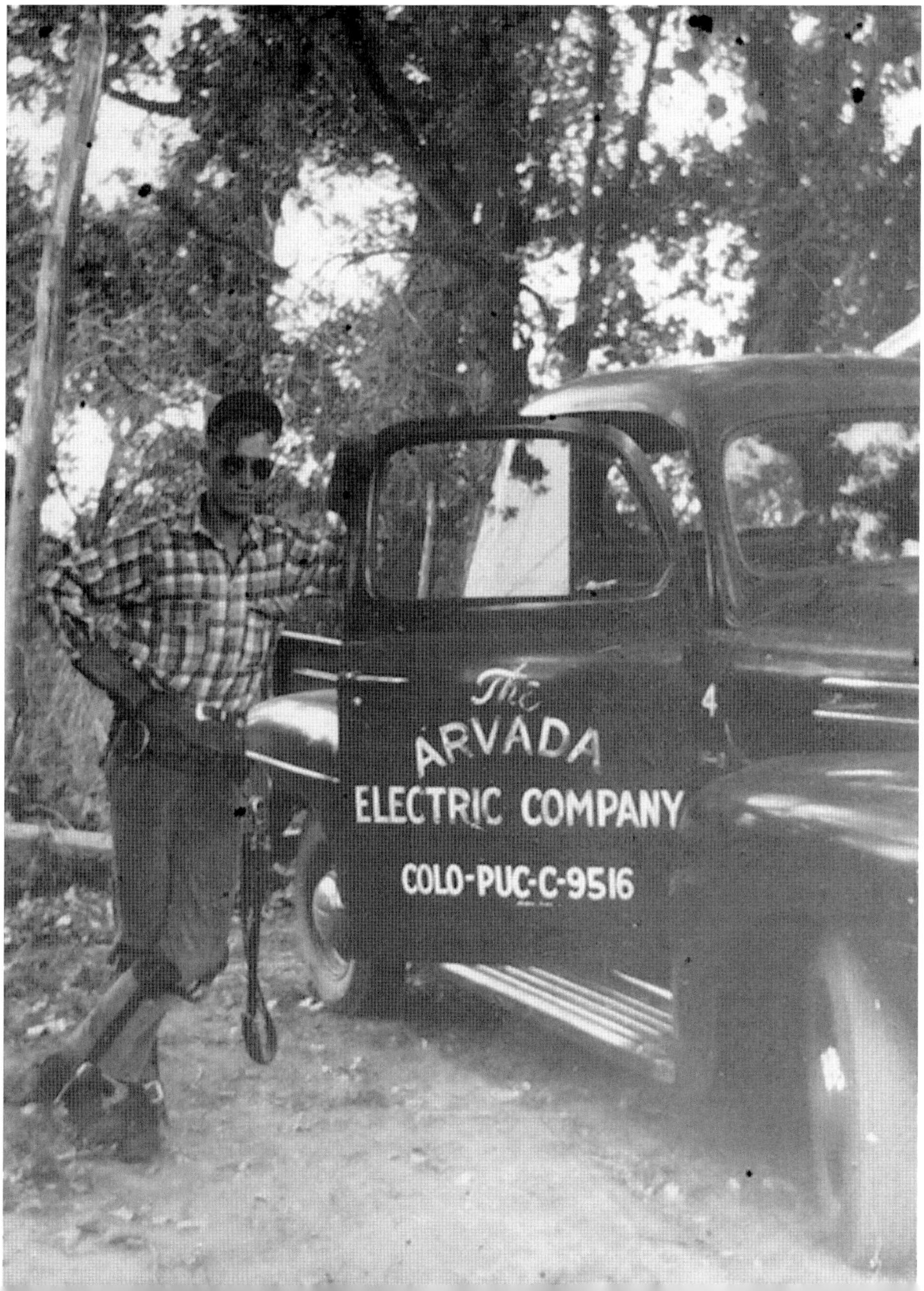

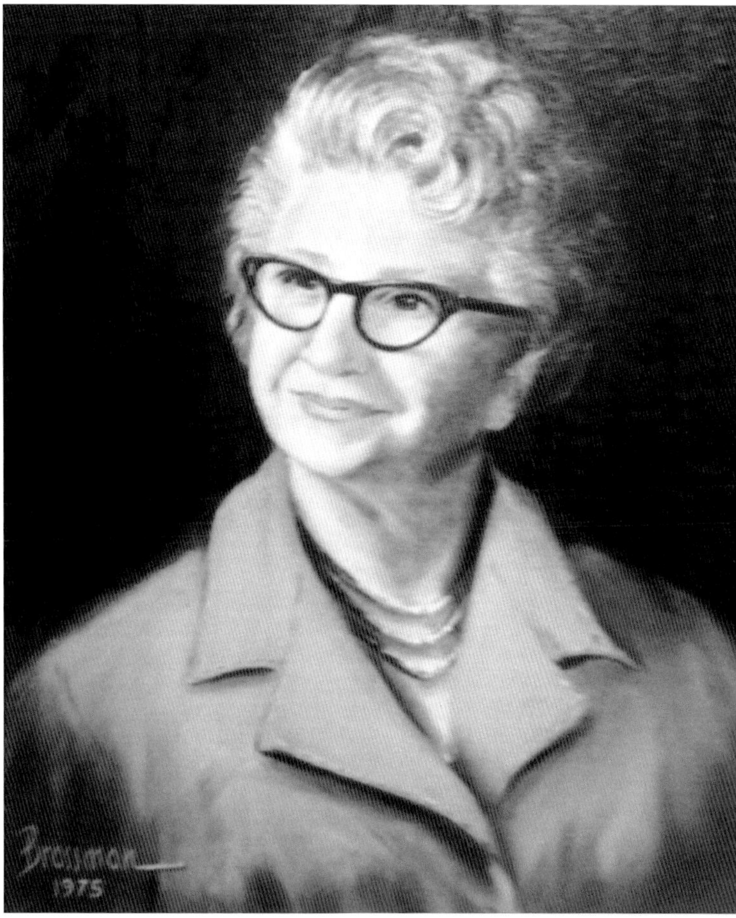

Zina Warder
Warder Elementary School in Arvada was dedicated in 1957 in honor of Zina Warder.

Born in Lund, Nevada, in 1906, Warder attended the University of Utah at Salt Lake. Her teaching career began in 1930 in Nevada. In 1941, she came to Pueblo, Colorado, to teach. She married her husband, Howard, that year. She moved to Arvada in 1947 and became a teacher at Lawrence Elementary School. Leaving Lawrence in 1958, Warder became principal at Fitzmorris Elementary the following year. Warder retired as principal of Fitzmorris in 1970. She served as a resources consultant for Jefferson County Schools in the late 1950s. Zina Warder passed away on January 13, 1983.

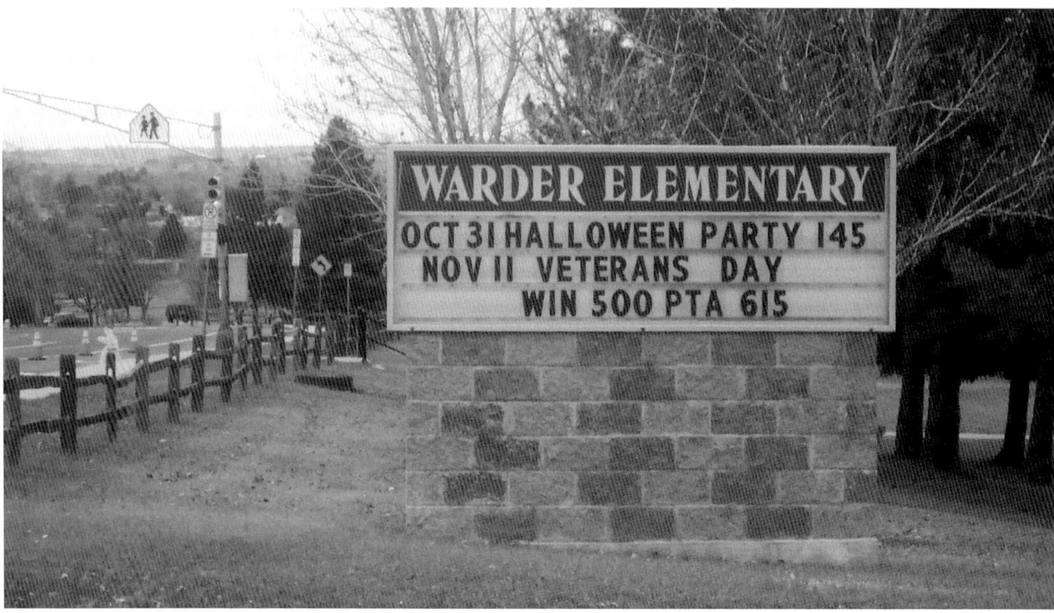

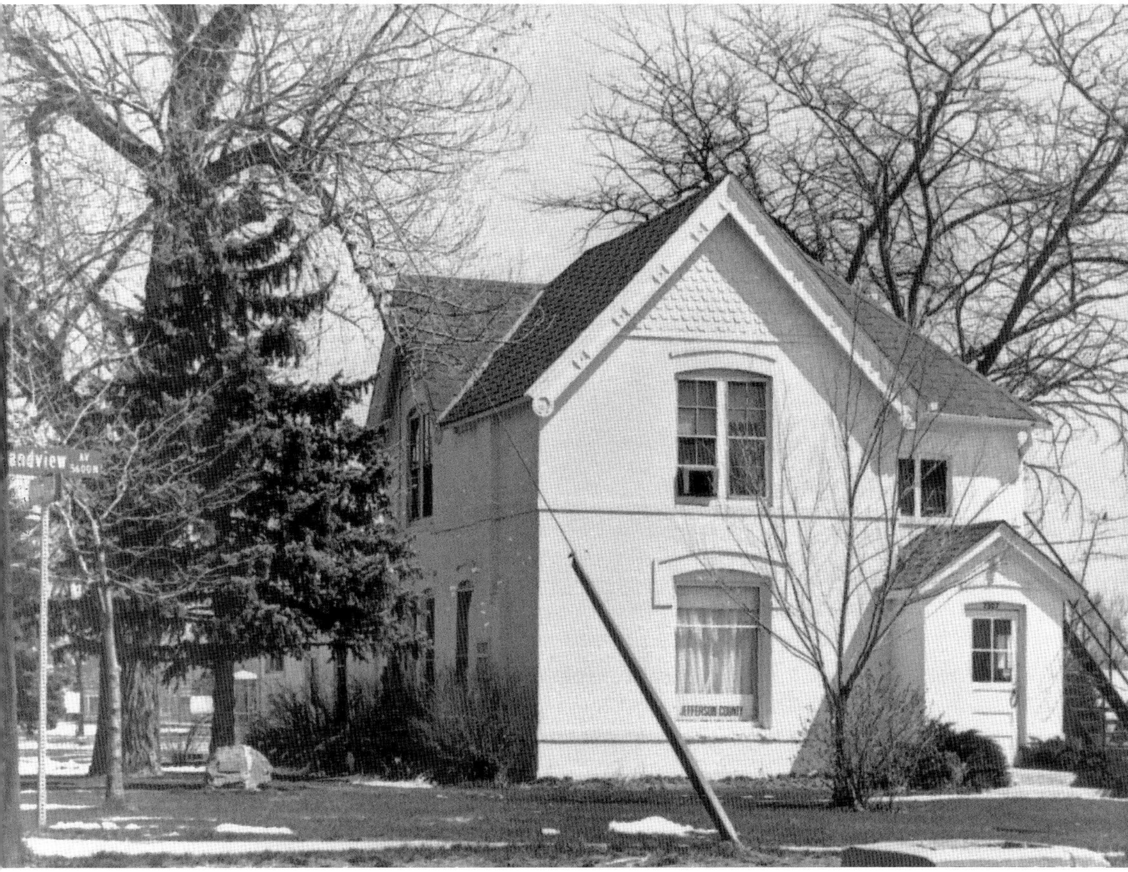

Murrell Gill

Beloved Arvada librarian for 17 years, Gill was Arvada's first Woman of the Year.

Murrell Gill was born on July 19, 1897, in Alma, Kansas. She was a schoolteacher in Kansas and Colorado before moving to Arvada in 1945 from Denver. Gill was hired as librarian for the Arvada Library in 1946. At that time, the library was in the Davis Block on Olde Wadsworth Boulevard. In November 1950, it was decided the library's new home would be the McIlvoy House on Grandview Avenue. The move was made in March 1951 under Gill's supervision. In a 1955 interview, Gill said that at that time, the library held 4,500 books and that she was looking to increase books for children and young adults. Named Arvada Woman of the Year in 1954, Gill had instituted many programs for young readers. Murrell Gill served as state vice president for the local Soroptimist Club and was a member of the Arvada Presbyterian Church and the Eastern Star. Gill retired from her librarian duties in 1964 and moved to Nebraska.

Murrell Gill passed away in April 1988.

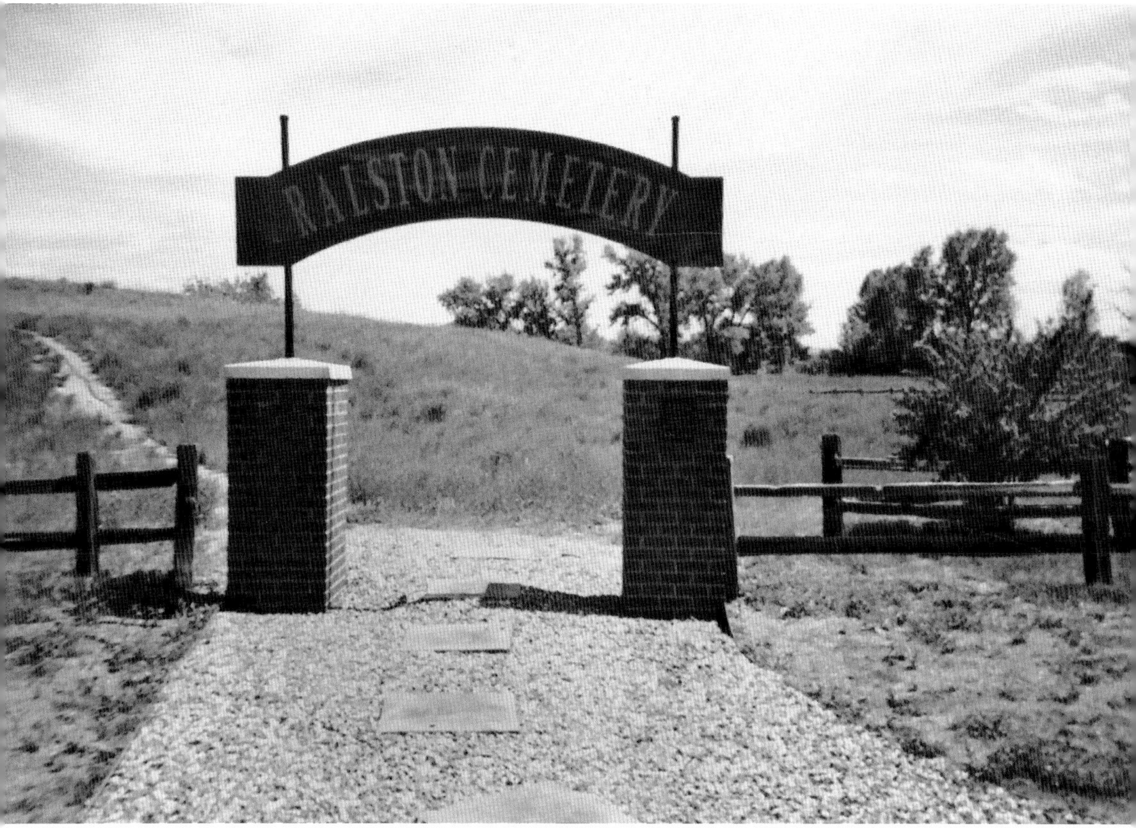

Matthew Prythero

Matthew Prythero's work led to the Ralston Cemetery being placed on the Colorado Historic Registry. As a teen, Matt Prythero came across a notebook on the Ralston Cemetery while volunteering at the Arvada Historical Society. The Ralston Cemetery's origins go back to the late 1850s. Prythero became involved in documenting all the headstones in the cemetery. Matthew formed the Ralston Cemetery Historic Association, and the City of Arvada, which owns the cemetery, gave Matthew custodianship. In 2010, the Ralston Cemetery was placed on the Colorado's Most Endangered Places list. The Ralston Valley High School graduate has received the Arvada Young Professionals' "Rising Star" award, as well as received an award from the Good News Coalition in 2011 for his preservation work. (Author's collection.)

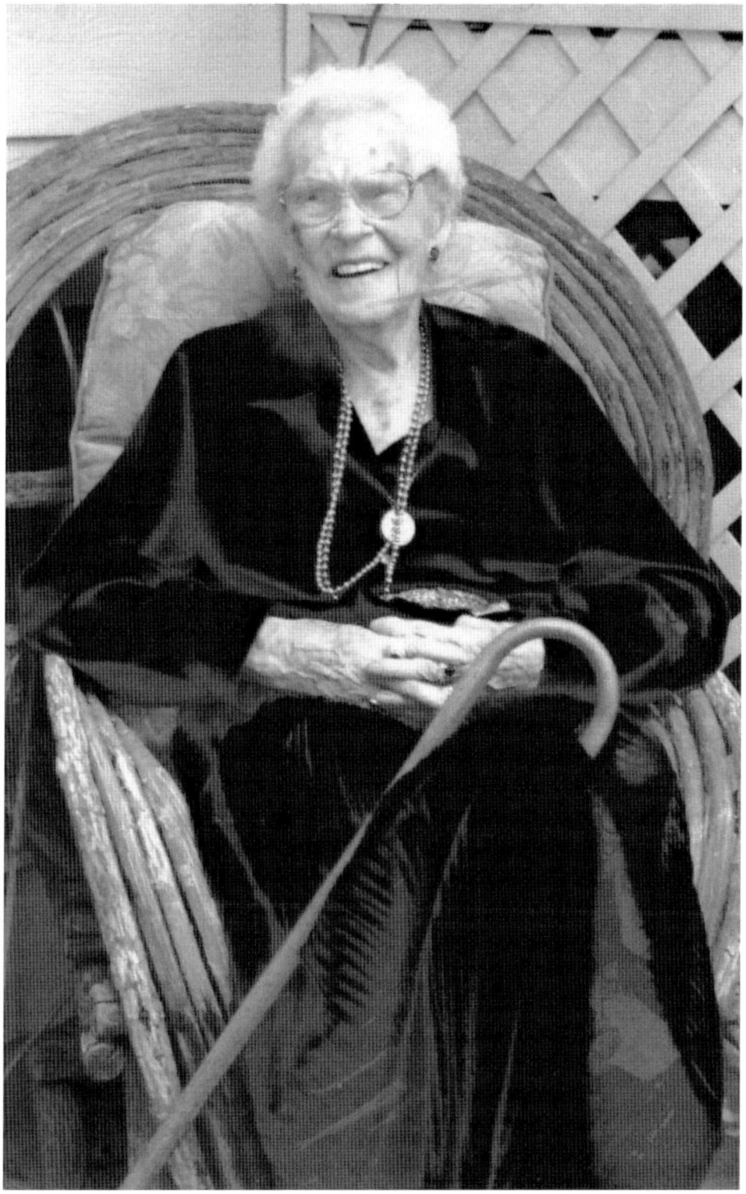

Jane Gardner
Historian Gardner was Arvada Woman of the Year for 1989.

Born on April 8, 1914, Gardner moved with her family to Colorado in the early 1920s. She graduated from Golden High School in 1933 and, from there, attended nursing school. In 1937, Jane married her husband, Russell. The Gardners moved to Arvada in 1948. She began volunteering at the Arvada Library and helped form the Future Librarians Association. When the library moved from the McIlvoy House to its new home on Fifty-seventh Avenue and Dover Street in 1966, Jane continued on as one of the librarians. Jane was a charter member of the Arvada Historical Society when it was formed in 1972 and was president of the society from 1981 to 1982. Gardner also served on the Jefferson County Historical Commission.

Jane Gardner died on June 22, 2011.

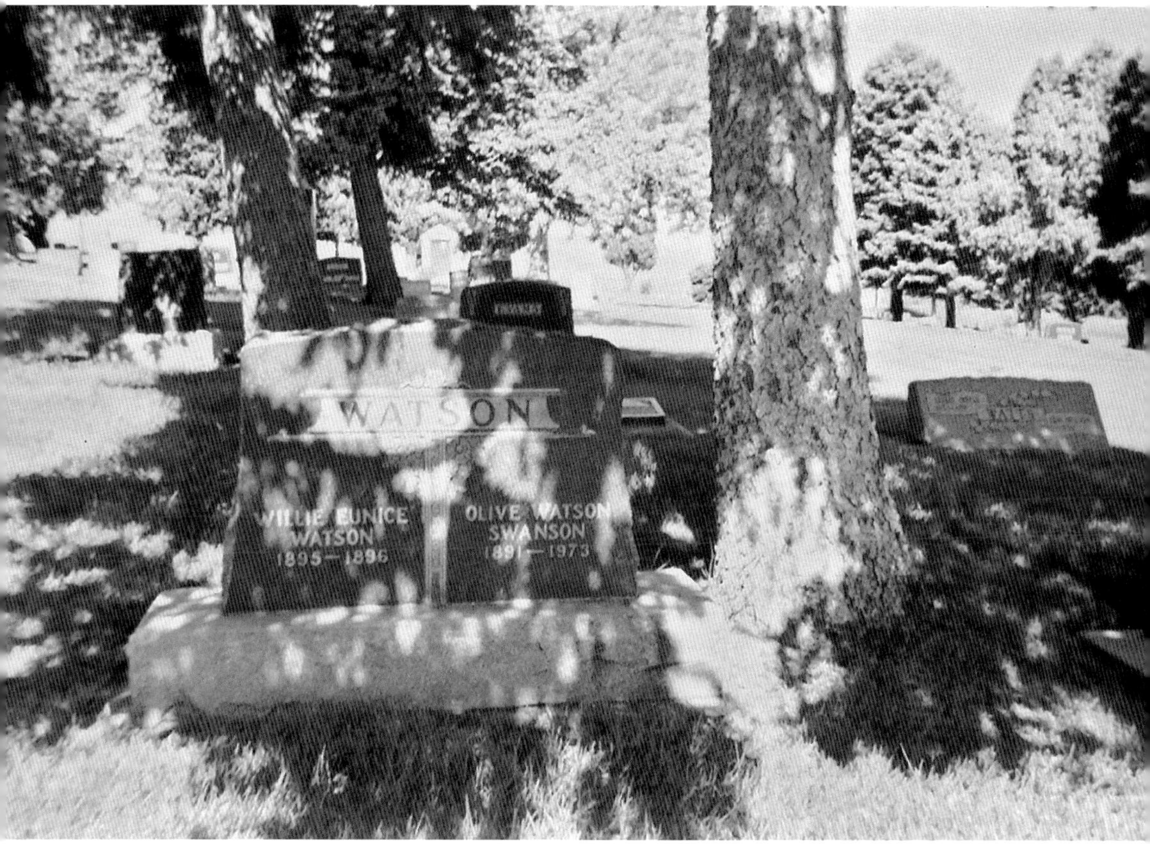

Olive Swanson

An Arvada native, Swanson was an educator who was honored with a school named after her.

Olive Swanson graduated from Arvada High School in 1906, a member of the second graduating class of that school. Olive attended Colorado Women's College and graduated in 1913 with a bachelor of arts degree. She also attended the University of California and the University of Denver. During her career, Swanson taught and was assistant principal in Las Animas and was the high school principal in Canon City. Olive taught seventh grade math and history at Arvada Junior High. She retired in 1957 after a 38-year career.

Swanson Elementary School at 6055 West Sixty-eighth Avenue in Arvada was dedicated in October 1963 in honor of Swanson.

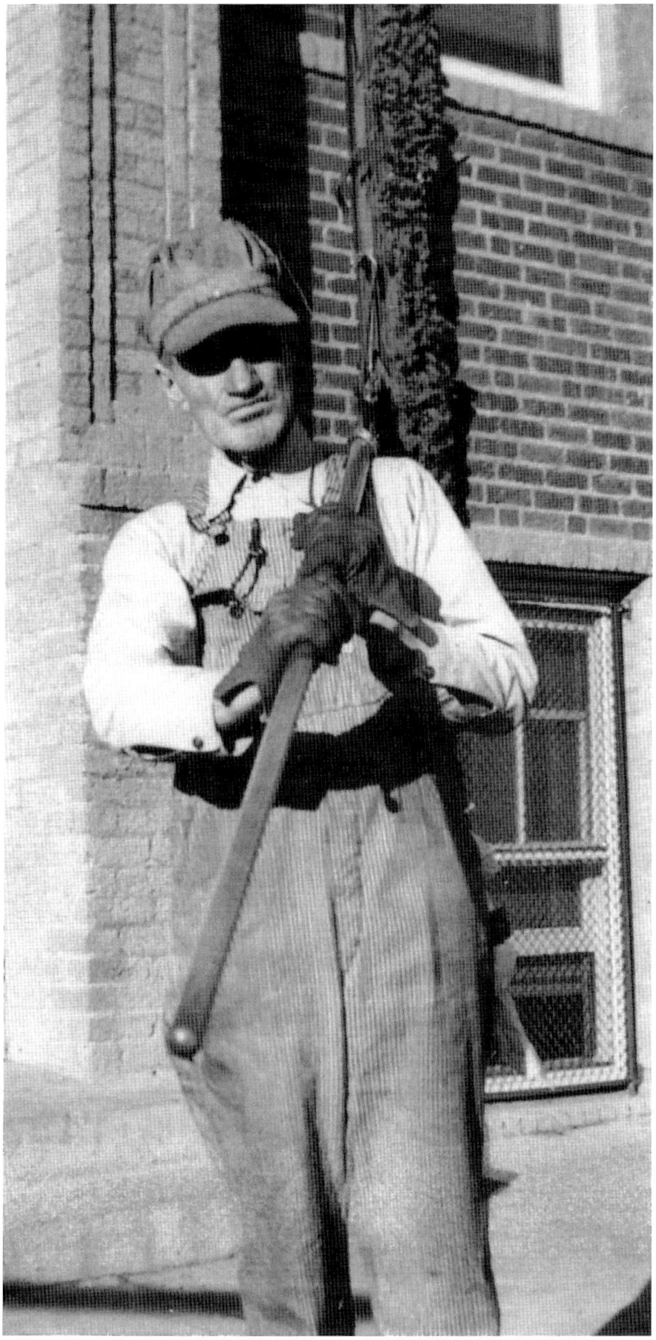

Berton Fields
Fields was the custodian for Arvada High School for 24 years and a friend to thousands of students.

Berton Fields was born in Rico, Colorado, on December 13, 1884. Berton was orphaned at a very young age and was shuffled between many different homes before he went to Ouray to work as a burro packer at the Camp Silver Bird mine. Looking for work on farms, Berton came to Arvada in 1906. While working at the Charles Davis farm, Berton met Mary Anne Davis. The couple wed on June 21, 1910. They had five children. After working at the Leyden mine for years, Berton was hired as janitor for the Arvada Grade School in 1932. The next year, he was hired as custodian for the high school. Berton was remembered as one who took the time to befriend the students who passed through the halls of the high school. Fields's daughter Dorothy Fields Galloway recalled, "He was such a friend to all of them. He respected them, and they respected him in return. They formed relationships with each other." Berton Fields also served as the first master of the Fremont (now Enterprise) Grange and was a member of the Odd Fellows Lodge, Woodmen of the World, and the Methodist Church.

Berton Fields passed away on March 4, 1976.

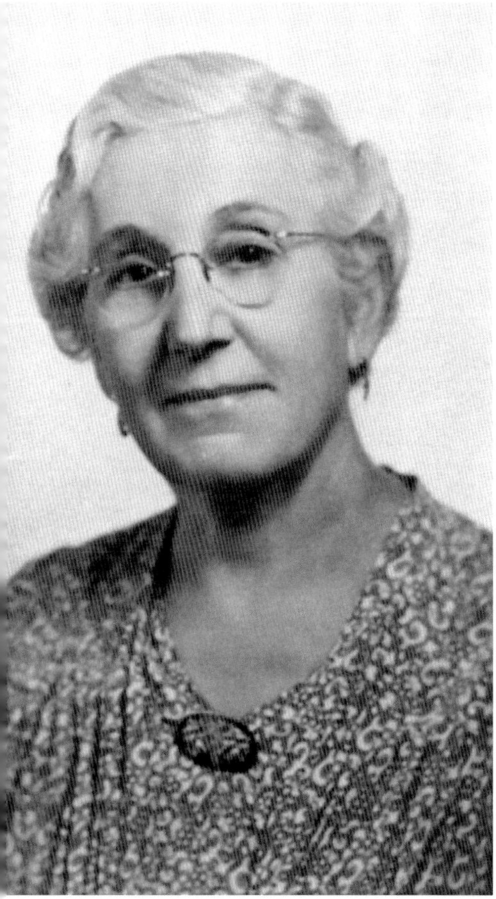

Hortense Foster

Hortense Foster, the wife of Dr. Edwin Foster, was known for her work in many local charities.

Hortense Brown was born in Reedsville, Missouri, on March 25, 1871. She wed Dr. Edwin Foster on June 17, 1891. The couple had four children, but two boys died in infancy. The Fosters moved to Colorado for the treatment of the doctor's tuberculosis. The family moved to Denver in 1902 and settled in Arvada in 1907. Dr. Foster set up practice and was soon volunteering at the Craig Colony, a tent city in current Lakewood for tuberculosis patients. Most of the residents of the colony were poverty stricken and unable to keep employment due to their conditions. In 1913, Hortense Foster, along with six other ladies from Arvada, founded the Craig Colony Aid Society. The group held many fundraising activities, with all proceeds going to aid the colony patients.

On November 8, 1913, the Arvada Women's Club was organized by Foster and six other women. Foster served as president of the Women's Club in 1919. In 1915, Foster served on the first Arvada Library Board. She was a charter member of the Arvada Garden Club, which began in 1937. In 1946, Foster, along with Estelle Russell, held an Arbor Day event honoring returning servicemen and women. Mrs. Foster was a member of the Daughters of the American Revolution, the Arvada Presbyterian Church, and the Woman's Christian Temperance Union. She also was the bookkeeper for her husband's practice.

Hortense Foster Brown died on April 19, 1960.

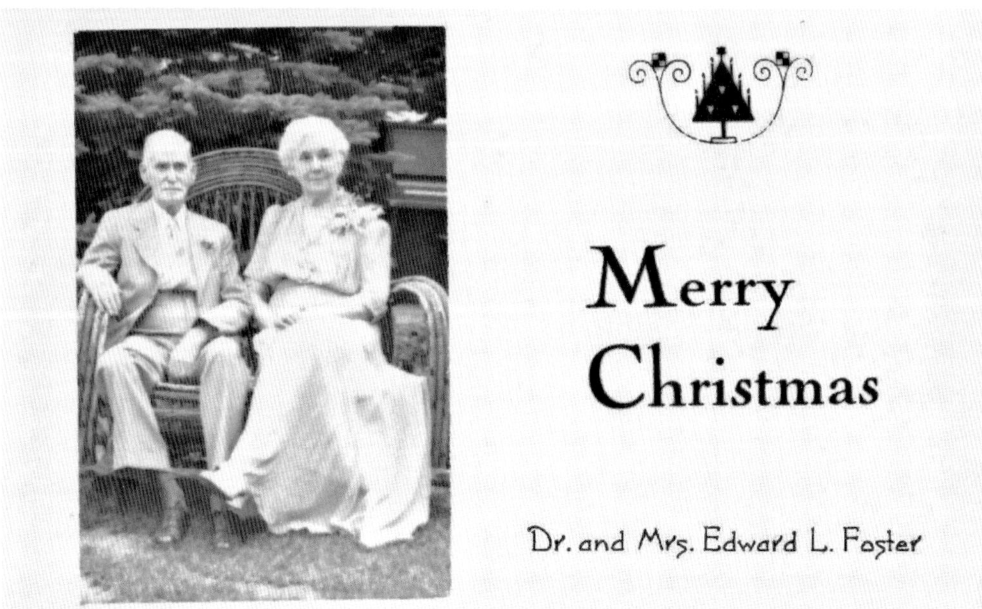

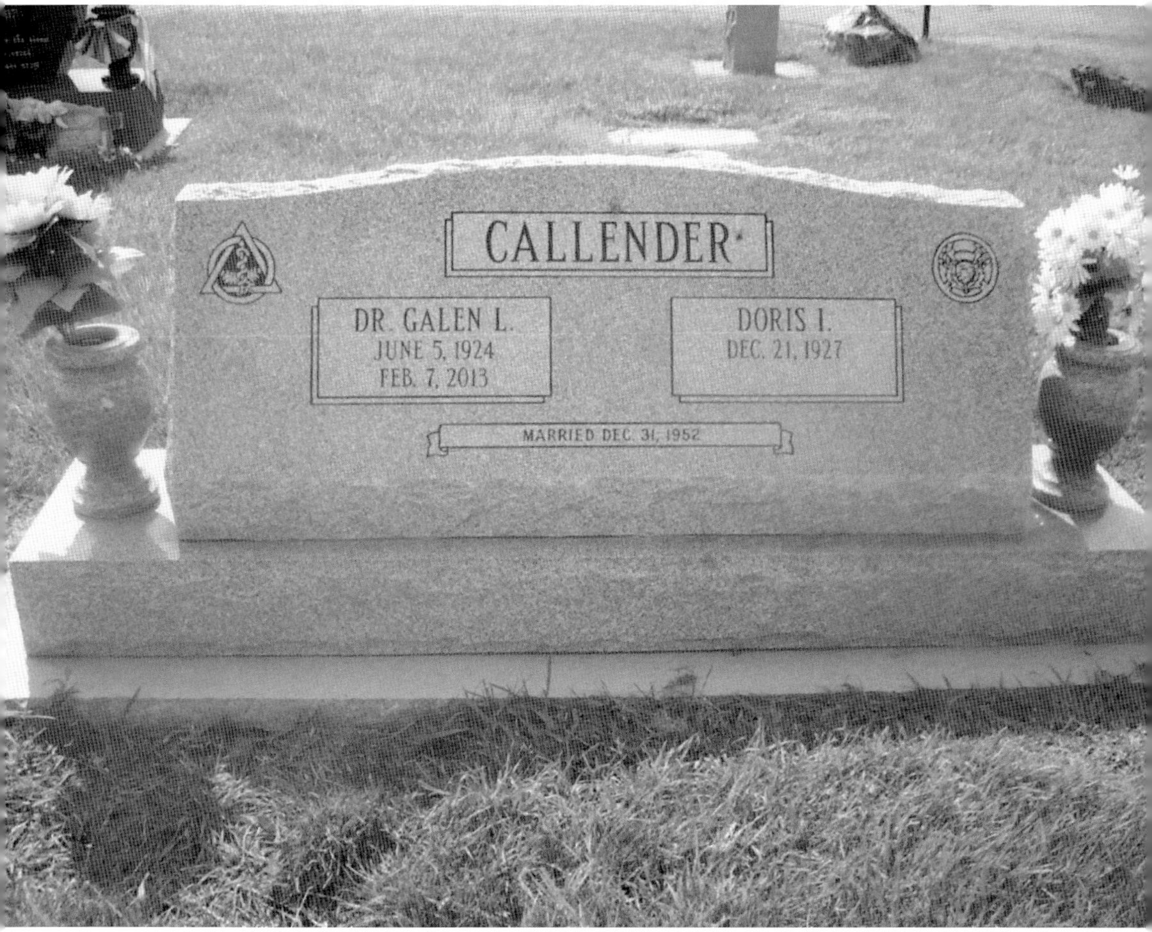

Dr. Galen Callender
In addition to being a local dentist, Callender contributed to Arvada in many ways.

Galen Callender was born on June 5, 1924, in Blue Rapids, Kansas. He graduated from Wyandott High School in Kansas City in 1939. During World War II, Callender joined the Army and trained as a dentist. In 1944, he joined the Navy as a medical corpsman. After the war, Callender returned to Kansas City and finished his dental studies, graduating in 1949.

Borrowing money from his younger brother, Galen bought a dental practice in Arvada. On New Year's Eve 1952, Galen married Doris Sylvester. Soon after the marriage, Galen was sent to Korea, where he served as a dentist for the air force. He returned from Korea to his dental practice. Galen and Doris had two children, Galen T., born in 1954, and Janice, born in 1956. Galen was active in the Arvada Historical Society, the University of Missouri at Kansas City Dental Alumni Association, the Masonic Lodge, and the Arvada Presbyterian Church. He also helped found the Colorado Dental Association Liability Trust.

Dr. Galen Callender passed away on February 7, 2013.

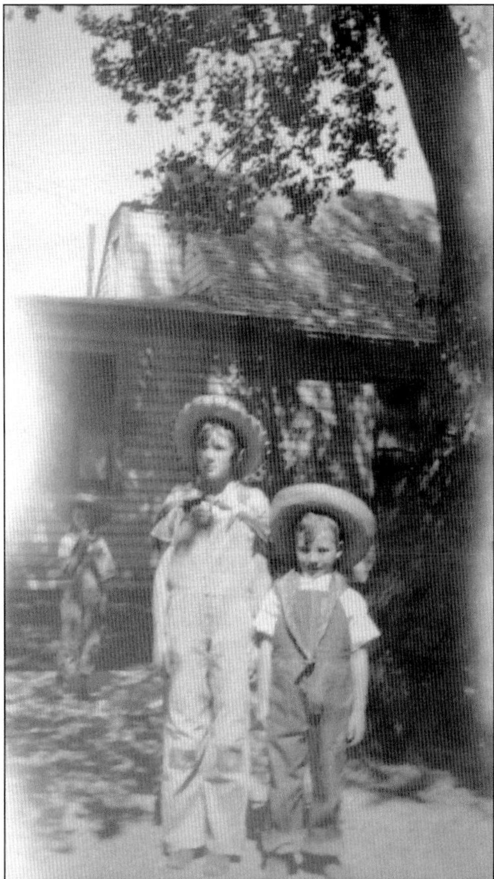

Dorothy Fields Galloway

Galloway was a fourth-generation Arvadan.

Born on August 22, 1918, in Arvada, Dorothy was the great-granddaughter of Arvada pioneers Harpin and Mary Davis and Soloman and Maryann Belgin. Dorothy attended school in Arvada and graduated from Arvada High School in 1936. Dorothy wed Francis Barton on August 29, 1941. Francis was killed in Italy during World War II in August 1944. In 1947, Dorothy married Mark Galloway.

Dorothy Galloway was a secretary at Pomona High School for 17 years and served as president of Secrest Elementary School's PTA. She was active in the Arvada Methodist Church. Dorothy was a charter member of the Arvada Historical Society, founded in 1972. She was involved in the annual Old-Timers Picnic sponsored by the historical society. Dorothy was the grand marshal for the Arvada Harvest Festival parade in 2005. Dorothy Fields Galloway passed away on July 28, 2008.

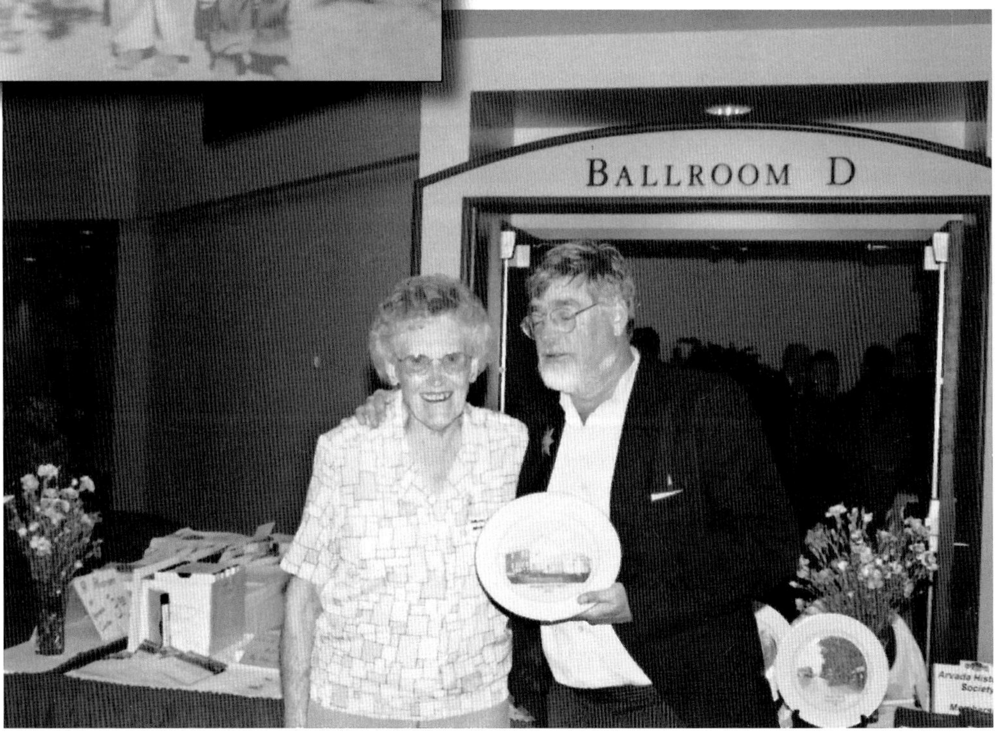

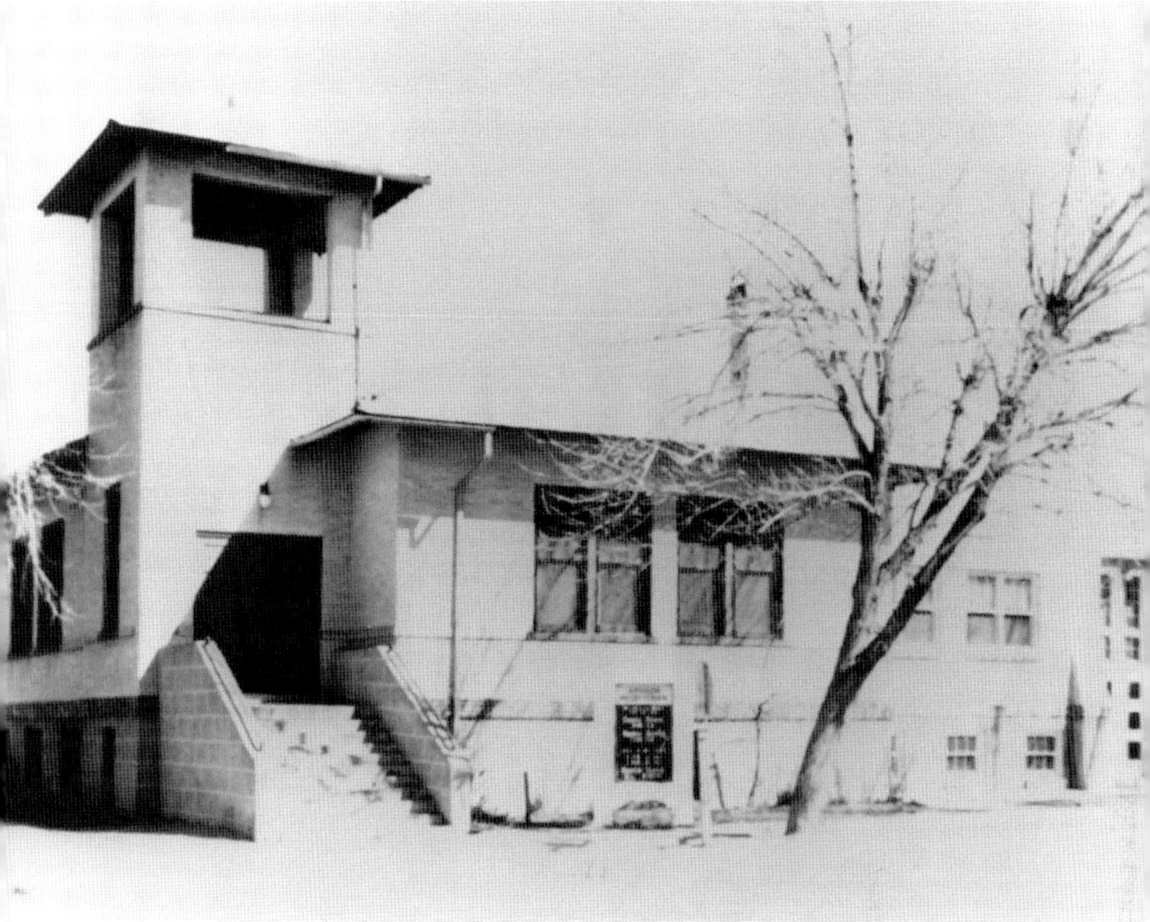

Rev. Clinton Reed
Reed served as pastor of the Arvada Presbyterian Church in the 1920s.

Born in Weeping Water, Nebraska, in 1874, Reed studied at Boston University. He spent 16 years with the Gospel Missionary Union in Morocco as a missionary. While in Morocco, Reed married his wife, Anna. The couple had two daughters. The Reeds returned to America because of Anna Reed's poor health. Reverend Reed served at a church in Strassburg, Colorado, before coming to Arvada in 1920.

Years later, parishioners would recall that Reed was a strict adherent to Presbyterian doctrine. While a very personable man outside the pulpit, when it came to giving sermons, Reed was all "fire and brimstone." The 1920s were a time of shifting social and moral standards in America, and Reed preached fervently against Darwin's theory of evolution, dancing, and gambling. In 1921, Reed was called to officiate over the funeral of beloved Arvada pioneer Clemancy McIlvoy. Reverend Reed resigned as pastor of the Arvada Presbyterian Church on April 8, 1930. He went on to pastor in Loveland, Colorado.

Rev. Clinton Reed passed away in 1944.

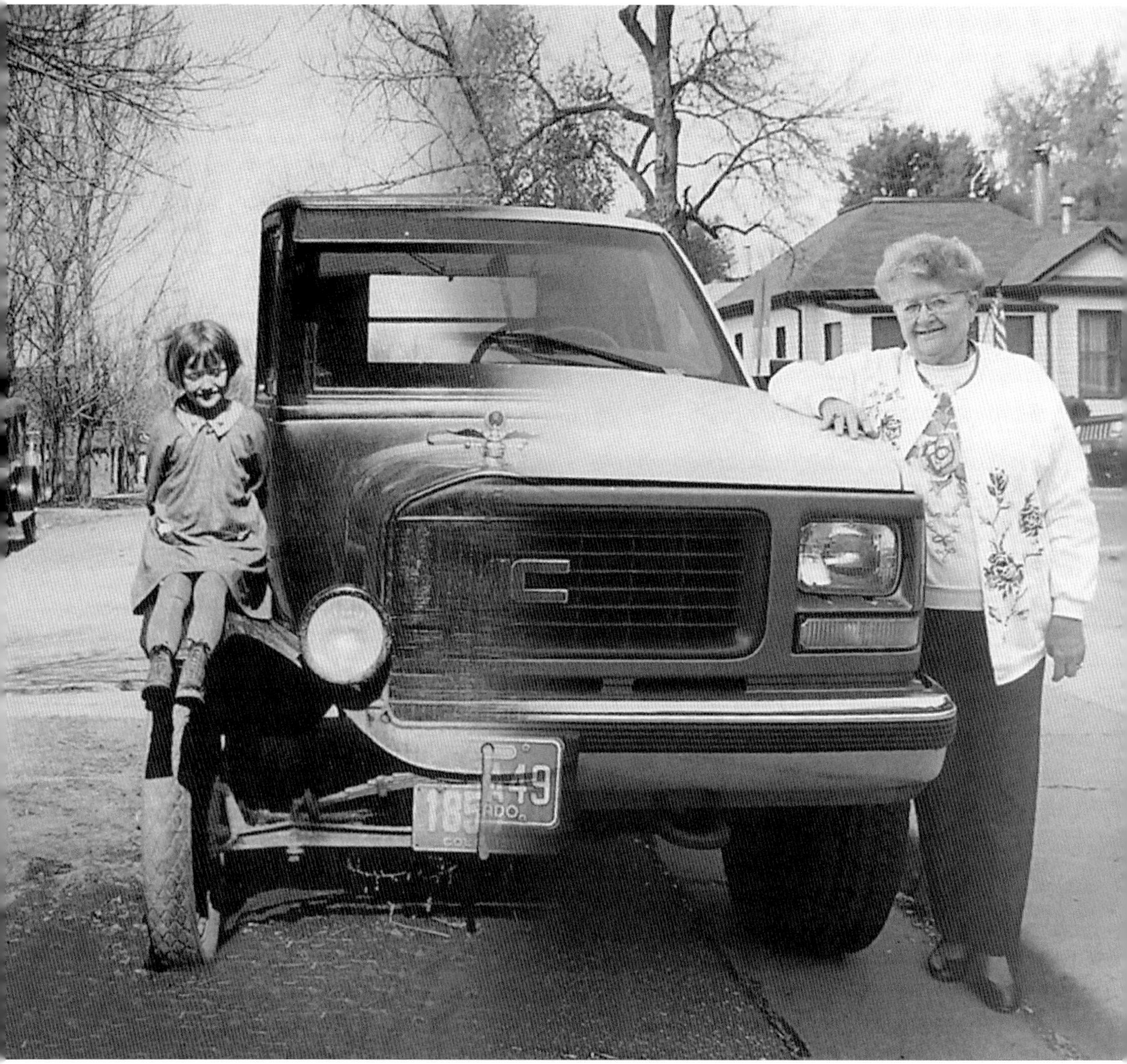

Billie Juchem Barton

Descendant of two pioneer Arvada families, Barton's career was in education.

Billie was born on December 22, 1919, in Costa Rica, where her father, Harold Juchem, was employed. Billie; her sister, Marguerite; and their mother came to Arvada in 1924. Billie graduated from Arvada High School in 1938 and went on to study at the University of Colorado. After earning her master's degree in special education, Billie spent 27 years as a special education teacher in Jefferson County. In 1957, Barton was voted Jeffco's Outstanding First Year Teacher.

Aside from her teaching career, Billie was active in the Arvada Presbyterian Church, was a Girl Scout leader, served as PTA president, and was secretary of Jeffco's Red Cross Board. Billie was a charter member of the Arvada Historical Society and assisted in the writing and publication of many of the society's books. She also served as president of the society.

Billie and her husband, Bob, had one daughter, Gail, and served as foster parents for many years.

Billie Juchem Barton died on December 13, 2006, in Lakewood, Colorado.

Oscar "Ozzie" Lutz

Lutz served as pastor of the Arvada Presbyterian Church for 22 years.

Born in Murphysboro, Illinois, on February 9, 1920, Lutz served as assistant minister at Denver's Central Presbyterian Church for eight years. On November 4, 1957, he was installed as pastor of the Arvada Presbyterian Church. Lutz came to be known for his "down home" style of preaching and endearing personality. Attendance at Arvada Presbyterian flourished under Lutz's leadership, enough so that there was soon a call for a larger facility for the church. On October 14, 1962, ground was broken for the new church sanctuary at Grandview Avenue and Independence Street. One year later, on October 13, 1963, the new $300,000 building was dedicated. Lutz was involved in the founding of the Inter-Church Arvada Resource for Ministry and Service program, which provides emergency financial aid to those in need.

After his 22-year call as pastor at Arvada Presbyterian, Lutz went to Houston, Texas, in 1979 to assist in organizing a church there.

Oscar "Ozzie" Lutz passed away in Las Cruces, New Mexico, on February 2, 2000.

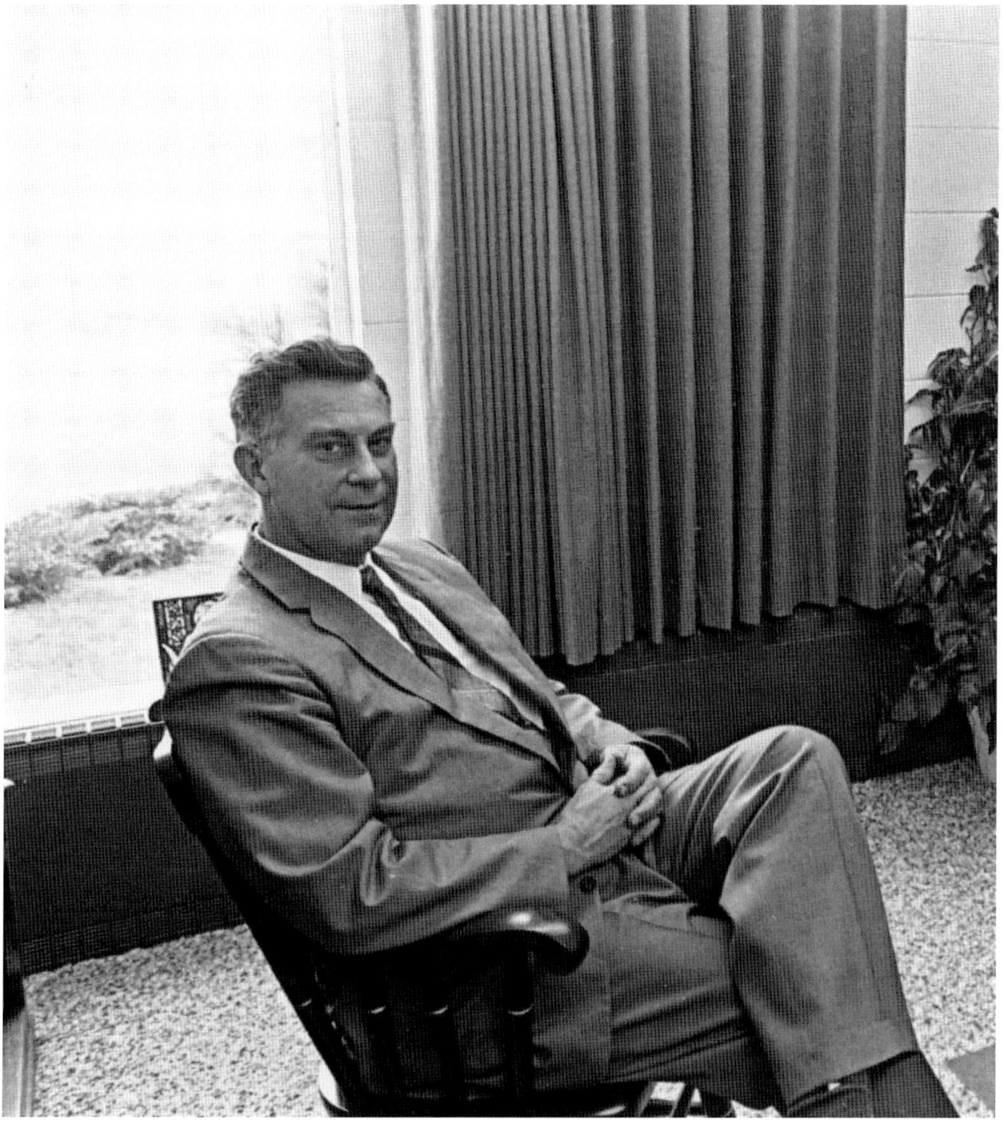

Bill Ashton

The son of businessman Ralph Ashton, Bill is passionate about preserving Arvada's history.

Born in Arvada on May 6, 1929, Bill graduated from Arvada High School in 1947. After attending the University of Colorado, Bill became a teacher. First teaching at Jefferson High School for three years, Bill moved on to the newly opened Arvada West High School in 1963. Ashton taught chemistry at the high school until his retirement in 1986. Bill was named 1987 Colorado Educator of the Year for the Arvada West Area. A charter member of the Arvada Historical Society, Bill served as society president from 1995 to 1997. Ashton was the Arvada Man of the Year for 1994. A member of the Arvada United Methodist Church, Bill is also involved in the Arvada West High School Foundation in the office of treasurer.

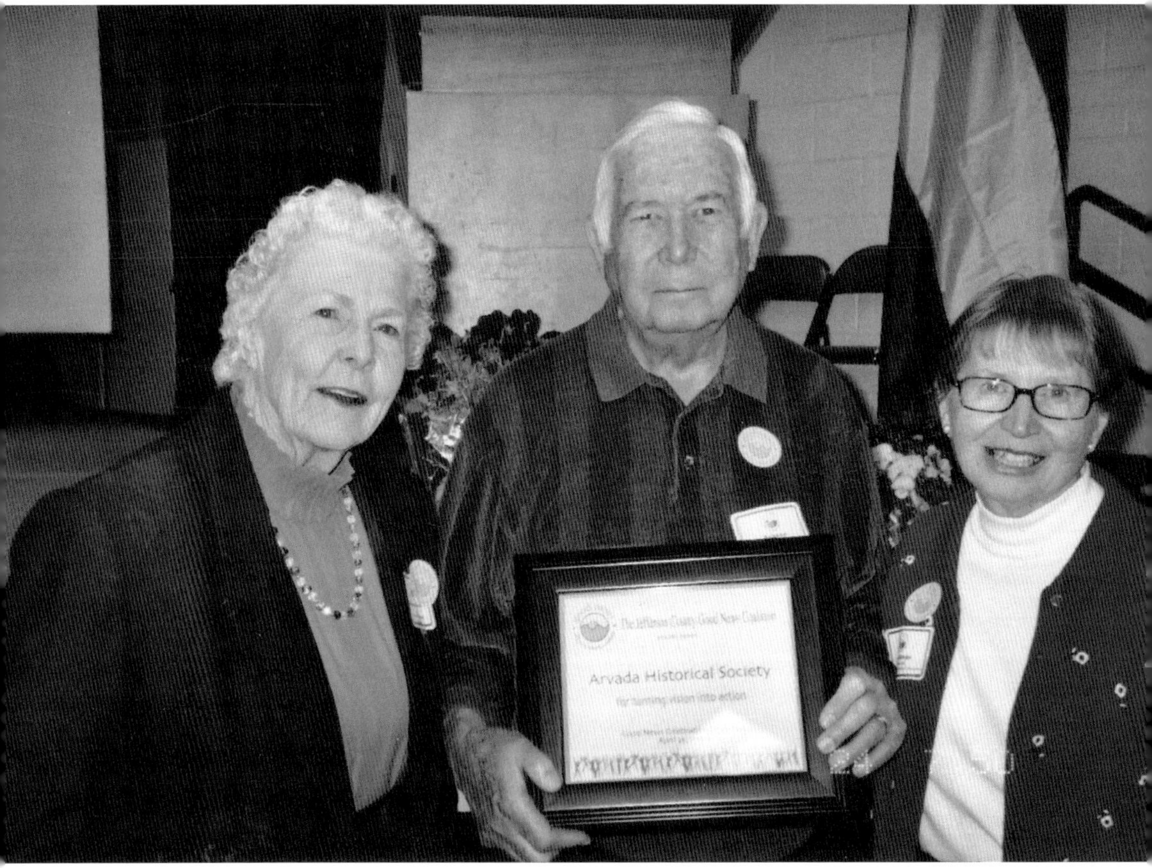

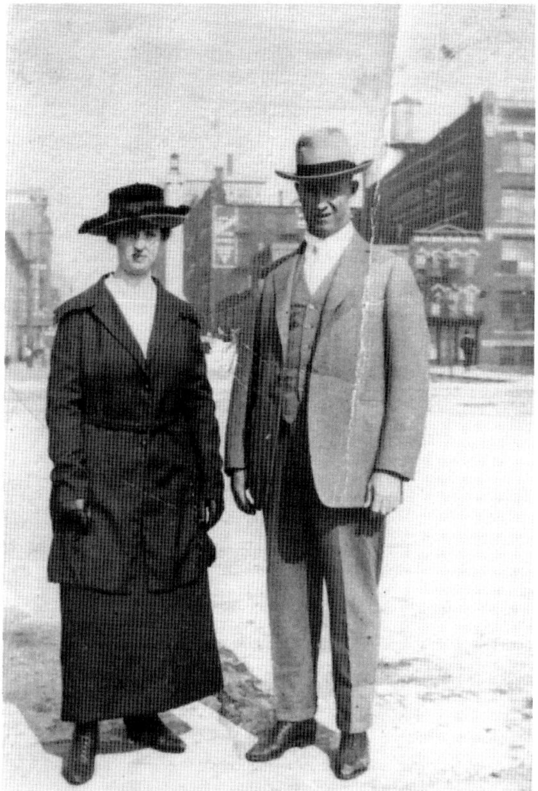

Viva Mahorney
Arvada's first chiropractor, Viva Mahorney, practiced in Arvada for 51 years.

Born in Kansas on November 5, 1889, Viva married Albert Mahorney in 1906. The couple attended Chiropractic College in Davenport, Iowa, and after graduation, they moved to Denver. Viva opened her practice in July 1925 on Grandview Avenue. She retired in January 1976. Viva Mahorney died on May 16, 1984 in Wheat Ridge.

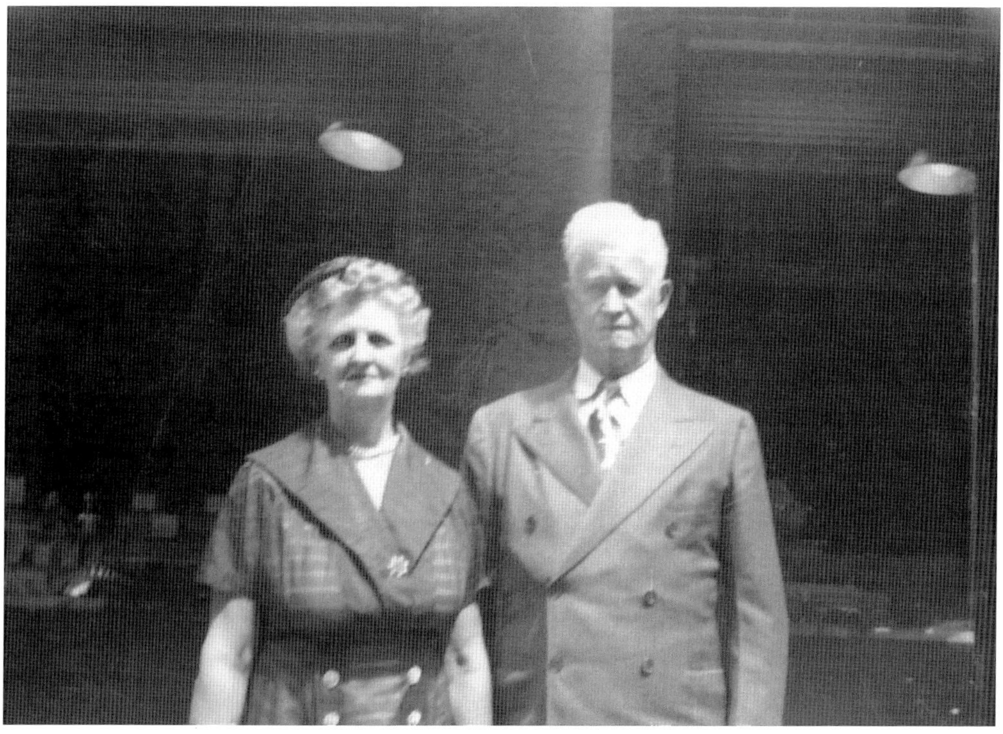

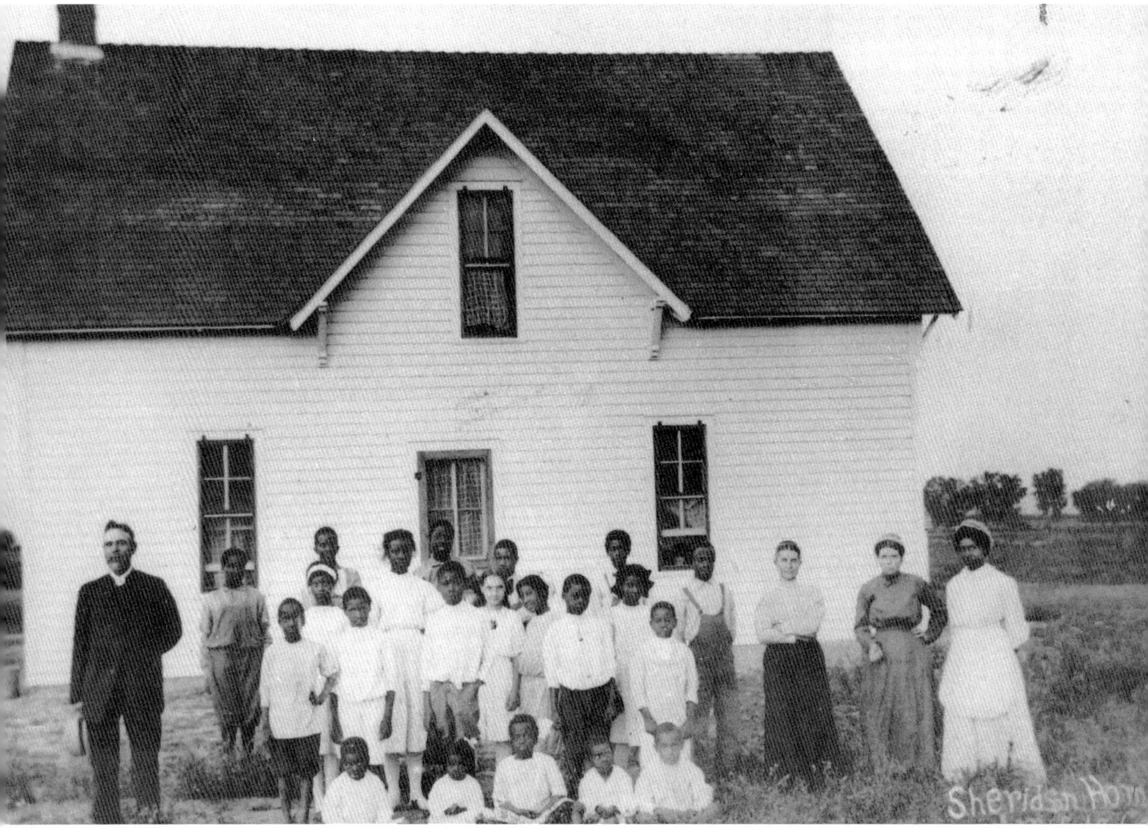

John Van Dyke

John Van Dyke ran the Sheridan Home for Negro Boys from 1913 to 1916.

In September 1912, the Sheridan Home for Negro Boys was established at in the area of current Sixty-sixth Avenue and Wadsworth Boulevard. The school was started by the Church of the Brethren and provided food, shelter, and educational and occupational training. Boys could stay until the age of 18. In 1913, John Van Dyke, along with his wife and daughters, came to Arvada to run the school. The building was located in a home built by Ralph Fields, who ran another school called Brightside northwest of Denver. The Sheridan Home closed in 1920, and records show that the Van Dyke family returned to the Grand Junction area.

Harry Hill

Arvada native Hill survived the infamous Bataan Death March during World War II.

Harry Hill enlisted in the Army in March 1941. He was sent to the Philippines in September 1941 with a field hospital unit. After Manila fell in January 1942, Hill, along with thousands of other American and Philippine troops, was taken prisoner by the Japanese. On April 9, the estimated 60,000 to 80,000 men began the Bataan Death March. During the 80-mile march, thousands of men died from starvation, illness, and acts of murder. Hill was ill with malaria and suffered from weight loss. Facing starvation, Hill caught and ate animals to sustain himself. Hill was classified as missing in action on May 25, 1942. It was another nine months before Hill's parents in Arvada heard any further information on their son. In a telegram dated February 25, 1943, Hill was reported as a prisoner of war. In February 1945, he was rescued and sent to San Francisco for medical care.

Two weeks later, Hill returned home to Arvada. Over 200 friends and family greeted Hill at his homecoming. Harry Hill went on to marry, have a family, and work as a cameraman for Channel 4 News in Denver.

Harry Hill passed away on December 5, 1975, in Arvada.

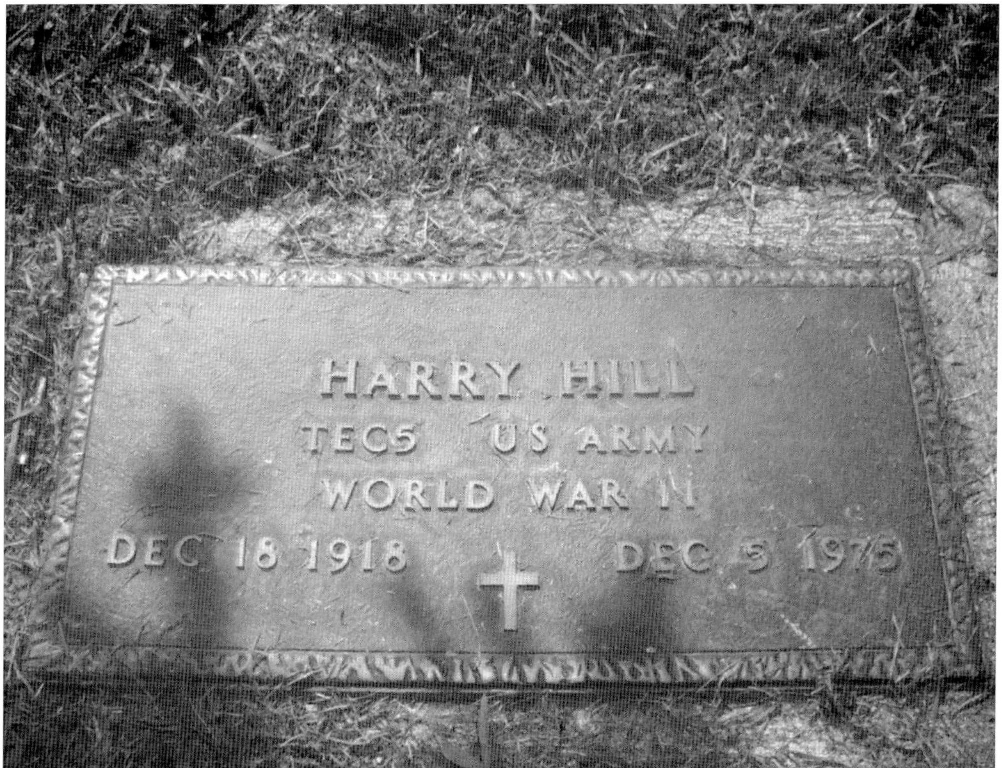

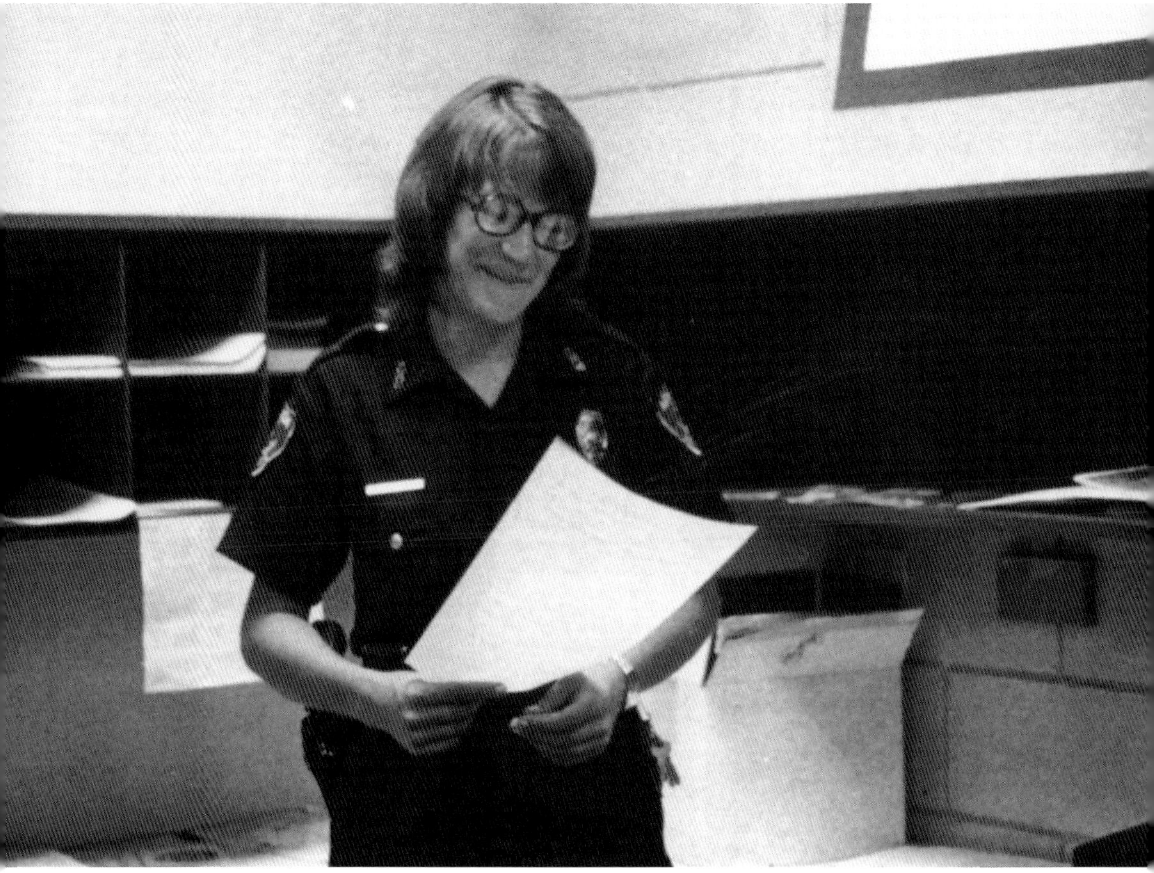

Regina Jo Gailus

Regina Jo Gailus was Arvada's first uniformed patrol officer.

An Arvada native, Gailus joined the Arvada police force in late 1973. She became the first woman in Arvada history to become a patrol officer. Gailus earned an associate degree in law enforcement from Metropolitan State College and graduated from the Colorado Law Enforcement Training Academy. In a 1974 interview, Gailus stated that she chose to become an Arvada officer for various reasons, but her main reason was because of "all the support the Arvada citizens give to police to maintain a superior department."

CHAPTER FOUR

Sports, the Arts, and Media

Arvada has always been known for its support and love of the arts and sports.

In the 1920s, the town had a Community Chorus and the Arvada Citizen's Band. Arvada's first movie theater, the Star, was only in operation briefly in 1911 before its demise. It was another 10 years before a movie house opened again, this time the Trivoli, later to be known as the Arvada Theater. In 1924, the Arvada Non-Theatrical Photoplays Company produced the first motion picture to be filmed in Arvada, *The Lure of the Scout*. Unfortunately, this film is lost to the passage of time. Also in 1924, Broadway actress Jessie Pringle retired to her Atlasta Ranch north of Arvada. And around the same time, future silver screen cowboy Bob Baker briefly called Arvada home.

Sports have also been a favorite pastime in Arvada since the early 1900s, when the town had its own Lone Tree Baseball Team. Two-time Cy Young Award winner Roy Halladay, along with Joel Klatt and Phil Heath, has carried in the Arvada sports tradition.

Roy Halladay

One of Major League Baseball's most prolific players, Roy Halladay called Arvada home as a youth.

Born in Denver on May 14, 1977, Roy Halladay spent his childhood and adolescence in Arvada, graduating from Arvada West High School in 1995. He started his professional baseball career as a pitcher with the Toronto Blue Jays in 1998. A two-time Cy Young Award winner (in 2003 and 2010), Halladay was traded from Toronto to the Philadelphia Phillies in 2010. Roy Halladay pitched the 20th perfect game in MLB history on May 29, 2010, against the Florida Marlins in Miami.

Roy and his wife, Brandy, have two children and reside in Florida.

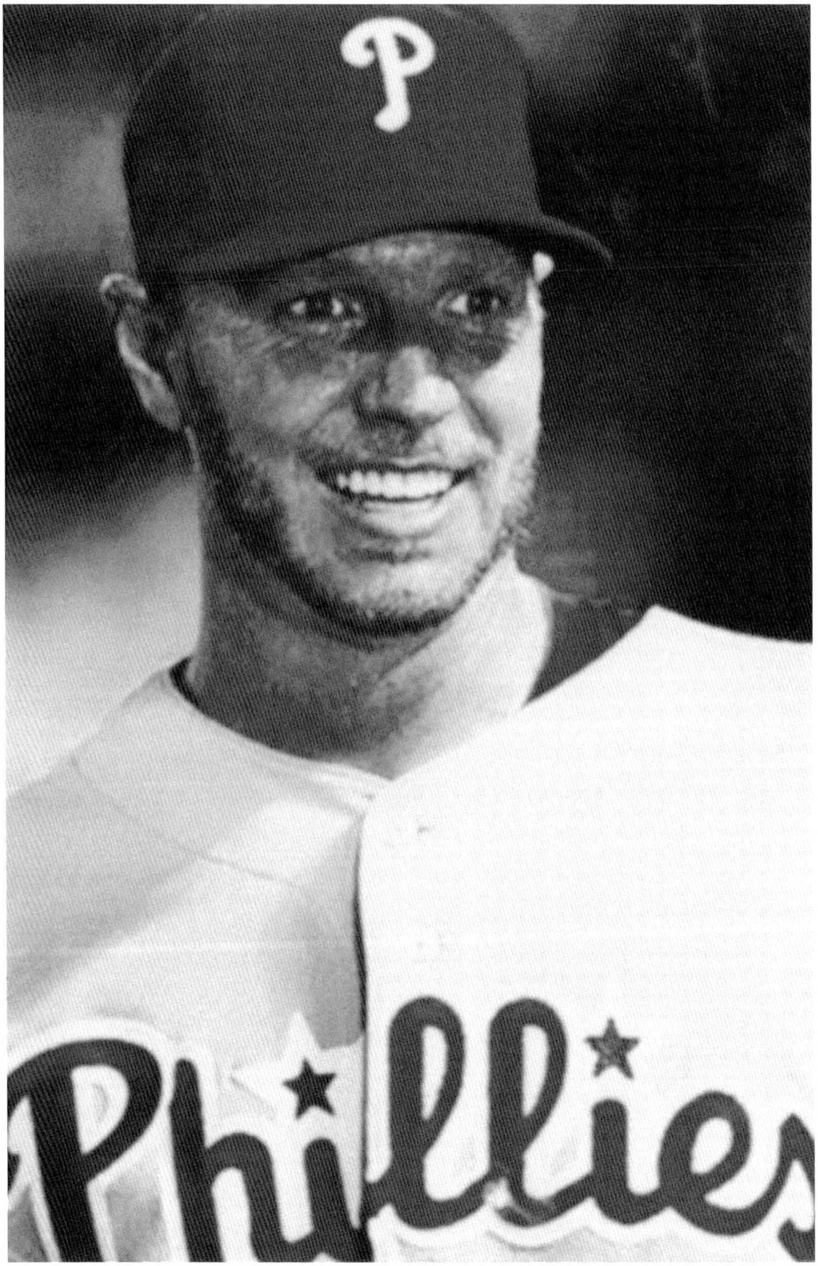

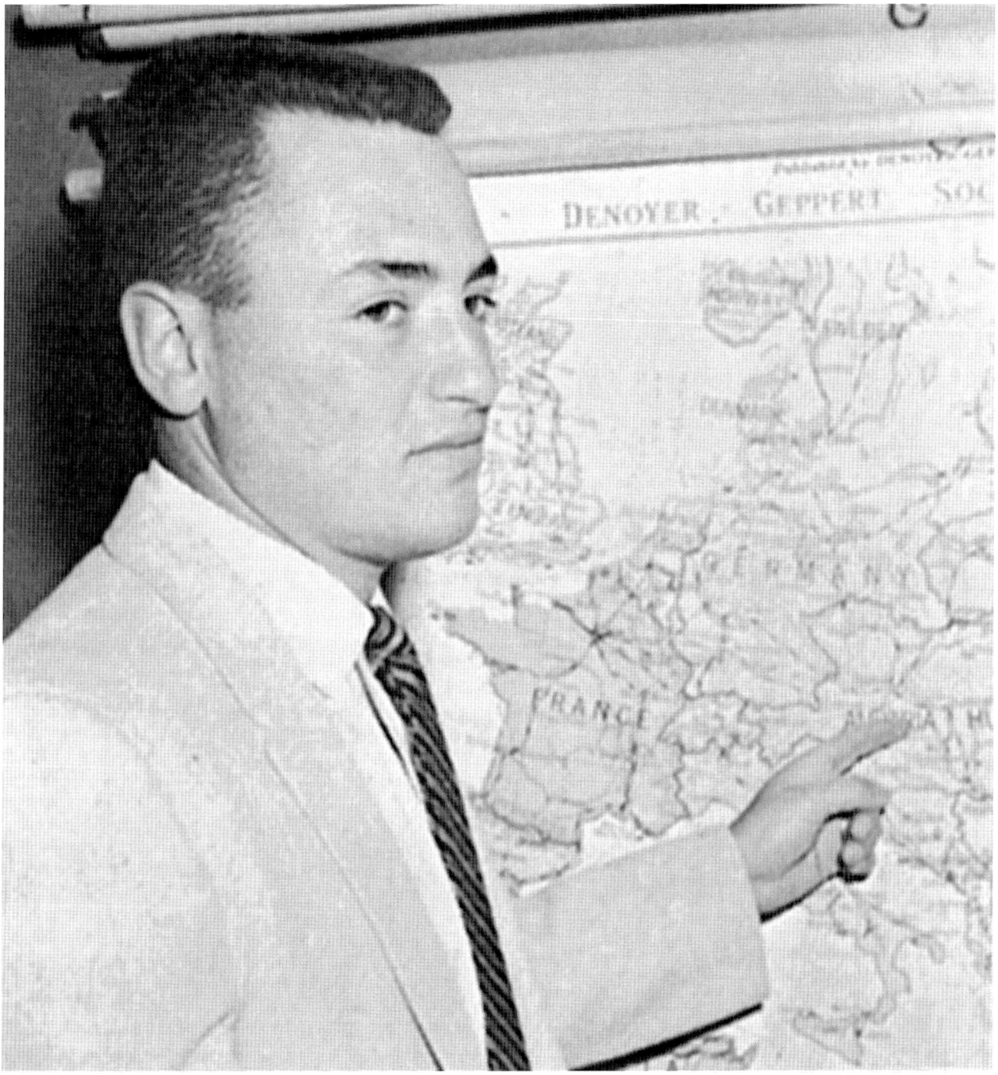

Irv Brown

A Denver native, Irv Brown is a Colorado sports legend.

Irv (Irving) Brown began his sports career at Denver's North High School in the early 1950s. After college graduation, Irv coached at Arvada High School from 1958 to 1969. Brown started as head wrestling and football coach and taught history. During those 11 years, Brown coached the football team to 10 conference football titles and 1 state championship. He also coached baseball at Colorado University and officiated in six Final Four championships.

In the late 1970s, Brown began his career as a sportscaster for KHOW. He coauthored *The Great Books of Denver Sports* with Joe Williams. In 1991, Irv Brown served as commissioner of the Colorado Athletic Conference and, in 1997, was inducted into the Colorado Sports Hall of Fame.

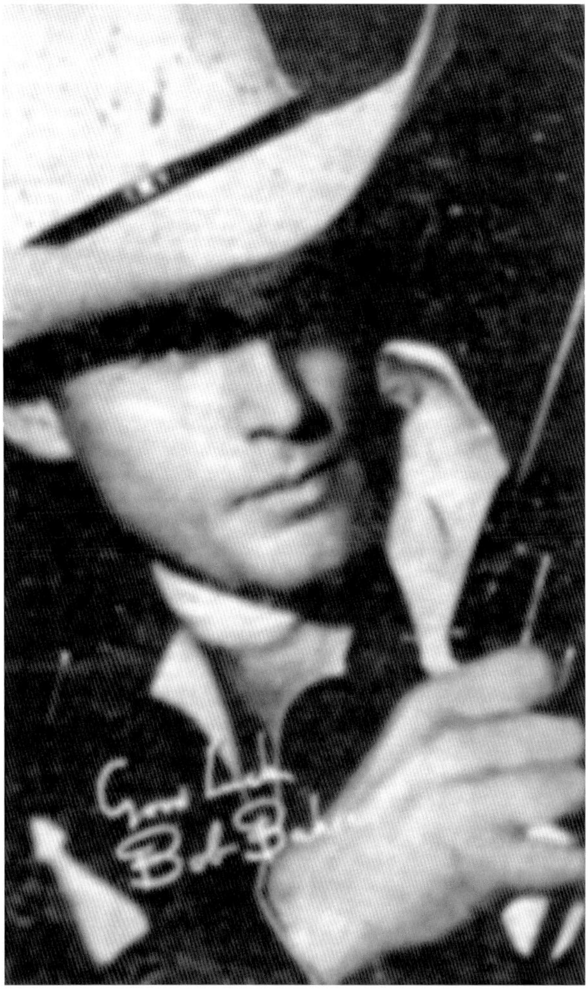

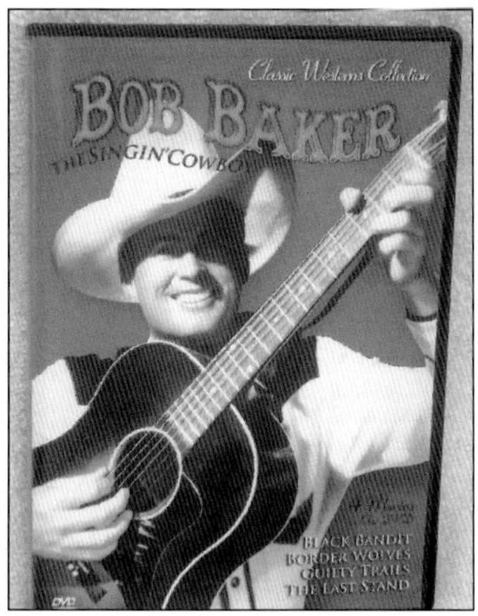

Bob Baker

A brief resident of Arvada in the 1920s, Bob "Tumbleweed" Baker rivaled Roy Rogers in popularity in the late 1930s.

Born Stanley Leland Weed on November 8, 1910, in Forest City, Iowa, Baker spent his teen years in Colorado and Arizona. It was in this period that he resided in Arvada, although the specific dates are unknown. While in the Army, Baker learned to play the guitar and acquired the nickname Tumbleweed. After leaving the service, Baker landed a job on the nationwide syndicated *National Barn Dance* radio show out of Chicago.

In 1937, Baker won a Universal Studios contract and made his first film, *Courage of the West*, that same year. In 1939, Baker ranked 10th on the list of "Top Ten Moneymaking Western Stars" poll. After his Hollywood career ended, Baker worked as a police officer in Arizona for a time and owned and operated a saddle shop.

Bob Baker passed away after years of ill health on August 30, 1975, in Prescott, Arizona. (Courtesy Stan Stewart.)

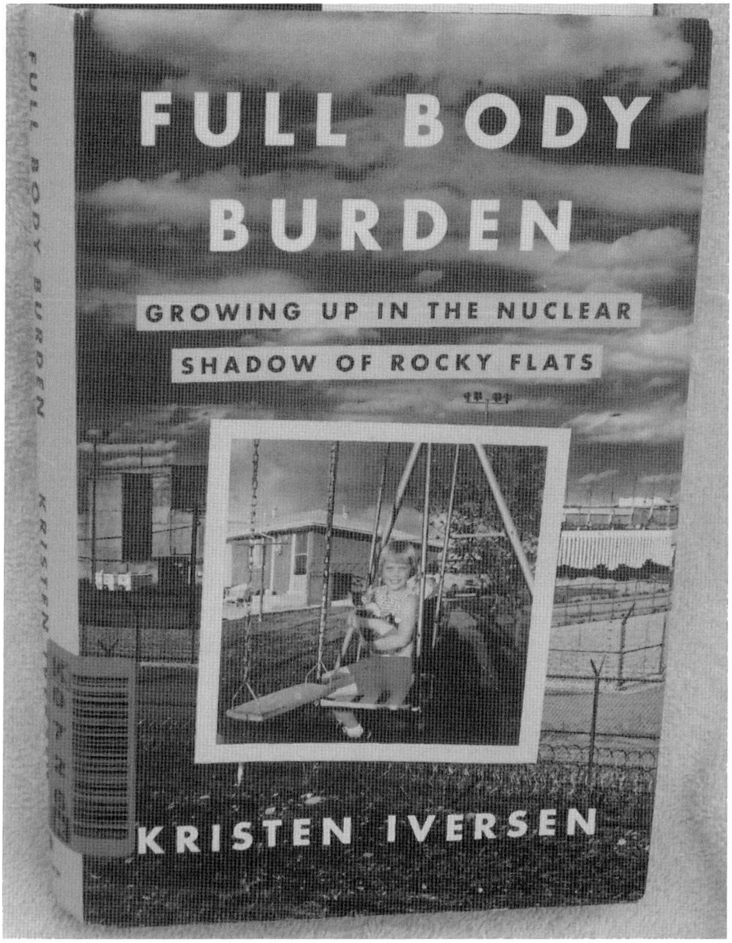

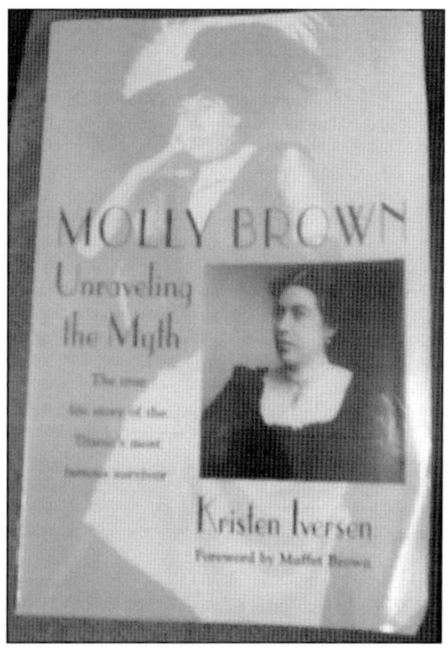

Kristen Iversen

An award-winning author, Iversen drew from her childhood in Arvada for one of her most popular books. In her 2012 book, *Full Body Burden: Growing Up in the Nuclear Shadow of Rocky Flats*, Iversen wrote of her youth living near the Rocky Flats Nuclear Plant that opened in 1953 west of Denver.

Iversen has a bachelor's of arts in English from the University of Colorado–Boulder. She has won many awards for her writing, including the Colorado Book Award for both *Full Body Burden* and for *Molly Brown: Unraveling the Myth*. Kristen also was a 1993 finalist for the Flannery O'Connor Award for Short Fiction. Currently, Iversen is director of the University of Memphis's MFA Program in Creative Writing. She is also a cofounder of Orphan Press.

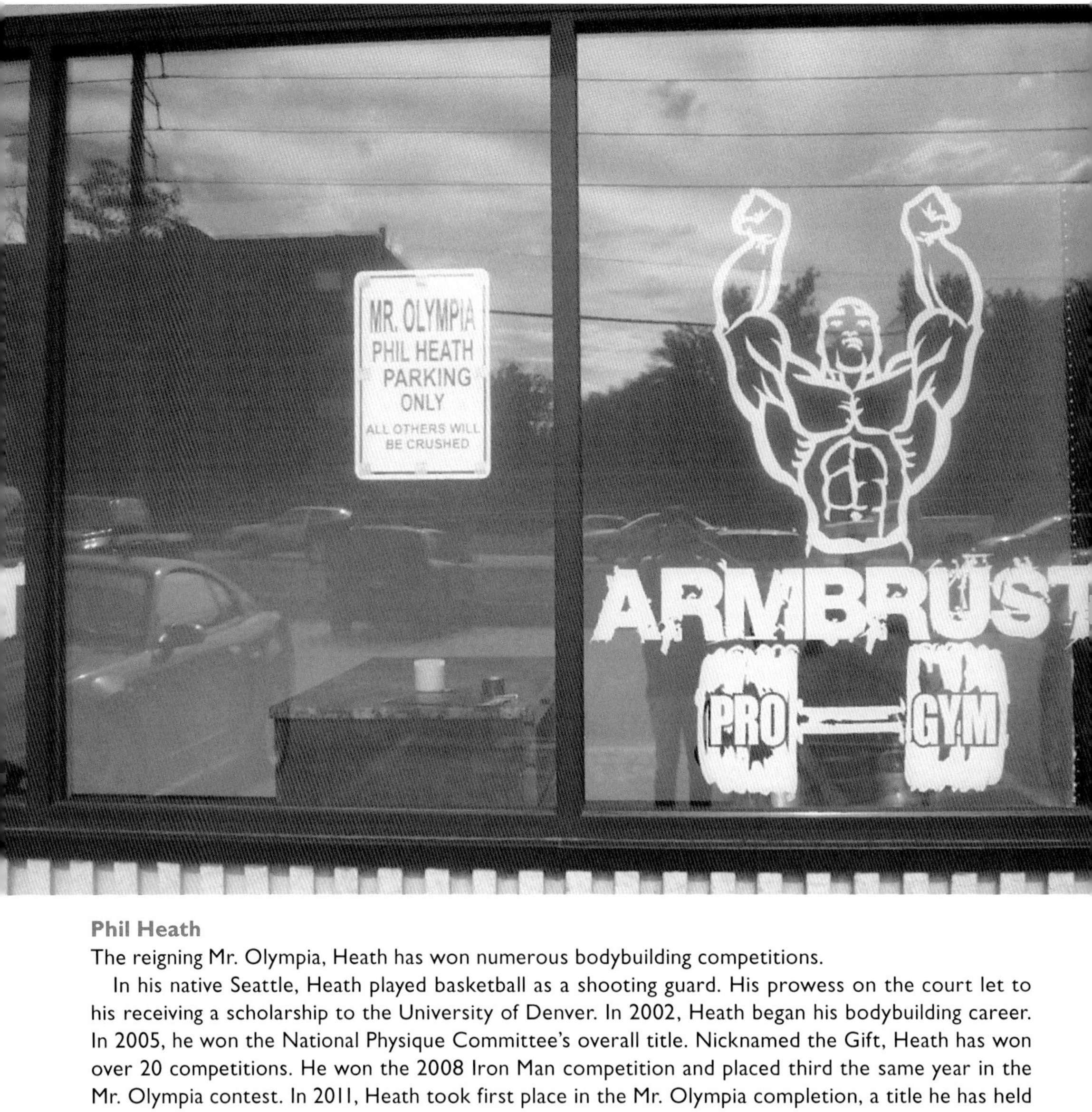

Phil Heath

The reigning Mr. Olympia, Heath has won numerous bodybuilding competitions.

In his native Seattle, Heath played basketball as a shooting guard. His prowess on the court let to his receiving a scholarship to the University of Denver. In 2002, Heath began his bodybuilding career. In 2005, he won the National Physique Committee's overall title. Nicknamed the Gift, Heath has won over 20 competitions. He won the 2008 Iron Man competition and placed third the same year in the Mr. Olympia contest. In 2011, Heath took first place in the Mr. Olympia completion, a title he has held for the last three years.

Phil Heath lives in Arvada today and trains in Wheat Ridge at Armbrust Pro Gym. He has been featured on the cover of *Flex* magazine.

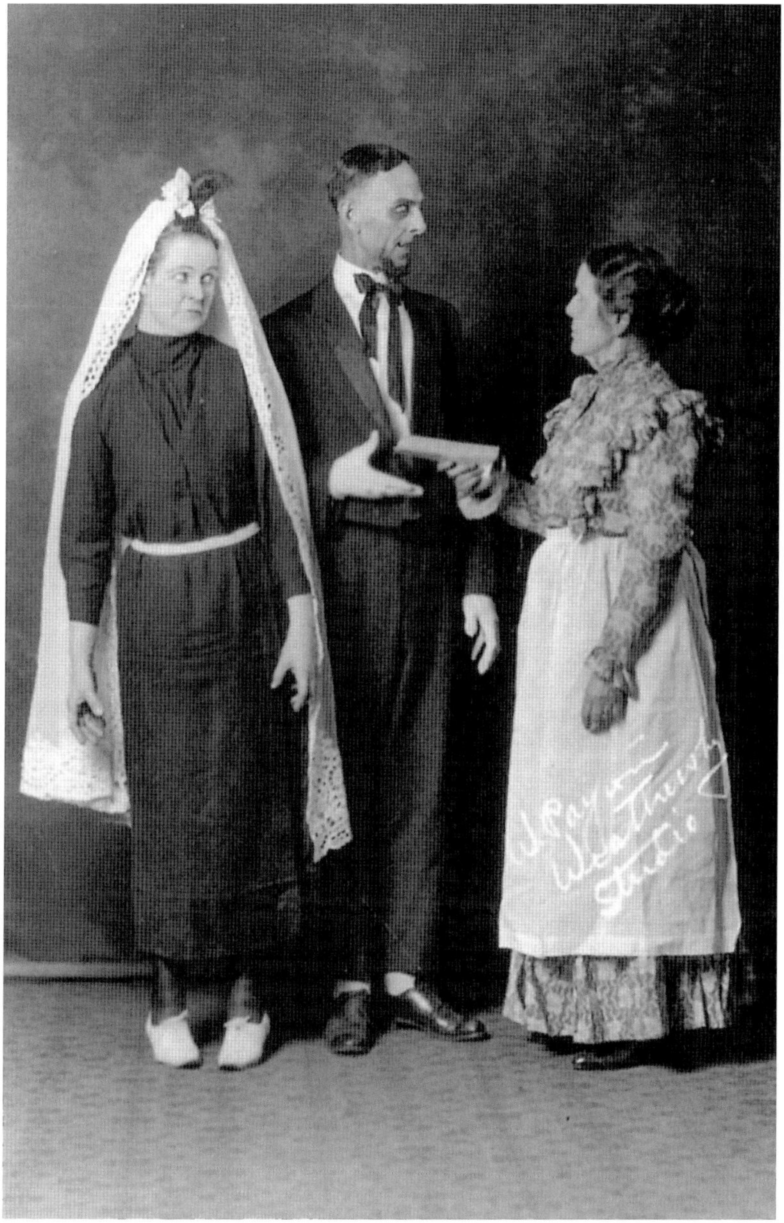

Jessie Pringle

Jessie Pringle retired from her Broadway career in 1924 to live at her ranch in Arvada.

Born Jessie Calvert in Iowa in 1866, she married William Pringle in 1889. Jessie struggled for years as an actress until she was discovered by producer John Golden in New Jersey in 1914. She went on to star in over 1,200 performances of *Lightnin'* on Broadway. Jessie had bought the ranch on present day Eightieth Avenue sometime in the early 1920s. She named her property the Atlasta Ranch, supposedly saying she was home at last. Pringle held acting classes for Arvada residents during her years there. Usually the classes took place at St. Anne's community room. Jessie sold the ranch to Clarence Lively in 1927, and the actress went on to make many movies in Hollywood during the 1930s.

Jessie Pringle passed away in 1953. (Courtesy Denver Public Library.)

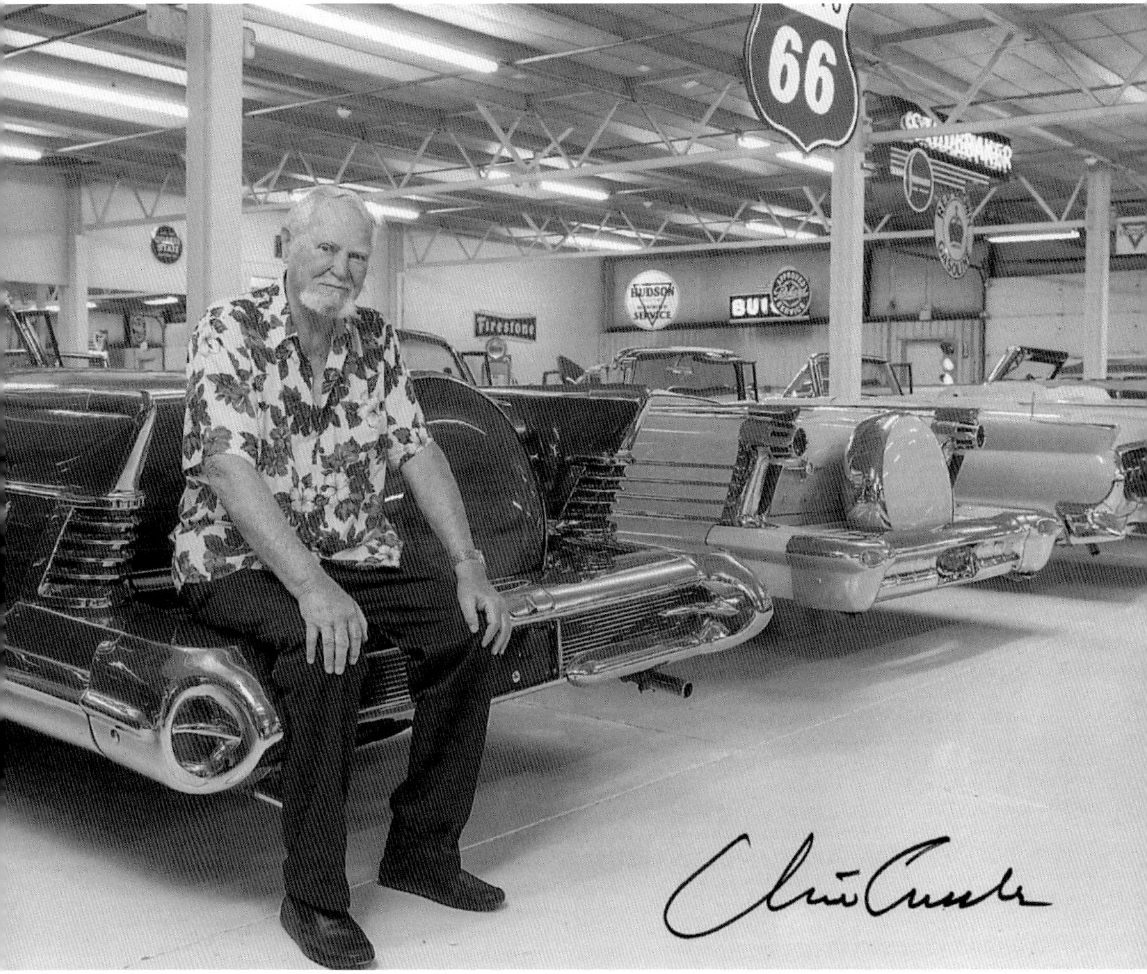

Clive Cussler

A bestselling author, Cussler has an auto museum in Arvada.

Born in Illinois in 1931, Cussler first achieved literary fame upon the publication of his book *Raise the Titanic* in 1976. Cussler became a *New York Times* bestselling author, with his main subject being marine adventures. One of Clive's passions is underwater exploration and searching for sunken ships. A love for antique cars led Cussler to open the Cussler Car Museum in Arvada.

THURSDAY

[T]HE DENVER POST

Voice of the Rocky Mountain Empire ★ Final Edition / 25 cents
35 cents in Designated Areas

Columnist Dick Connor dies

[B]y Todd Phipers
[D]enver Post Sports Writer

"You're a good deal poorer this morning, [D]enver. I wonder if you really know yet just [h]ow much."

So did Dick Connor start his tribute to Bob [M]artin, his longtime friend and associate, [w]hen the Denver broadcaster died of cancer [i]n 1990.

Now, less than three years later, the [w]ords tragically and ironically fit again.

The man who wrote them is gone.

Richard James Connor Jr., 62, lost his val[i]ant, 27-month-long battle against cancer

▪ **LOOKING BACK:** A review of Dick Connor's career /**6-7D**

yesterday. He died at 7:10 p.m. at home, with all his children and his beloved wife, Mary Kay, at his side.

Life isn't fair. Dick Connor was.

A sports-writing career that began in 1961 — when he left his job as director of public information at Regis College to join the Rocky Mountain News — has been silenced, more than three decades and countless awards later. Through two terms at the News and two at The Post, the honors poured in, culminating in his induction into the National Sportscasters and Sportswriters Hall of Fame earlier this year.

But it won't be the awards that will be remembered by his vast and appreciative reading public. It will be personal honesty and linguistic dignity he brought to the task.

"I'm not going to use vague words — like gallant and brave and determined — to describe the way he spent more than two years battling cancer," he wrote of Martin.

Please see CONNOR on 11A

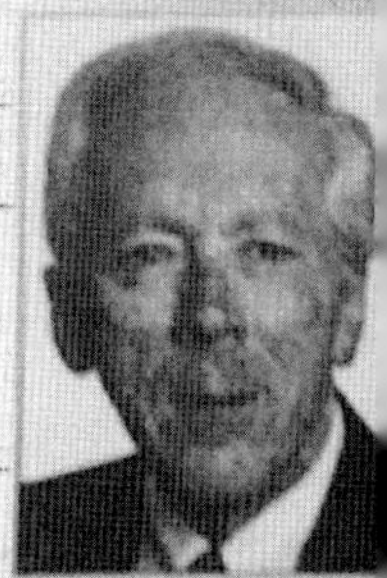

DICK CONNOR: 1930-199[2]

Dick Connor

One of Denver's most legendary sports writers ever, Dick Connor lived in Arvada for 30 years.

Dick Connor was born in 1933 in Iowa. After serving in the Korean War, Connor attended Regis University in Denver, where he earned a degree in English. In 1961, Dick got a job with the *Rocky Mountain News* as a sports reporter. Four years later, he moved to the *Denver Post* in the first of his two stints at that paper. In 1982, Dick returned to the *Rocky Mountain News* only to go back to the *Post* six years later. In all of those years, Connor covered a multitude of Denver sports history. He also won Colorado Sports Writer of the Year 23 times over his career, among many other awards.

After a two-year battle with cancer, Dick Connor passed away on December 30, 1992.

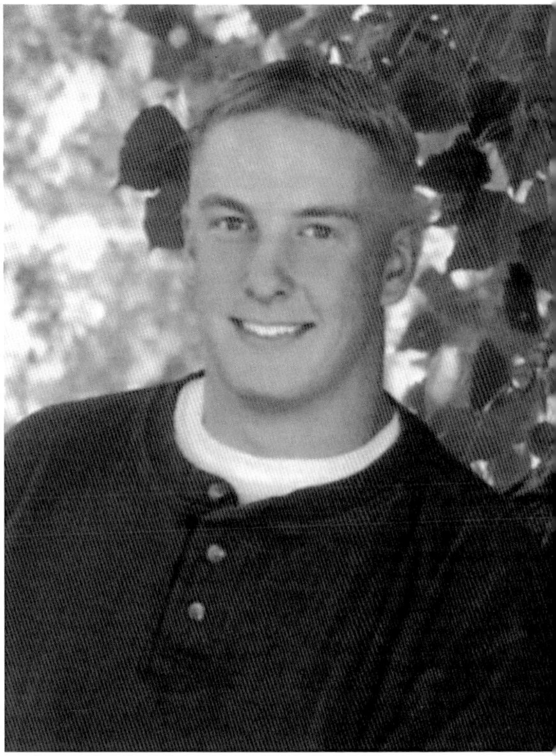

Joel Klatt
A sports broadcaster, Klatt has played both football and baseball.

Born in Arvada in 1982, Klatt played high school football for Pomona High School. Klatt excelled in basketball and baseball during his high school years. In 2000, he was drafted by the San Diego Padres. He played for Class A Peoria that year. After two years of not making it to the majors, Klatt moved on to college football.

In 2003, he was the starting quarterback for the University of Colorado (CU) Buffs. He earned CU's Offensive Player of the Year and was honored as National Player of the Week in August of 2003. Klatt's football career ended when he suffered a concussion in the Big 12 Championship game against Texas in 2006.

Joel Klatt now has a sports talk show on 104.3 FM in Denver.

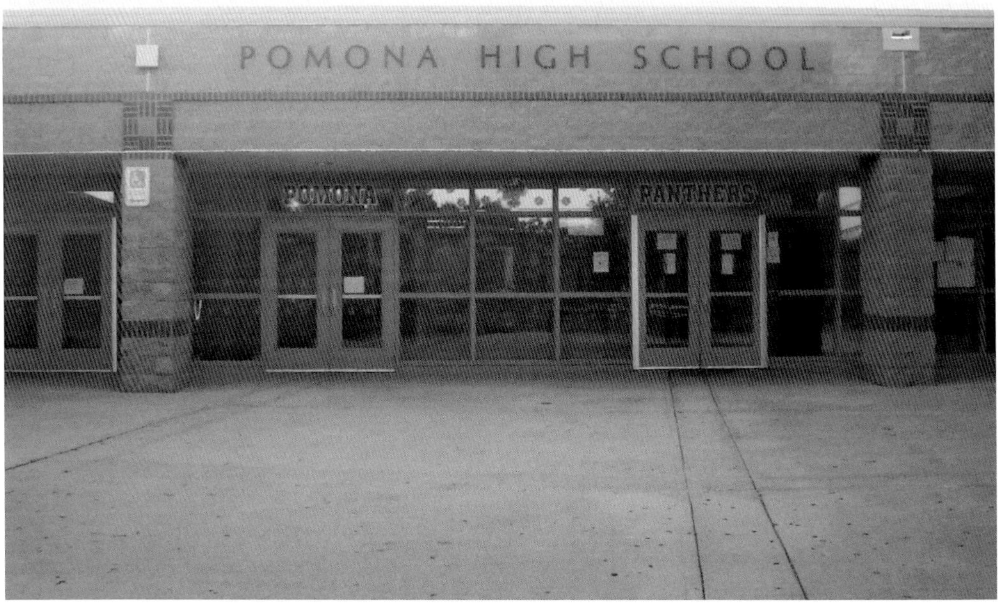

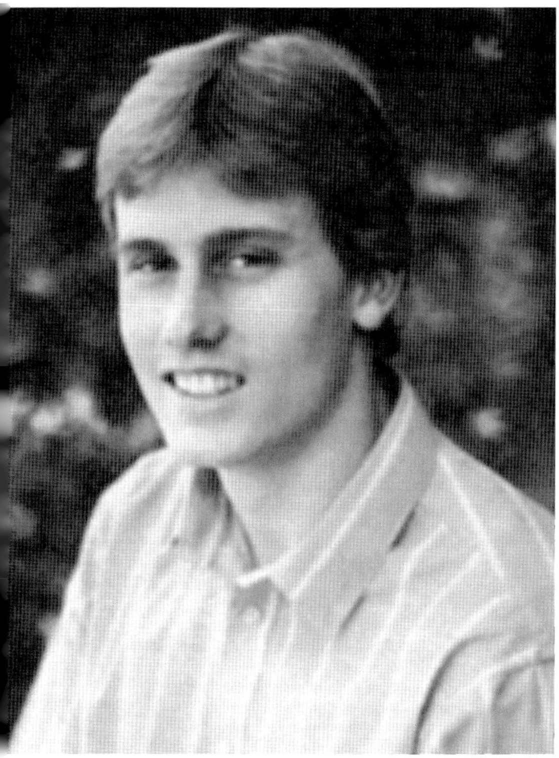

Barry Kooser

A well-known animator, Kooser worked on some of Disney's most popular films.

Born in Wheat Ridge on December 23, 1968, Kooser graduated from Arvada West High School in 1987. After earning a bachelor's degree in fine art from Kansas City Art Institute in 1991, Kooser was hired by Disney Studios in Orlando Florida.

His first Disney project was 1993's Roger Rabbit short *Trail Mix-Up*. The next year, Kooser worked on Disney's 32nd animated film, *The Lion King*. He was also a background artist for the Disney films *Pocahontas*, *Mulan*, *Lilo & Stich*, and *Brother Bear.* After his Disney career, Kooser taught at the Rocky Mountain College of Art + Design. He is now chief creative officer for Worker Studio Animation in Centennial, Colorado.

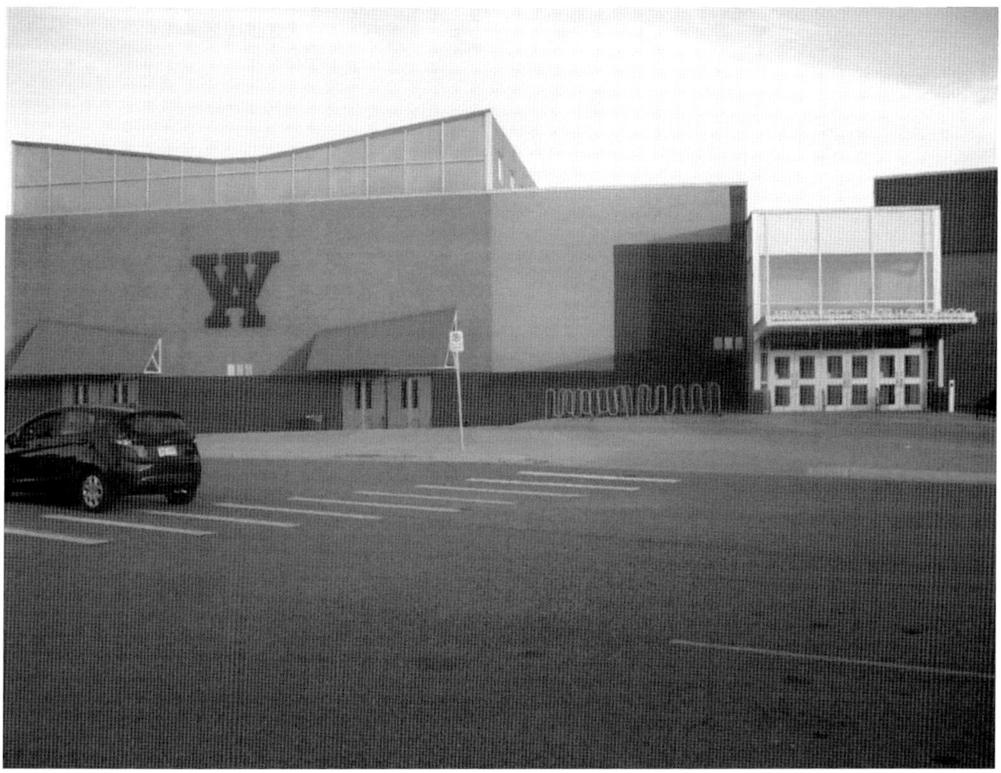

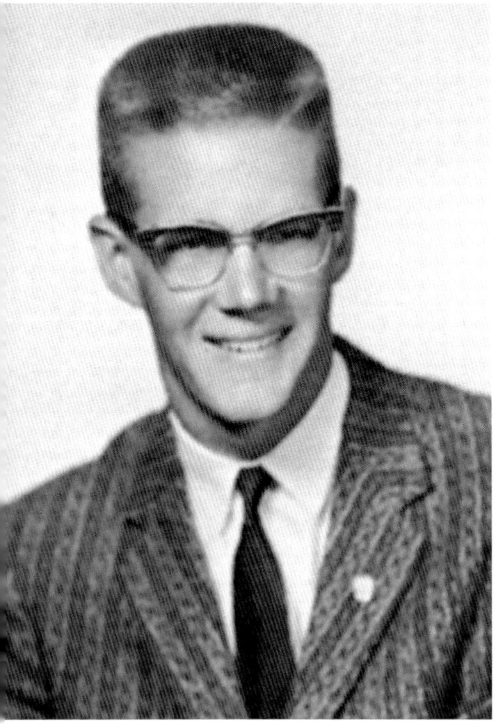

Jack Price

Jack Price was both an outstanding athlete and student.

Jack Robert Price was born March 12, 1943. His parents were Robert and Dorothy Price. Jack had two siblings, Carol and Scott. The Price family moved to Arvada in 1947 from Rifle, Colorado. Robert Price served as principal of Lawrence Elementary School from 1947 to 1949.The Prices resided at 5608 Yarrow Street in Arvada. Jack started high school in 1958 and played on the B squad football team for the Redskins. He also played that year for the B squad basketball. The 1960 school year school year saw Jack on the A squad football team. Jack was also a member of the National Honor Society and was both basketball and football Second Team All Conference. In his senior year, Jack Price made All Conference again, this time in baseball, football, and basketball. In a game played against Golden on October 22, 1960, Price, a halfback, scored two touchdowns for the Redskins, aiding in the teams 13-6 win. Jack Price was named Outstanding Athlete of the Year for Arvada High School in the 1960–1961 season. After graduating in 1961, Price went on to play halfback for two years for the University of Colorado–Boulder Buffaloes. Jack Price later moved to Stayton, Oregon.

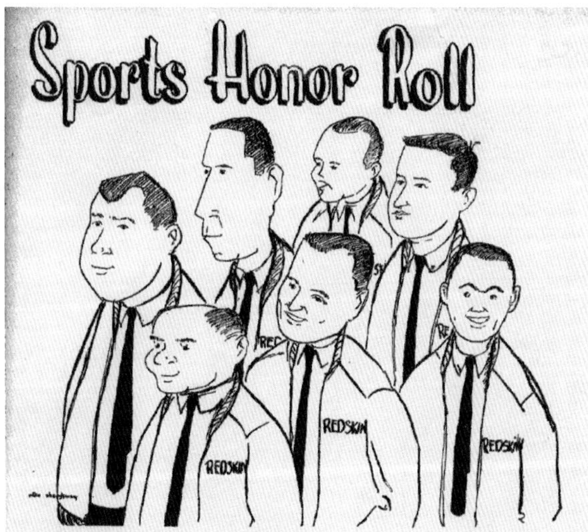

Sports Honor Roll

KEN BORING	Wrestling; District Champion, 2nd state.
TOM DILDINE	Tennis; 2nd State, 1st Singles.
CURTIS ELLIOT	Wrestling; District Champion.
BOB ELSTON	Wrestling; 2nd District, 2nd State.
JIM FOTHERGILL	Wrestling; District Champion, 3rd State.
RICK HAGAMAN	Football; All Conference; Wrestling; District and State Champion.
DUANE HARRIS	Basketball; All Conference.
HAROLD HUDSPETH	Baseball; All Conference (1960).
ADRIAN MOHR	Basketball; All Conference.
DENNY PARDEE	Wrestling; 2nd District.
JACK PRICE	Football; All Conference, All Metro, All State; Basketball; All Conference; Baseball; All Conference (1960).
GORDON ROWLEY	Football; All Conference, All Metro, All American, Tom McAn Award.
DICK SHEPHERD	Wrestling; 2nd District.
TOM VAUGHN	Wrestling; District Champion, 2nd State.
JOE VINNOLA	Football; All Conference.

99

Redskins to Play In North Tourney Friday, Saturday

Arvada high school's undefeated basketball team will be one of the four participants in this weekend's North tournament which will be held at the Lakewood high school gym.

The tournament schedule is as follows:

FRIDAY—7:30 p.m., North Denver vs. Westminster; 9:00 p.m., Lakewood vs. Arvada.

SATURDAY—7:30 p.m., Friday night's losers; 9:00 p.m., Friday night's winners.

The tournament orginally was scheduled to be played in the new North high gym, but because the gym is not completed the tourney was moved to the Lakewood site. The Lakewood high school is located at West Eighth avenue and Kipling street.

On the same two days the "B" squads of the participating schools will cnduct their own tournament at the Westminster gym. First round games will be played at 1:30 and 3:00 Friday afternoon and the finals at the same time Saturday afternoon.

The Redskins maintained their undefeated schedule last week by defeating Littleton 52-43 Friday night and Sterling 53-50 Saturday evening. Both games were played in the Redskins gym.

Jack Price led the Arvada scoring Friday night with 14 points; while Rick Sankey scored 17 points Saturday night to lead the Redskin cause.

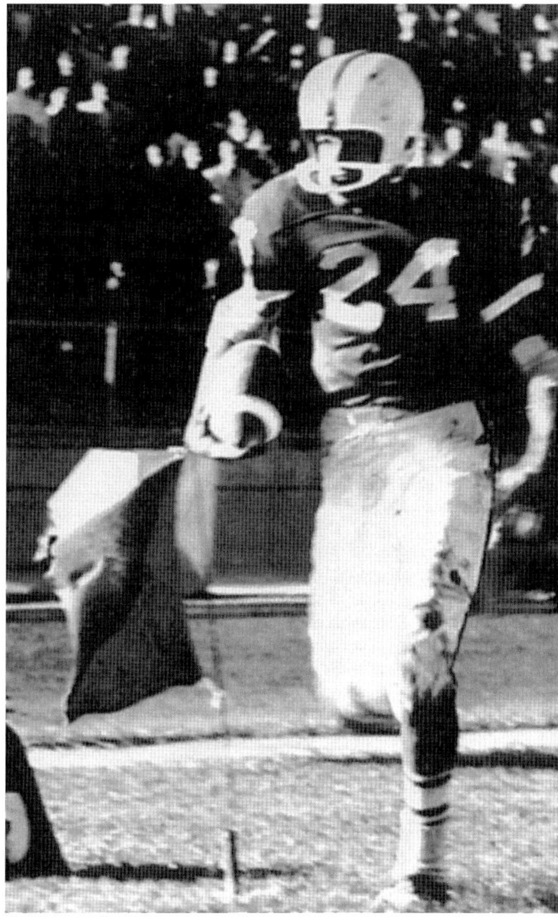

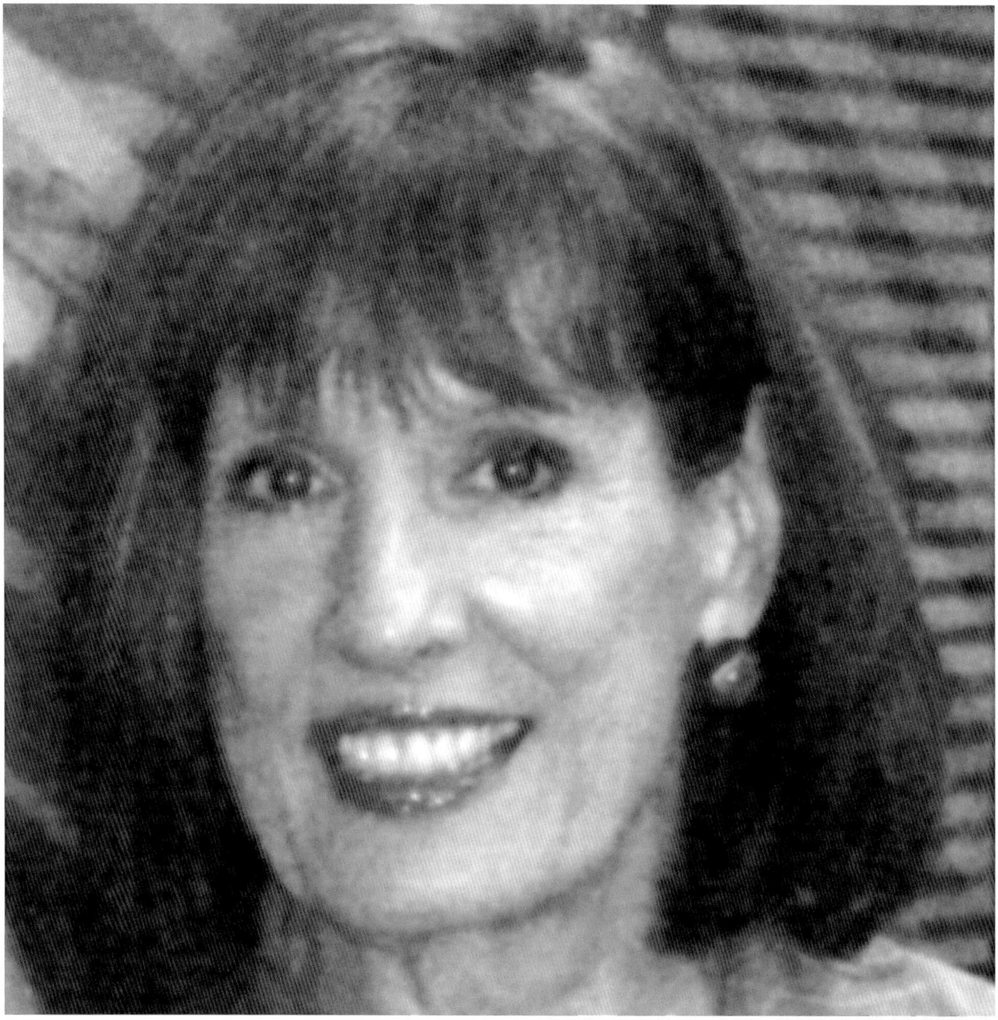

Cynthia Hessian

Arvada West graduate Hessin is an award-winning journalist.

Cynthia Hessian is host of *Colorado State of Mind*, a weekly news program on Rocky Mountain PBS. Hessian is also executive producer on the show. Hessian's career with RMPBS began in 1995. Before that she was with KHOW radio. She was hired by KCNC in 1979 and moved to KMGH in 1984. Cynthia has won five regional Emmy Awards and served as the Denver Press Club's first female president from 1996 to 1997. Her job at RMPBS has included work on the documentary *Losing Ground: The Cliff Effect* in 2013. Hessin was the 2013 winner of the Silver Circle Award from the Heartland Emmy Awards. (Courtesy Cynthia Hessian.)

CHAPTER FIVE

The Political Arena

On August 24, 1904, Arvada was incorporated. This move led to the formation of the Arvada Town Board by the town's first mayor, Dr. Richard Russell. In the 110 years that have followed, Arvada has seen many changes to its political landscape.

Finley C. Murchison, an Arvada businessman, became a state senator in the 1920s. Tom Tancredo has served in congress and has also run twice for the Colorado gubernatorial seat. Ann Jackson was Arvada's first female mayor, elected in 1963. Although Jackson's mayoral term was contentious, she blazed a trail for other women in city politics, such as Vesta Miller and Arvada's first transgender politician, Joanne Conte. James Biggin Jr. and Oliver North Evans both served in offices for Jefferson County in the 1920s and 1930s.

Arvada's political climate has often been volatile, but it has been the desire of all who have served in office to make Arvada a better place to live.

Vesta Miller

"You have to give back to the community where you live. You have to be a contributor, not a taker-part of the solution, not the problem," Vesta Miller said in 1987, and it is certainly a clear example of Miller's life. Vesta Miller and her family moved to Arvada in 1960. She taught as a substitute teacher from 1966 until 1975. In 1972, Miller led the Arvada Goals Task Force, a group of citizen calling for community resources. Miller was elected to the Arvada City Council in 1973. She served as mayor from 1979 to 1981. Vesta has also sold real estate.

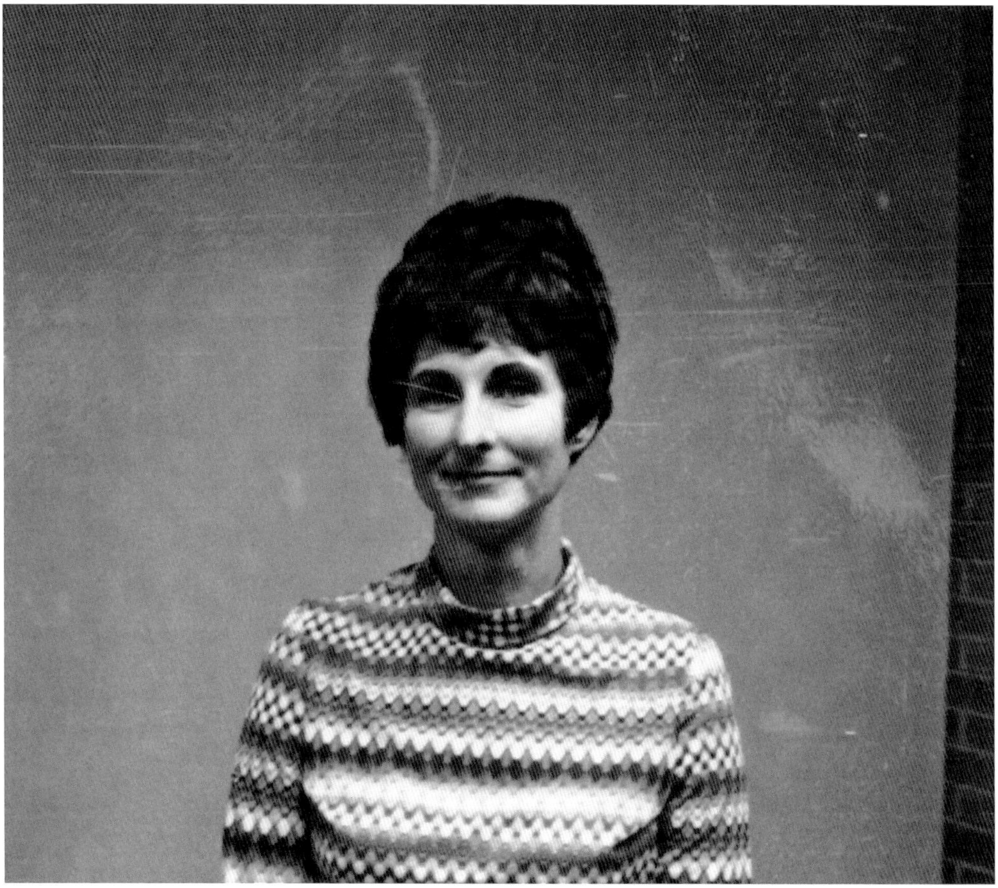

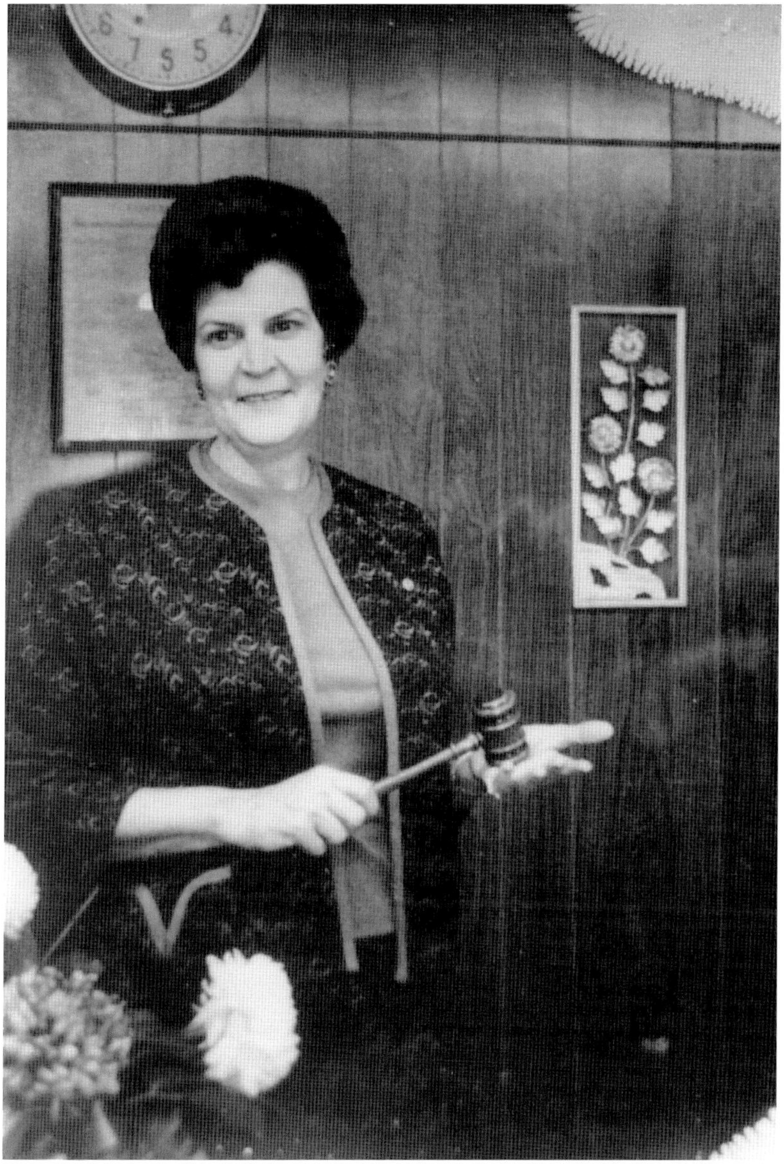

Ann Jackson
Arvada's first female mayor was the city's Woman of the Year in 1960.

"Arvada gets first lady mayor" was the headline in 1963 when Ann Jackson was elected to her controversial 21-month term. From the start, due to Jackson's stand against a proposed shopping complex in historic Olde Town Arvada, controversy dogged the mayor. Within a few months, a recall election against Jackson was in full swing. Gossip about Jackson's divorces and business dealing fueled the recall firestorm. In the end, the mayor prevailed, winning the recall and continuing in office for another year. But the recall had taken its toll on Jackson, and on August 12, 1965, she resigned from the office of mayor. "I have done nothing dishonest, but have reached the end of my endurance with respect to the insinuations of my integrity," Jackson stated in her resignation letter.

After leaving office, Ann Jackson lived in Germany and Missouri before settling in Idaho to be closer to family. Ann Jackson died on March 6, 1976, in Boise, Idaho. She was laid to rest in the Arvada Cemetery.

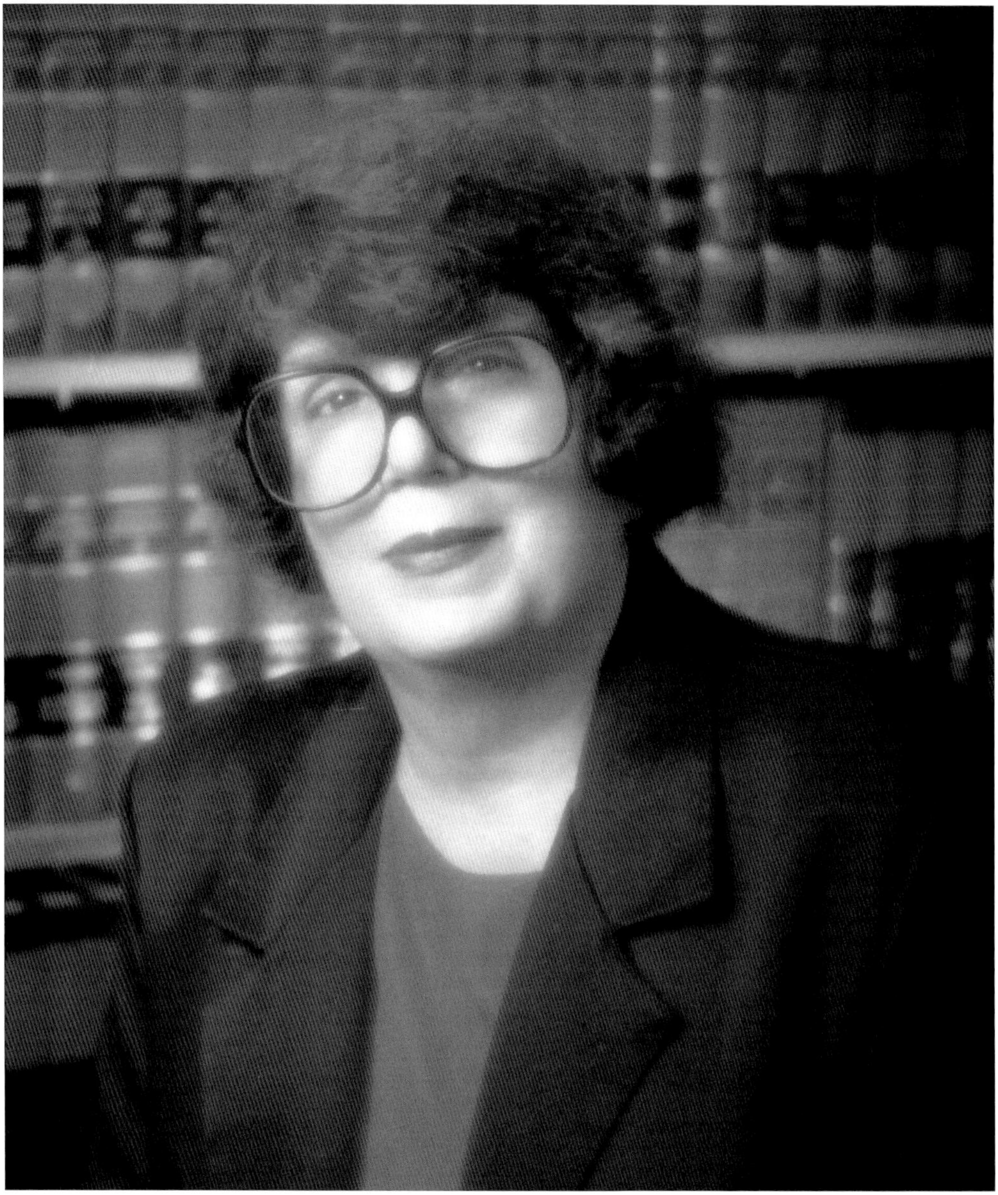

Joanne Conte

Arvada's first transgender city council member, Conte served for two terms.

Born Joseph Baione in Rochester, New York, in 1933, Conte served in the Korean War. In 1972, after changing her legal name, Conte underwent sex reassignment surgery. In 1991, she ran for and won a seat on Arvada City Council. In 1993, *Westword* newspaper planned to reveal Conte's surgery to the public. Acquiring knowledge of the upcoming article, Conte, in a public statement on March 5, 1993, acknowledged her surgery 20 years earlier. Unfortunately, the confession ruined Conte's political career.

After Conte's term on city council was over, she became a local activist, leading many causes against local government. She also enjoyed a radio career, volunteering and becoming an investigative reporter for KGNU in Boulder.

Joanne Conte passed away in January 2013. (Courtesy KATV.)

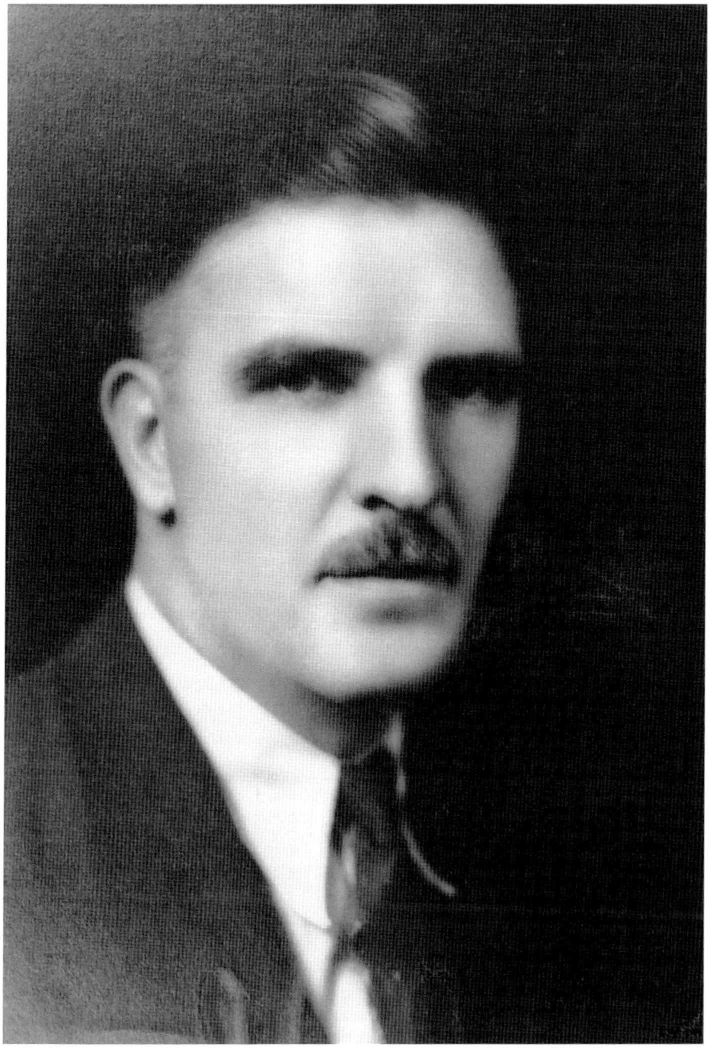

James Biggins Jr.
Biggins made his mark on Jefferson County by serving in many political offices.

Hailing from Illinois, Biggins moved out west to work in the coal mines. When America entered World War I, Biggins answered his country's call. After the war, James worked at the Leyden coal mine west of Arvada from 1921 to 1923. James married Janice Ayer in late 1927, and the couple's only child, James, was born in 1928.

Biggins held the first of his many political offices from 1927 to 1931 as Jefferson County deputy assessor. In 1930, he won his bid for the office of Jefferson County sheriff, an occupation he held until 1935. Those were the days of Prohibition, and Biggins uncovered many illegal stills and bootleg operations in the county. Next on the list of Biggins's public service jobs came when he was elected Arvada's mayor in 1936. In 1939, the Biggins family moved out of Arvada city limits, resulting in James resigning from the mayoral office.

Remembered as a somewhat solemn man, Biggins did have a great sense of humor as family members recall. He was active in the Arvada Chamber of Commerce and the VFW and was a Master of the Masonic Lodge in Arvada.

James Gibson Biggins Jr. passed away in 1964.

Dr. Richard Russell

Dr. Richard Russell became Arvada's first mayor.

Russell led the movement for Arvada's incorporation in 1904 and was elected mayor upon incorporation. In 1907, Russell moved to Westminster, where he became that town's first mayor. Russell moved back to Arvada in 1916 and served eight terms as Arvada's mayor. He also helped organize the First National Bank of Arvada.

Dr. Richard Russell died on April 12, 1934.

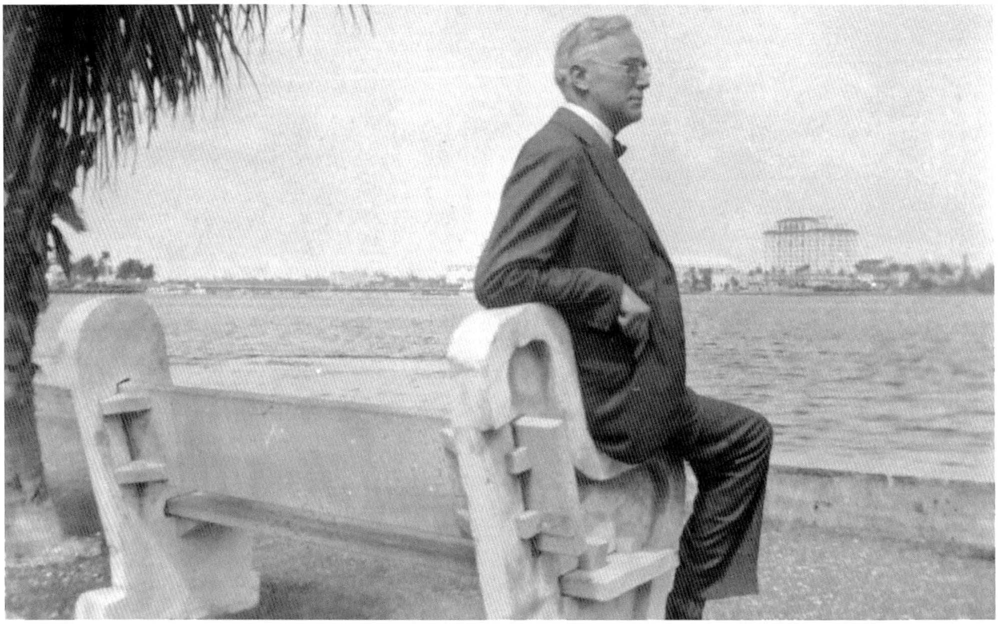

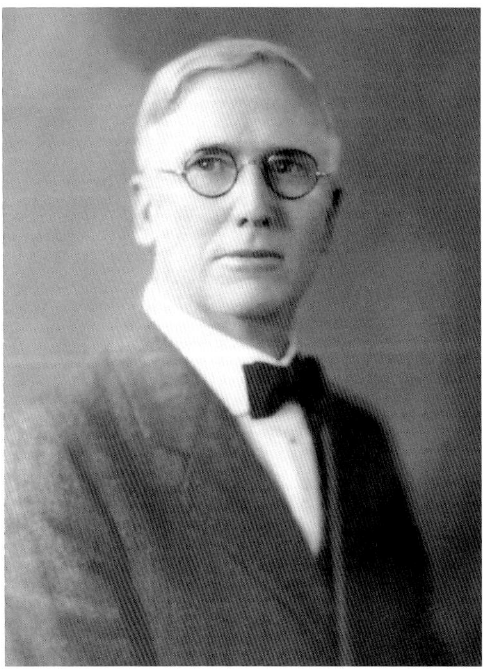

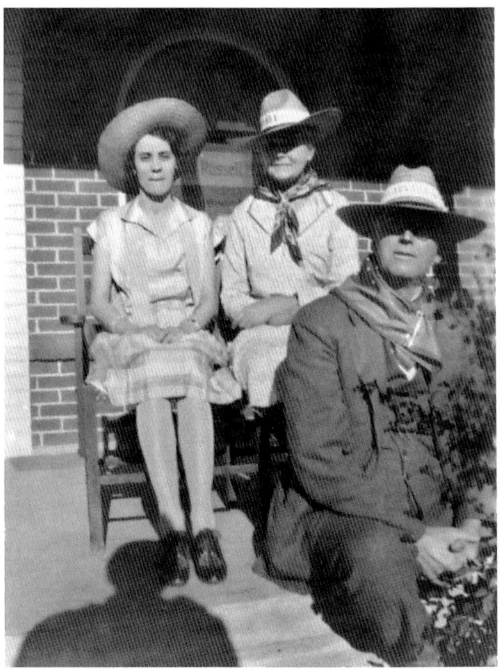

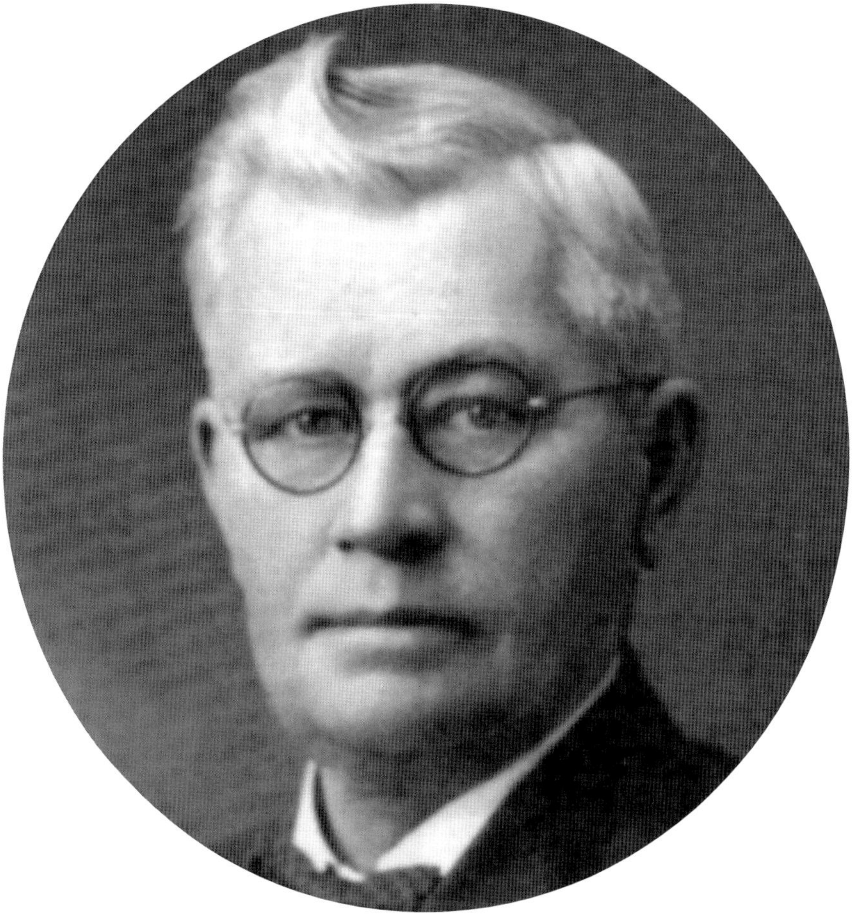

Finley C. Murchison

A man of many hats, Murchison was one of early Arvada's most prolific residents.

In 1902, Murchison and his family moved to Arvada from Kansas. An enterprising man, Murchison opened a livery stable on Grandview Avenue. His clientele included not only local residents but also out-of-town visitors who arrived on the train. Murchison also rented a horse-drawn hearse. In addition to the livery business, Murchison ran a hay and grain business in town.

In a primarily "dry" town, Murchison ran on the "Pro-Saloon" ticket in the 1907 election for mayor. He lost to Morton Alexander, a Prohibitionist. Finley continued on with his political aspirations, serving as a Colorado state senator from 1925 to 1930 and as Arvada mayor from 1923 to 1925. Irene Murchison in 1975 described her father as a "self-educated" man with a high moral character.

F.C. Murchison passed away in the 1950s.

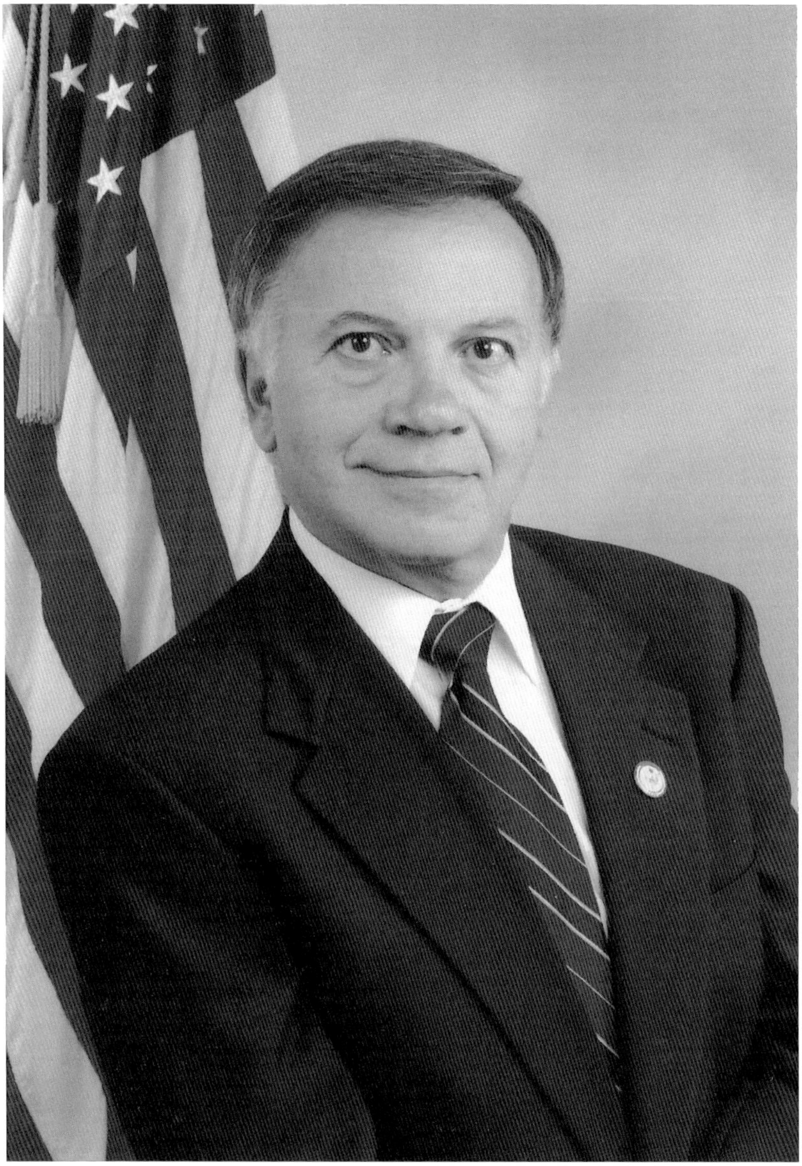

Tom Tancredo
A 2014 Colorado gubernatorial candidate, Tancredo once taught at Drake Junior High.

Born in Denver on December 20, 1945, Tancredo graduated from the University of Northern Colorado with a degree in political science. In 1976, while teaching civics at Arvada's Drake Junior High, Tancredo won a seat in the Colorado House of Representatives. He won reelections in 1978 and 1980. In 1981, Tancredo was appointed by President Reagan as the secretary of education's regional representative. He was reappointed to the office by President Bush. In 1993, Tancredo became president of the Independence Institute in Golden. During his time with the Independence Institute, Tancredo became a regular on the TV shows *Independent Thinking* and *Colorado Inside Out*. In 1998, Tancredo won a seat representing the Sixth Congressional district of Colorado. He ran for the 2008 Republican nomination for president but dropped out. Tom Tancredo is now running for governor of Colorado in the 2014 primary. (Courtesy Tom Tancredo.)

Don Feland

Feland served as the Arvada mayor from 1973 to 1977.

Donald Feland was born in Arvada on January 8, 1937. After graduating from Arvada High School in 1955, Don served in the army. His job with Continental Airlines sent Don and his family to El Paso and Los Angeles. Upon the family's return to Arvada, Don was elected to the city council in 1971. He became mayor in 1973. It was during Feland's tenure as mayor that the Arvada Center for the Arts and Humanities was built and 22 city parks were developed.

Feland also served five years on the Arvada Urban Renewal Authority Board in the late 1980s and served on city council once again from 1985 to 1993.

Donald Feland passed away on May 29, 2009.

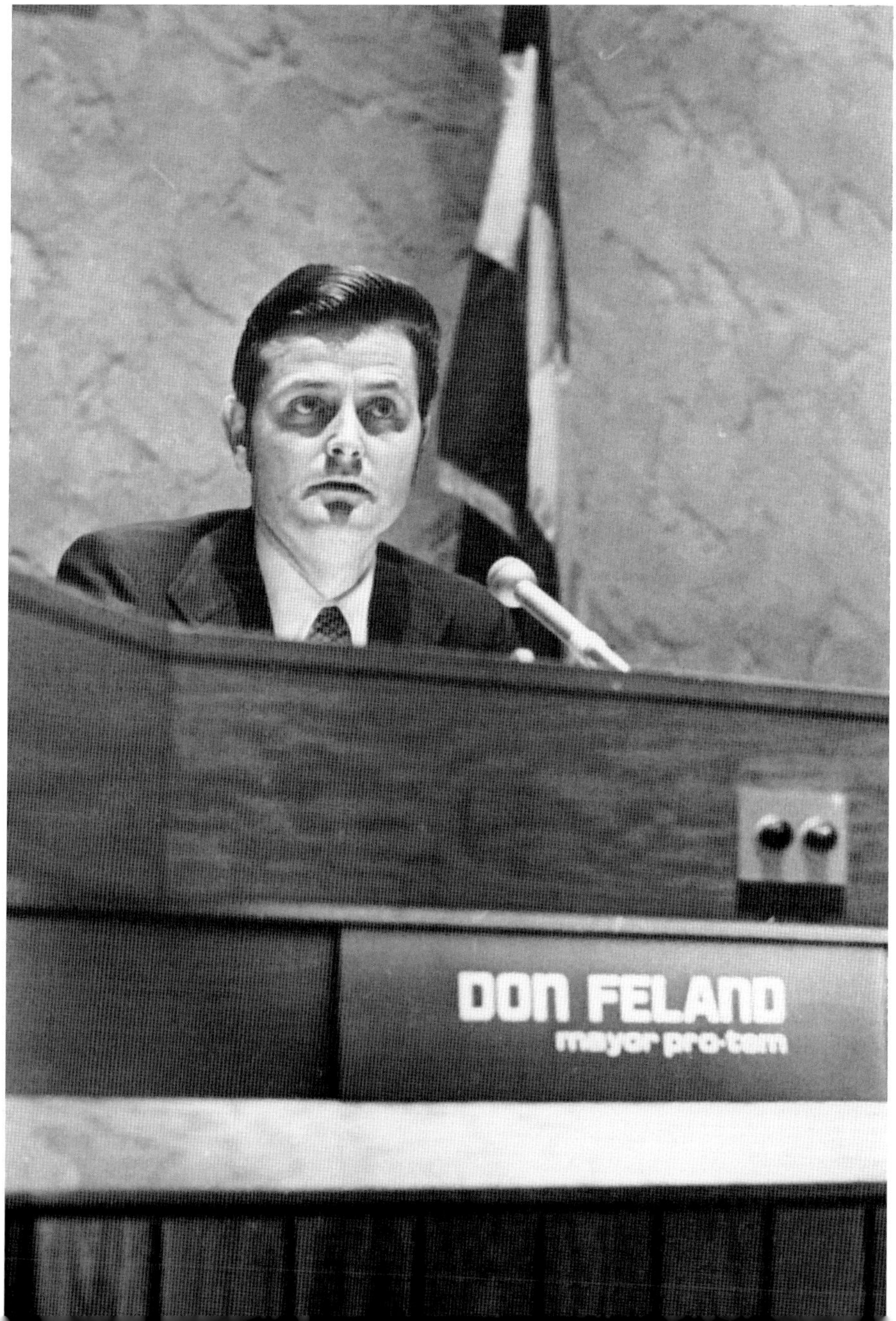

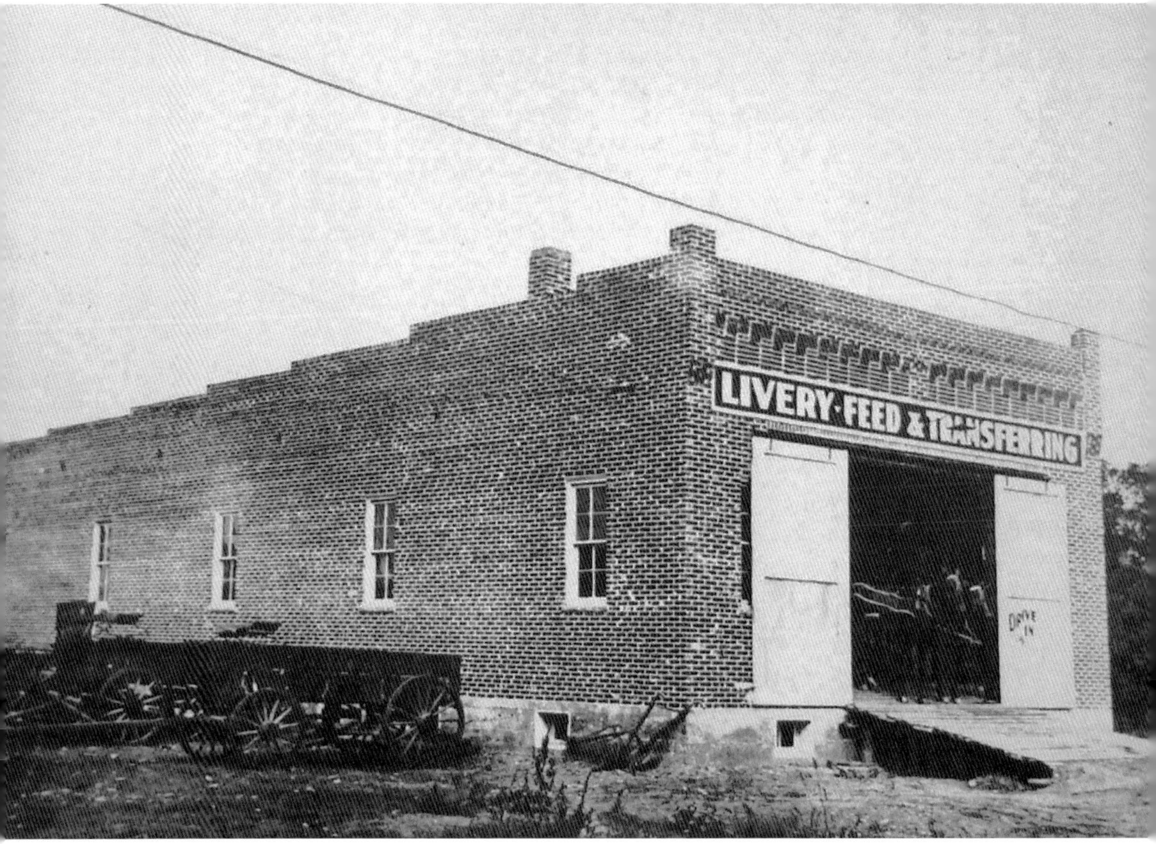

Oliver North Evans

Evans was prominent in politics and business in the early 1900s.

Born in Pennsylvania in 1869, Evans came to Colorado as a child and farmed until 1911, when he moved to Arvada. That year, the Evans and Bennett Feed and Coal store opened on Grandview Avenue, where it would stay for 25 years. Evans served three terms on the town board starting in 1914. In 1921, Evans was elected county commissioner for District 1, an office he held until 1929. A 45-year member of the Arvada Community Methodist Church at Fifty-seventh Avenue and Webster Street, Evans served in many different roles over the years in service to the church. He was also a member of the Arvada Masonic Lodge, the Woodmen of the World and the IOOF Lodge. In 1927, after a typhoid outbreak, Evans and his partner, William J. Bennett, were hired by the city to supply clean water to the town water tower via a reservoir using chlorination. The two were also hired that same year to provide mail service to Arvada by auto from Denver.

Oliver North Evans died in Arvada in April 1945. He is buried at the Arvada Cemetery.

Ted Terranova

Local businessman Ted Terranova has served on city council.

Coming to Arvada in 1969, Terranova is an Arvada High School graduate. He attended Faith Bible College in Arvada. He is the owner of Aaark Total Home Services in Arvada. He served on the Arvada City Council from 1989 to 1993 and served as president of the Arvada Chamber of Commerce in 1989. Ted has also served on the Arvada Planning Commission and is vice president of the Arvada Fire Protection District Board of Directors. Ted has always been a supporter of continuing economic growth in Arvada. In 2013, Ted ran for another term on city council but lost his bid for the seat.

Ted Terranova and his wife, Jeannie, had two sons: Titus and Levi. (Courtesy Ted Terranova.)

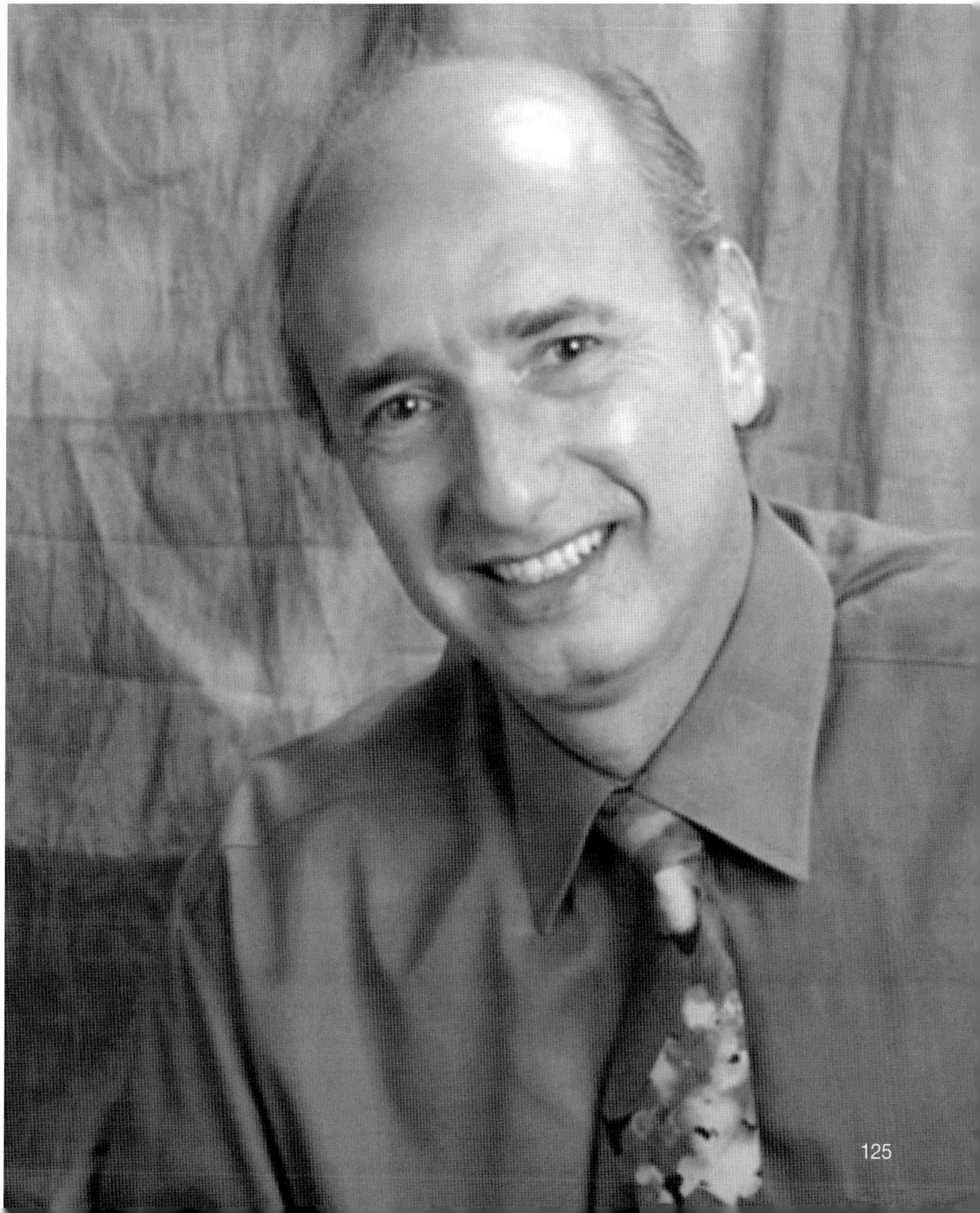

BIBLIOGRAPHY

Arvada Enterprise

Arvada Historical Society. *Arvada Comes of Age*. Westminster, CO: Publishing House, 2002.

———. *Arvada, Just Between You and Me*. Boulder, CO: Johnson Publishing Company, 1985.

———. *More Than Gold*. Boulder, CO: Johnson Publishing Company, 1976.

———. *Waters of Gold*. Arvada, CO: Arvada Heritage Printers, 1973

Arvada Historian

Arvada Press

Arvada Profiles. Stories of the People Who Most Influenced Our First 100 Years. Arvada Sentinel, 2004.

Arvada Sentinel

Denver Post

Lindstrom, Lois Cunniff. *Footprints on the Way. Arvada Presbyterian Church 1904–1984*. Arvada Presbyterian Church, 1986.

INDEX

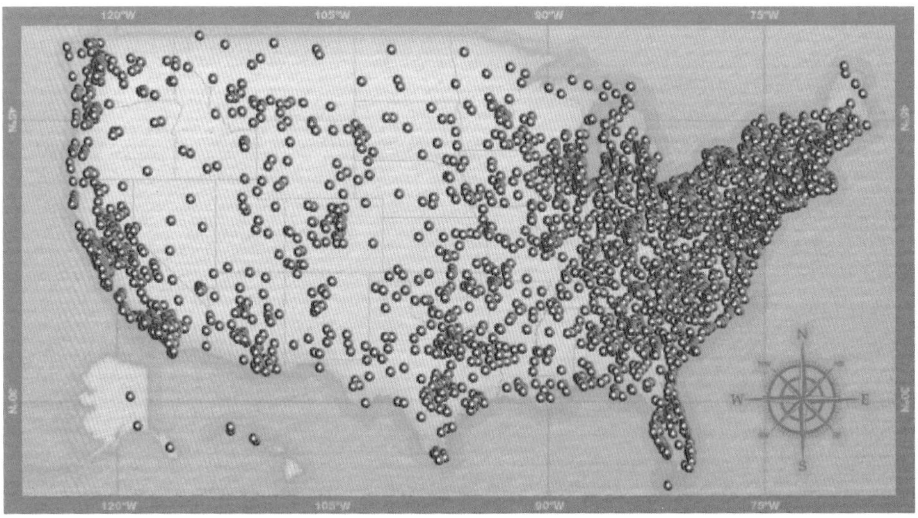